HISTORY OF PSYCHOLOGY

THE MACMILLAN COMPANY
NEW YORK · BOSTON · CHICAGO · DALLAS
ATLANTA · SAN FRANCISCO

MACMILLAN AND CO., Limited
LONDON · BOMBAY · CALCUTTA · MADRAS
MELBOURNE

THE MACMILLAN COMPANY
OF CANADA, Limited
TORONTO

History of Psychology

FROM THE STANDPOINT OF A THOMIST

Robert Edward Brennan, O.P.

UNIVERSITY OF MONTREAL

THE MACMILLAN COMPANY • NEW YORK

1945

150.19
B 838

Nihil Obstat

    CHARLES JEROME CALLAN, O.P., S.T.M.
    JOHN AMBROSE McHUGH, O.P., S.T.M.

Imprimi Potest

    TERENCE STEPHEN McDERMOTT, O.P., S.T.Lr.
            Provincial

Nihil Obstat

    CESLAUS MARIA FOREST, O.P., S.T.M.
          Censor deputatus

Imprimatur

    ✠ JOSEPH CHARBONNEAU, D.D.
          Archbishop of Montréal

BF81
B68
Cp2

PRINTED IN THE UNITED STATES OF AMERICA

"Tenebras illuminare, vias dirigere, latibula manifestare, differentias rerum ostendere."

Thomas Aquinas

A
Monseigneur Olivier Maurault
Prêtre de Saint Sulpice et Prélat domestique
Recteur magnifique
de
l'Université de Montréal
je dédie ce volume
en témoignage de ma profonde gratitude
pour son inépuisable bonté
envers moi
et tous les autres professeurs
qui trouvent
dans son souriant accueil
et dans son bienveillant encouragement
une source permanente
d'inspiration

PREFATORY NOTE

Dear Father Brennan,

Please excuse me for making shorter than I would have liked the preface I promised you; you know that my health has been in poor condition for some months.

I read your book with great interest and I am convinced that a historical survey, as you have conceived it, of the efforts of the human mind to know its own inner functioning and its own depths is of very valuable help to the students in psychology and brings a new stimulus to those already acquainted with the matter. As a rule, the succession of opinions and conflicting theories in the realm of knowledge is not to be seen without some sadness and discouragement. Yet you tell this story in such a way that we have a heartening feeling of the real progress toward truth which has been accomplished both in the field of philosophical and of experimental psychology, and even of the possibility of a converging between these two quite different ways of approaching the secrets of the human self.

Of course, the brevity to which you have constrained yourself made it necessary to outline in a very summarized manner the great philosophical doctrines on the human soul, and thus it seems to me that the second part of your book, dedicated to the development of modern scientific psychology, is a picture in which the authors mentioned would find they had received a most favorable treatment; for the particular trends of a scientific school suffer less from being epitomized than the all-pervading outlook of a philosophical one. This was inevitable. The great fact, however, is that, on the one hand, the student will realize, with regard to the philosophical approach, how Thomistic psychology manifests itself as being the most realistic and the most comprehensive, and, on the other hand, he will be able to do justice both to the philosophical approach and to the scientific one, if he applies the epistemological principles which you have so timely stated at the beginning of your book. Thus he will interpret better than is usually done and follow with greater interest the historical development of two kinds of psychological scrutiny — the ontological and the empiriological one — that are essentially different in method, and complement one another.

Though I cannot say that I am entirely in agreement with all the particular statements contained in your history of psychology, I am happy to congratulate you on your undertaking.

When the philosopher comes to the end of your book, the great problem with which he is confronted is that modern scientific psychology — all the while tending toward the pure type of scientific knowledge, in which reality is analyzed, conceptualized and defined, not in terms of intelligible being, but in terms of observable and measurable sense-data, and empirical ways of verification — cannot, nevertheless, undergo full mathematical symbolization and systematization, as physics does, because psychological phenomena, even observed from a merely empiriological point of view, are imbued with the vital unity and totality, dynamism and finality of the ontological reality they express, and cannot be scientifically grasped without at least some indirect consideration of these characters. As a result, scientific psychology, while developing on its own empiriological level, must take into account, in its own language and by means of some equivalents, the deeper reality which philosophy looks upon from its ontological point of view. Thus we may understand those two facts, that modern psychology has not to use the strictly ontological conceptualization of Thomistic philosophy — and even manifests an old positivist-minded distrust toward it — and that nevertheless modern psychology, in its general mood and inspiration, makes a kind of growing affinity with this philosophy appear, as you point out at the end of your book. The task of Thomist philosophers will be to bring to light the reasons for this affinity, to make clear the inconsistencies of the positivist prejudices, and to achieve, in the psychological field as in the other fields of human knowledge, the rapprochement and reconciliation between science and metaphysics.

JACQUES MARITAIN

CONTENTS

PAGES

Chapter 1. PROLOGUE 1–7
1. A Word of Introduction 1
2. The Household of Human Knowledge 3
3. The Moments of Human Knowledge 4
4. The Role of Philosophy 6
5. The Special Task of Psychology 6

Chapter 2. THE OLD WISDOM AND THE NEW SCIENCE 8–14
1. The Goals of Human Knowledge 8
2. How Science and Philosophy Are Related 9
3. Types of Experience 10
4. Two Ways of Looking at Human Nature 11
5. What Is Psychology? 13

Chapter 3. THE PIONEERS OF PSYCHOLOGY 15–26
1. The Animism of Early Man 15
2. The Causes of Primitive Animism 16
3. Oriental Beginnings 16
4. The First Greek Thinkers 17
5. A Great Truth in Embryo 18
6. The Manifoldness of Nature 20
7. The Tradition of Democritus 21
8. Psychologists of the Sophist School 22
9. Socrates 22
10. The Tradition of Plato 24

Chapter 4. THE ARISTOTELIAN SYNTHESIS 27–38
1. The Founding of a New Tradition 27
2. The Psychosomatic Approach in Psychology 29
3. The Body-Soul Problem 30
4. The Dynamic Picture of Life 31
5. Vital Phenomena 32
6. The Life of Sense 33
7. The Life of Reason 35
8. Nature of the Intellectual Faculties 36
9. Meaning of Aristotle's Synthesis 37
10. Philosophy Separated from Superstition 38

PAGES

Chapter 5. DECLINE OF THE ANCIENT WISDOM . 39-44
  1. Eclectic Psychologists   39
  2. An Early Medical Psychologist   40
  3. Philo the Jew   41
  4. Plotinus the Mystic   42
  5. The Great Transition   42
  6. In the Year of Our Lord   43

Chapter 6. AUGUSTINE AND THE FATHERS 45-53
  1. Pauline Psychology   45
  2. The Genius of Augustine   46
  3. The Nature of the Soul   47
  4. The Augustinian Man   47
  5. The Doctrine of Recollection   48
  6. Human Freedom   49
  7. The Practical Man   50
  8. The Doctrine of Illumination   50
  9. The Influence of Augustine   51
  10. The Trend of Patristic Psychology   52

Chapter 7. THE SCHOOLMEN 54-60
  1. Renewal of Learning   54
  2. The Meeting of East and West   55
  3. The Flowering of the Scholastic Movement . . .   57
  4. Forerunners of Modern Science   59

Chapter 8. THE THOMISTIC SYNTHESIS 61-79
  1. Sources of Inspiration   61
  2. Core of the Thomistic Psychology   62
  3. The True Nature of Man   63
  4. What Is the Soul?   65
  5. The Ladder of Life   65
  6. How Our Knowledge Arises   66
  7. What the Senses Know   67
  8. The Birth of Our Ideas   70
  9. The Order of Human Knowledge   71
  10. The Life of Desire and Action   72
  11. How We Perfect Our Powers   74
  12. The Person of Man   75
  13. The Spirit of Man   76
  14. Appeal to Experience   77
  15. Philosophy Separated from Revelation   78

CONTENTS

PAGES

Chapter 9. THE DECLINE OF MEDIEVAL WISDOM . 80–85
  1. At Loggerheads with Aquinas 80
  2. A Little Learning 81
  3. The Psychology of Occam 82
  4. The Fruits of Misunderstanding 83

Chapter 10. THE DEVELOPMENT OF MODERN
         PHILOSOPHY 86–119
  1. A Turning Point 86
  2. The Cartesian Philosophy of Human Nature . . . 87
  3. The Beginning of Chaos 88
  4. Like Father Like Son 90
  5. The Gentle Pantheist 90
  6. British and French Empiricists 91
  7. Phrenological Interlude 95
  8. The Idealists 95
  9. In Praise of Process 98
  10. A Résumé and a Transition 100
  11. The Sage of Königsberg 101
  12. The Light That Failed 104
  13. After Kant 105
  14. Psychologists of the Scottish School 107
  15. French Psychology in the Nineteenth Century . . 110
  16. Champions of Associationism 113
  17. Evolution and Psychology 114
  18. In Retrospect 116

Chapter 11. THE RISE OF SCIENTIFIC PSYCHOLOGY 120–38
  1. Psychology and the Other Natural Sciences . . . 120
  2. Facts and Findings 120
  3. Start of the Experimental Period 124
  4. The Genetic Approach 132
  5. The Problem of Heredity 134
  6. Individual Differences 135

Chapter 12. THE ESTABLISHMENT OF PSYCHOLOGY
         AS A SCIENCE 139–47
  1. The Wundtian Tradition 139
  2. Further Trends in Experimentation 143
  3. How We Learn 145
  4. Interest and Apathy 146

Chapter 13. ACT PSYCHOLOGY 148–57
    1. A New Angle of Vision 148
    2. The Failure of Content Psychology 150
    3. Higher Mental Activities 150
    4. Imageless Thought and the Thomistic Teaching 152
    5. Studies in Volition 155

Chapter 14. MIND AS STRUCTURE 158–64
    1. An Ardent Wundtian Disciple 158
    2. Atoms of Consciousness 159
    3. The Problem of Attention 160
    4. The Field of Orexis 161
    5. Bones to Pick 161
    6. Further Findings of the Introspectionists 162

Chapter 15. THE OUTLOOK OF FUNCTIONALISM . . 165–72
    1. The Dean of American Psychologists 165
    2. The Problem of Emotion 166
    3. The Stream of Consciousness 167
    4. The Value of Performance 168
    5. Interest in Adolescence 169
    6. Naturalism in Psychology 170
    7. The Functional Ideal 171

Chapter 16. PSYCHOLOGY AND ITS CLOSE RELATIVES 173–91
    1. Connection of Psychology with Other Sciences 173
    2. Further Contributions of the Physiologists 174
    3. Functions of the Autonomic Nervous System 176
    4. Brain Physiology 177
    5. Experiments on Animals 180
    6. How the Psychopathologists Helped 186

Chapter 17. THE FIELD OF PSYCHOMETRICS . . . 192–201
    1. Mental Tests and the Experimental Method 192
    2. Trail Blazers in Mental Testing 193
    3. Early American Workers 194
    4. Testing Comes of Age 195
    5. Factorial Psychology 197
    6. What Is Intelligence? 199
    7. Psychometrics and the Doctrine of Faculties 200
    8. The Fruitfulness of Psychometric Research 201

CONTENTS

PAGES

Chapter 18. BEHAVIORISTIC PSYCHOLOGY 202–13
1. The Spirit of Rebellion 202
2. The Father of Behaviorism 203
3. The Outside Way of Looking Inside 203
4. The Principle of Reflex Action 205
5. Intellectual Behavior 205
6. Disciples of Watson 206
7. The Battle Over Instincts 207
8. The Progressive Aspects of Behaviorism 208
9. Oversights in the Watsonian Technique 209
10. Motorized Consciousness 210
11. Response Psychology 211
12. Failure of Behaviorism as a System of Psychology . . . 212

Chapter 19. GESTALT PSYCHOLOGY 214–21
1. The Pendulum Swings Back 214
2. Historical Antecedents 215
3. The Phi Phenomenon 216
4. Further Developments 216
5. A Vote of Disapproval 219
6. Evaluation 220

Chapter 20. PSYCHOANALYTIC PSYCHOLOGY 222–35
1. The Empirical Approaches to Psychology 222
2. The Genesis of Freudian Psychology 223
3. The Function of Symbols 224
4. A Case in Point 224
5. The Omnipotence of Sex 226
6. The Watchman Who Never Sleeps 227
7. The Psychoanalytic Technique 229
8. Men at Cross-purposes 230
9. Evaluation 233

Chapter 21. TRENDS OF THE MOMENT 236–50
1. Further Lands to Explore 236
2. Psychic Research 237
3. In English-speaking Lands 239
4. Totality Psychology 240
5. Understanding Psychology 241
6. Eidetic Psychology 242
7. Personalistic Psychology 244

                                                                    PAGE
    8. European Functionalism   24
    9. Italian Research   24
   10. Progress in France   24
   11. Russian Psychology   24
   12. The Perspective of Seventy Years   24

Chapter 22. THE THOMIST TAKES STOCK 251–6
    1. Main Streams   25
    2. The Study of Human Nature   25
    3. Modern Issues   25
    4. Troubles of the Scientist   25
    5. The Anthropological Approach   25
    6. Where Things Have Gone Awry   25
    7. Man in Truth and Reality   26

INDEX 265–7

HISTORY OF PSYCHOLOGY

CHAPTER 1

PROLOGUE

I

A Word of Introduction

Tell the average person that you are a psychologist and the odds are ten to one that he will ask you to read his mind or psychoanalyze him. It is doubtful if the first of these two tasks has any reference to psychology at all; it is certain that the second pertains to only a small segment of the total field of mental science. In neither case could one say that either mind reading or psychoanalyzing is synonymous with the study of human nature which is the real business of psychology. If the story set down in the following pages has the effect of correcting notions such as these, it will have accomplished one of its purposes.

But, it has other ambitions, too. The story of psychology has been told before. One could point to numerous stout volumes that give accounts of how this vast and intriguing body of knowledge, which studies human nature from so many different and often opposing angles, has grown to its present stature. So far as I know, the book now offered to the student is the only one that attempts to relate the tale of psychology in a strictly traditional manner. By this I mean an interpretation or a point of view that Aristotle or Thomas Aquinas might have given us, were they able to look back, like ourselves, over the perspective of nearly three thousand years' development.

Moreover, the story of psychology has a philosophic as well

as a scientific background. Indeed, it has far more of a philosophic than of a scientific history. Yet, the fact would be hard to discern from most of the chronicles that are written about it today. This, I am quite sure, is due to a positivistic prejudice; that is to say, to a conscious or unconscious attitude, on the part of certain scientists, which presumes that philosophy has nothing to contribute to the field of psychology. For such men, the philosophy of human nature is something utterly remote from reality, a set of ethereal principles that have no more connection with life than the Milky Way or the Hanging Gardens of Babylon. If the present volume instills the faintest doubt as to the reasonableness of such an attitude, it will have realized another one of its ambitions.

Finally, let me say that I have no illusions about the shortcomings of my work. It is folly to think that so long a story could be adequately told in so short a space. All I want to do here is to declare my dissatisfaction with the way that the story of psychology has been told heretofore, and to point out the possibility of a new way of approaching its content. Let me go a step further and say that all the factual data that have accumulated in the laboratories and clinical chambers over the past half century, can be placed only in one tradition, so far as their philosophic significance is concerned; and that is the tradition of Aristotle and Thomas Aquinas. I may be wrong in this judgment, but my book is an attempt to prove that I am right.

Following the advice of good authority, I have labored to be brief, and in so doing have undoubtedly fallen into the vice of obscurity. There are dark patches in the portraits of some of the great figures in psychology as I have drawn them. There are lines left out that would complete the picture and make it the interesting pageant that the story of psychology should be. On the other hand, if the student is earnest about mastering the contents of this book, he will have, I daresay, a fairly good idea of what the science and philosophy of human nature look like in the long section. From that point on, he must fill in by his own deeper reading of the scrolls.

2

The Household of Human Knowledge

In the drama of man's intellectual history, three knowledges have played a significant role, corresponding to the three periods of development in human experience. The knowledges are philosophy, theology, and science. The ages are ancient, middle, and modern. In the first period, which reached its zenith with the wisdoms of Plato and Aristotle, philosophy was separated from superstition. In the second period, represented most perfectly in the work of Thomas Aquinas, philosophy was disengaged from theology. In the third period, the age in which we are now living, philosophy was distinguished from science.

The glory of the ancients was to have perfected philosophical knowledge; that of the medievals, to have brought theological knowledge to its highest degree of excellence; that of the moderns, to have cultivated and applied science in the interests of humanity. Each of these knowledges, philosophy, theology, and science, is a rightful heir in the household of human progress. Each has made a profound contribution to the advance of human culture and human happiness. Just as the birth and growth of theology did not imply the dispossession of philosophy, so the appearance of science must not mean the dispossession of either philosophy or theology.

3
The Moments of Human Knowledge

In the ancient world, there was practically no distinction between philosophy, theology, and science. If we were to note a difference, it would be in terms of orientation. Thus, the wisdom of Democritus and the early cosmologists was focused on matter. It was phenomenal in its direction and scientific in its outlook. The wisdom of Plato and the Academicians was fixed on form. It looked to heaven and was theological in its ultimate bearings. The wisdom of Aristotle and the Peripatetics was philosophic, but with a shifting vision: now casting its glance toward matter and science, now toward form and theology. It was in its Aristotelian aspects that the knowledge of the ancients was most mature. This means, of course, that philosophy was the most highly perfected form of human knowledge before the rise of Christian scholarship. The philosophy of this first moment, in fact, may be said to have fairly well discerned the three different directions along which the mind of man could develop.

The medieval world and its culture represented a highly polarized period of human progress. Its polarization arose from the religious influence exerted by the truths of revelation. Human knowledge, in its philosophic aspects, had only an incidental function to perform; but, having achieved a separate character in the ancient world, it was bound to reassert its own personality, despite the claims of patristic and medieval theology. For the first thousand years or so of its coexistence with revelation, it wore a Platonic mask, because that seemed to be most suited to the demands of Christian asceticism. But philosophy could not continue to submerge itself in the vast expanses of theological knowledge. Aristotle was remembered and brought to life again in the West. The happy denouement was reached when Thomas Aquinas, in the thirteenth century, christianized Aristotle and achieved the perfect distinction of philosophy and theology. Whatever its attitude toward science, it was now quite clear that the philosophic wisdom of the Greeks was a separate branch of human learning which could be cultivated in independence of the theological wisdom of the Fathers. Now, as never before, the two disciplines understood each other; and out of their sharp distinction came a union and a compatibility that was never possible before. If the glory of the first moment, then, was the glory of Plato and Aristotle, the glory of the second moment was distinctly that of the Angelic Doctor. The Thomistic synthesis was really an advance in human knowledge, because, by its very separation of philosophy from theology, it enabled the former to reach a maturity that was hitherto impossible.

In the modern world, science occupies the center of the stage. The gifts of the philosophers and theologians have not been forgotten; but science opens up fresh vistas with new and undreamed of worlds to conquer. Now philosophy is torn between theology and science. In its effort to solve the dilemma, it is trying to be all things at once. It is reaching once more for its mask, but this time it is a Democritean rather than a Platonic mask, because that is the guise under which it is most easily reconciled with the claims of science. Philosophy made a mistake of this sort before when it courted the affections of theology and became idealistic in its outlook. Now the lure is in the other direction — toward the altar of scientific progress and the cult of the material. Unless it looks back to the Aristotelian rock from which it is hewn, philosophy will be locked again in the arms of positivism.

4

The Role of Philosophy

In the synthesis which Aquinas achieved, philosophy and theology were well united because they were well distinguished. So, in the synthesis which the modern mind will accomplish, the same critical tasks of union and distinction must be wrought in the interests of philosophy and science. On the mounting ranges of human knowledge, the wisdom of philosophy occupies a median and therefore a strategic position. It looks downward as its glance sweeps over the vast limits of matter with which science is concerned. It looks upward, as it envisions the limitless reaches of spirit with which theology is mainly occupied. In thus broadening its world view, it will come to a better understanding of itself.

The rise of science has multiplied the tasks that philosophy is now called upon to perform. The fruits of wisdom can be brought to fuller maturity by the very existence of the errors against which it must struggle, such as the positivism of the scientists; just as theological knowledge has been made more perfect by the presence of doctrines that militate against the deposit of faith. The understanding of theology brought about a better comprehension of the philosophy of Aristotle. In like manner, the understanding of science will result in a better comprehension of the philosophy of Aquinas.

5

The Special Task of Psychology

Of all the branches of philosophy, that of psychology has, perhaps, the most crucial offices to perform. For one thing, man must understand himself and his true spirit and the manner in which his intellect operates, before he can hope to correct the mistakes which the extremes of idealism and positivism have imposed on his thinking. Unless the philosophy of psychology is sound and reassuring, the science of psychology can hope for no real progress. Unfortunately, much that is proclaimed today as scientific psychology has no claim whatever to the title of science. The misfortune, here, would not be so great if the falsehoods and unfounded presumptions were confined to the area of pure theory. But they are not! For psychology has made its way into the practical world where it has only too often been the cause of untold disorder in education, ethics, religion, and politics. Its very ability to reach out in all directions shows its extreme importance. It is the theoretic root of all the moral disciplines.

To look at man scientifically, without studying him in his philosophic nature, must inevitably result in a false purview of his real being. And of the two approaches, surely the philosophic is the more important. We can neglect the scientific analysis and still have a basically correct notion of human nature. But I doubt if we can ever neglect the philosophic analysis and still retain a sound notion of what man really is. Thus, for Aristotle, who knew very little about our modern science of mind, man was a rational animal. For Aquinas, who was also unacquainted with the techniques of experimental psychology, man was a person. Both these views were fundamentally right. But for Watson, or Koehler, or Freud, man is an animal regulated by reflexes, or configurations, or libidinal impulses; and all these views are fundamentally wrong.

CHAPTER 2

THE OLD WISDOM AND THE NEW SCIENCE

I

The Goals of Human Knowledge

Human knowledge is useful both in the control of natural phenomena and in the management of human conduct. Science is practical in the first way; philosophy in the second. Science gives us mastery over the workings of nature as means to a physical end. Philosophy, and more specifically moral philosophy, provides us with rules of wisdom about human actions as means to an ethical end. Because it is paramount that we be good men, irrespective of our scientific achievements, it is clear that the usefulness of philosophy is absolute in the natural order; whereas the usefulness of science is only relative. Thus it falls within the province of philosophy to discuss human goods and their proper ordering to the full measure of human happiness. Science has nothing to do with this question. *Aristotle's goal in the Ethics*

All the scientific knowledge that has accumulated since the sixteenth century does not change, in any essential detail, the basic analysis of man's moral nature, his intellectual and moral virtues, and the natural happiness which is the goal of such virtues. Science, to be sure, can serve the ends of human happiness when it is cultivated for ethical purposes and prudently employed in the interest of humanity. Science is productive of fruits that become values when they are regulated by moral principles. The directive task of philosophy becomes more difficult in proportion to the greater advances made by science and technology.

2

How Science and Philosophy Are Related

Certain difficulties are encountered when we attempt to distinguish between science and philosophy. Two points of view present themselves.

On the one hand, there are those who say that science and philosophy are two distinct species of knowledge. Thus the material object, or the thing known, is the same for both disciplines. It may be described as the physical order of reality; that is to say, the order of nature which exists sensibly and under conditions of mobility and change. Within this material object, however, we can discover certain formal distinctions of things which are sought out for special purposes of analysis and which constitute particular aspects of the material object. The scientist of nature is concerned with the phenomenal or empiriological order of corporeal substances, that is, with the sensible accidents or properties of matter and their correlation. The philosopher of nature deals with the noumenal or ontological order of corporeal substances, that is, with the essential nature of physical reality. He studies not only the essence of physical substances, therefore, but also the essence of physical accidents. According to this view, science and philosophy operate on the same generic level of abstraction, though they are specifically different. Both deal with sensible matter, but from different angles. We can contrast them and differentiate them, first, because they have something in common, namely, the same material object; second, because they have something distinct, namely, diverse formal objects.

On the other hand, there are those who declare that no formal distinctions are discoverable within the material object of science and philosophy. Both constitute one doctrine or one species of knowledge, that is to say, one *scientia* in the traditional meaning of the term. Both aim to understand mobile being, even though science, in the modern meaning of the term, is concerned chiefly with accidents; whereas philosophy is occupied mainly with substance. Both operate on the same specific level of abstraction. The goal, here, is the understanding of nature in its sensible or mobile aspects; and such a goal includes a knowledge of both substance and accidents, since the latter are really intelligible only in relation to the former. With one end in view, the student employs every tool at his disposal the better to grasp the meaning of physical nature: every kind of reasoning working on every kind of fact culled from every kind of observation.

3
Types of Experience

Apart from the kind of distinction that exists between science and philosophy, there is a further difference of backgrounds which may help to clarify the position of each within the household of human knowledge. It is the difference between common and special experience. Both science and philosophy begin with the data of induction. But science, with its instruments of precision, is able to discover a wealth of detail that is hidden from common experience. Philosophy, on the other hand, employs no tools except the naked senses. It should be noted, at once, that special experience does not alter common experience, but merely refines it. Thus, if experience in the vulgar sense is the source of philosophic information, experience in the experimental and clinical sense is the source of scientific information. Experience, in both cases, is empirical, which means that philosophy, as well as science, is empirical. From the data of common or public experience we derive the general truths of philosophy. From the data of special experience we derive the facts or inductive generalizations of science. Note, however, that philosophy can also begin with the data of special experience, though there is no strict necessity of its so doing. Science, on the other hand, cannot neglect special experience or rely solely on general experience.

Is science, then, more certain because more specialized in its experience? Not at all! The certitude of philosophy rests on first principles and its interest is in ultimate causes. The certitude of science is more remotely related to first principles. Its interest is in proximate causes. Further, scientific descriptions lack the immediate and easy control which is peculiar to common experience, even though they are of greater value by reason of the number and precision of their details. Still, the addition of these details is irrelevant to philosophic truth in its essential aspects.

4

Two Ways of Looking at Human Nature

The proper subject matter of psychology is man in his human nature. Its adequate subject matter is every besouled organism. Man, by his essence, is an intellectual creature. Man, by his powers is also a sensitive and vegetative creature. In him, therefore, we find the basic capacities of all living corporeal substances. Man manifests himself, like every other creature, through his operations. His operations, in turn, exhibit his powers and habits. In approaching the study of psychology, then, we must first analyze the acts of man before we can investigate his powers and habits; just as we must first study his powers and habits before we can determine his nature or essence.

When we say that the proper subject matter of psychology is man, we include the analysis of the acts, powers, and habits of man. This subject matter can be approached from two angles, giving rise to a distinction between the science of psychology and the philosophy of psychology. The former limits its investigation to acts, powers, and habits, all of which are accidents belonging to the phenomenal order of man's being. It considers these accidents from the point of view of a purely phenomenal analysis, dealing only with the characteristic relations that exist between observable or measurable data. The latter advances its analysis beyond the data and facts of induction and does not repose until it has reached the ontological depths of man's nature. Scientific psychology, accordingly, is peripheral in its goal; philosophic psychology is central. The science of human nature is interested primarily in laws of operation and their relationship; the philosophy of human nature is concerned primarily with laws of essence and being. Science, here, studies what a man does; philosophy studies what a man is.

We can show further differences between the two disciplines by reference to the methods that are appropriate to each. Thus, philosophic psychology is grounded on the data of public experience, data in which all men can share by virtue of their possessing the same kinds of senses which are exercised on the same kinds of material. Scientific psychology, on the other hand, is based on the data of special experience, exemplified in what is called the "experimental procedure," wherein the senses are implemented by tools and artifacts for making refinements of analysis that would be impossible to the naked powers. Whereas, then, the methods of the science of human nature are investigative and created to yield special forms of experience, those characteristic of the philosophy of human nature are simply observational, designed to produce the reflective types of experience in which all men, with their five wits about them, can participate. There is no conflict here since special experience does not alter common experience, but merely supplements it with more abundant detail. Moreover, philosophy can arise, through reflection, from any kind of experience, as we have already said. This being the case, philosophy and science tend to complement each other, both in content and in method. Thus psychology should unite both philosophic analysis and scientific research in one continuous doctrine, in which philosophy answers the fundamental questions about the nature of man, and science resolves in detail the problem of those human phenomena that can be experimentally observed and classified.

5

What Is Psychology?

There is a proper subject matter of psychology which is man. There is also a twofold manner of approaching the study of man: (a) from the scientific point of view, basing our analyses on special experience and striving to express the operational relationships that obtain between the acts, powers, and habits of man; and (b) from the philosophic point of view, grounding our analyses on general or public experience and striving to determine the entitative relationships of man's acts, powers, and habits to his nature or essence or being. We may define psychology, therefore, under this twofold aspect, as *the study of the acts, powers, habits, and nature of man*. In this definition we can discern both the scientific and the philosophic ambitions of psychology; that is to say, what is phenomenal or empiriological and what is noumenal or ontological in the study of man. Notice, however, that the philosophy of psychology is not necessarily dependent upon the science of psychology, as already pointed out; that the ancients, and especially, Aristotle, created a body of philosophic knowledge about man and his nature without the assistance of modern experimental science.

If the proper subject matter of psychology is man, it is

obvious that psychology constitutes a very peculiar branch of knowledge inasmuch as the subject of the knowledge is also the object of the knowledge. This peculiarity allows the employment of an introspective technique that is legitimate nowhere else. Introspection is the analysis of one's own consciousness. It implies that every man's mind is a sort of laboratory in which he can investigate the data peculiar to psychological experience. Yet, despite the nearness of man to himself (for surely nothing is more intimate to a man, after his being, than his own consciousness) there have been more mistakes and less general agreement about the introspectible data of human consciousness than about any other subject of knowledge. If there is one thing every person could be, it is a psychologist, that is to say, a student of human nature; but if there is one thing that very few people are capable of judging correctly, it is the highly intricate and finely poised organization of what we call "the human mind."

CHAPTER 3

THE PIONEERS OF PSYCHOLOGY

I

The Animism of Early Man

The story of Genesis shows that man, at the beginning, had a clear idea of the existence and meaning of his soul. But as the descendants of Adam multiplied and spread over the earth, and as races drew further and further away from the primitive Revelation, the true notion of a soul, as the life-giving principle of human action and an entity distinguishable from the body, was more or less lost. In recent times, men have sought to wipe out altogether the concept of living matter as distinct from nonliving matter; so, in early times, men sought to endow everything with life. Rivers and oceans, clouds and heavenly bodies were supposed to be set in motion by spirits that dwelt within them.

For the ancient hylozoists, there was no distinction of animate and inanimate matter because everything was living. For the modern materialists, similarly, there is no distinction of animate and inanimate matter because nothing is living. To say that the ancients regarded everything as somehow filled with the breath of life does not mean that they had a limpid idea of the distinction between material and immaterial substances. It would seem likely that their notion of soul as the source of life did not extend beyond the concept of something thin and tenuous with physical properties like those of a body, though of a more refined and intangible character. This sort of naïve belief is not uncommon among the savage tribes of the world today.

2
The Causes of Primitive Animism

There were two very likely reasons for the appearance of primitive animism. The first was the tendency of the un-educated or unreflective mind to confuse self with environment. This is a characteristic of very young children and was quite manifest at the infantile levels of human culture. In early times, people projected their sensations, feelings, and ideas into the world about them. They were anthropomorphic, in the sense that they sought to invest animals, plants, and even lifeless objects with the traits and habits of human beings.

The second reason arose from the personal equation with which men approached the solution of their practical problems. Primitive people struggled to exist. Natural environment meant much more to them than it does to us today. Their thinking was largely patterned in terms of the effect of the surroundings on their personal lives. As a result, they developed a feeling of intimacy with nature, an intimacy that expressed itself by endowing nature with vital and even conscious attributes such as they themselves possessed.

3
Oriental Beginnings

The teachings of Oriental thinkers about such problems as the origin, nature, and destiny of man are matters of religious belief rather than of rational explanation. For this reason, it is difficult to separate the philosophic additions which they made to the content of human knowledge from the forms of worship which they cultivated. Their psychological doctrines are impregnated with so much superstition that they are practically valueless from the analytical point of view. Two points, however, are worthy of notice in this connection:

first, the solid defense of the existence of a soul in man; second, the consistent belief in the immortality of this soul.

To most Oriental minds, the idea of the soul's ever coming to an end would have seemed so absurd as to call for no demonstration. Here is a striking contrast between Eastern and Western attitudes toward one of psychology's most crucial questions. With the idea of immortality we find the notion of metempsychosis commonly associated, especially in the Hindu religions. For the most part, the Orientals failed to make a clear distinction between the facts of experience and the fictions of mythology. Their genius, as thinkers, did not run along dialectical lines — a habit of thought that was to characterize the later Greek philosophers. If they discussed things at all, it was in friendly nonargumentative modes. Yet it is very likely that they exerted an influence on the early philosophic efforts of the Greeks.

4

The First Greek Thinkers

Men really began to be philosophers when they first attempted to understand the world in an objective way and to interpret its events in terms of natural causes. The Greek naturalists of the seventh century before Christ are definitely to be considered wise men in this sense. There were several favorable factors that brought about the cultivation of philosophy in Greece. For one thing, the Greek state was composed of many wealthy and independent citizens who had both the means and the leisure for speculative thought. Moreover, as a maritime nation, Greece had commercial relations with outside peoples and was therefore in a position to profit by an exchange of ideas with scholars from the Orient. Again, the civil strife that afflicted many of the Greek cities really proved a boon for philosophy since it turned thoughtful men away from public affairs and inspired a search for the more peaceful and cultured ways of human living, such as the pursuit of wisdom.

The first Greek philosophers sought for an elemental substance from which everything living and nonliving was supposed to be made. Their outlook on reality was hylozoistic, since they tended to see all nature as alive. They differed little, then, from the primitive animists. At this stage in their thinking, there was no clear distinction between mind and matter, and any psychological doctrines that they developed were simply part of their larger philosophy of the cosmos. *Thales* believed that water was the basic element. *Anaximander* thought that the fundamental constituent of the universe was something boundless or unlimited, an infinite material substance. Life sprang from moisture, and the first animals were fishlike in form. *Pythagoras* introduced the doctrine of transmigration into Greek philosophy. He probably derived it from an Eastern source. The doctrine holds that the spirit of man passes on into another body after death. It presupposes a belief in the immortality of the human soul. Pythagoras was the first to use the word "philosophy" which means "a love of wisdom." He also coined the term "cosmos" which, to the Greek mind, symbolizes "a world full of order and physical loveliness"; so that, when philosophers of a later date referred to man as a "microcosmos" they meant to imply that man's nature sums up every kind of perfection: the beauty and order of the material universe as well as the spiritual beauty which is unique and proper to itself.

5

A Great Truth in Embryo

Heraclitus postulated change as the first principle and ultimate goal of nature. Change, indeed, is the only changeless thing. Fire is the universal cause of things. In its subtler form, it is also the soul of human beings. Sensory experiences are the grosser aspects of fire and, by comparison with the more delicate and refined fires of intellectual experience, are essentially inferior and untrustworthy. The theory is interesting because it exemplifies one of the earliest attempts to distinguish between the rational and animal aspects of man's nature. *Parmenides* opposed the views of Heraclitus with his doctrine of the essential changelessness of nature. Change, in fact, is an illusion. Man, like the other objects of the universe, consists of a blend of qualities, such as heat and cold, light and dark, moist and dry. Of these qualities, heat and cold are the most important for life and reason. Monistic views, such as the early Greek thinkers exhibited, were bound to encounter difficulties. Their description of the universe and its imposing array of objects in terms of a single substance or a single principle of explication became meaningless, since it left no ground for the distinction of things that are obviously separable from each other.

The argument between Heraclitus and Parmenides was battled out in the courts of philosophy. As with so many other disputes of the pioneer thinkers, we find truth and falsehood on both sides. The elements of this particular controversy are significant because, when the dust finally settled and the merits of the case for change and changelessness were examined dispassionately, a new principle was brought into being that revolutionized man's outlook on nature. I am referring to the principle of potency and act which Plato evolved into a clear statement and which Aristotle finally purged of all internal contradiction and made the cornerstone of his entire philosophy.

6

The Manifoldness of Nature

The next group of philosophers were more pluralistic in outlook. *Empedocles* maintained that earth, air, fire, and water were separate cosmic elements. Love, or the principle of good, unites these elements; hate, or the principle of evil, tears them apart. In man, earth forms the solid parts, water the liquid organs, air gives rise to life, and fire produces reason. External objects discharge emanations or small material replicas of themselves which enter the blood through the pores of the body and produce an awareness of the outside world. This is the process of sensitive cognition. Thought, too, like every other vital activity, depends upon the mixture of the four elements. Empedocles contrasted the untrustworthiness of sense knowledge with the higher and more reliable forms of reflective experience. Still, he did not consider the soul as an entity apart from the body. Man is the result of a general organic evolution, since the superior types of life can arise only from the inferior. He seems to have approved of the Pythagorean doctrine of transmigration.

Anaxagoras, born about the same time as Empedocles, taught that there are numerous elements in the universe. He was the first philosopher among the Greeks to develop the idea of the supersensible. Thus *nous* or mind, which is the moving power that formed the world, is something simple and unmixed with matter, a self-ruled principle with knowledge about everything and supreme power over everything. The *nous* of man is the faculty of true knowledge, the principle of understanding which is also the principle of man's higher psychic life. Here for the first time we find the germ of a dualistic doctrine, manifest in the separation of mind and body. This doctrine was to be more completely expanded by Socrates and Plato and brought to perfection by Aristotle.

7

The Tradition of Democritus

Leucippus founded the school of atomism, but his importance is overshadowed by the brilliant talents of his pupil *Democritus*. Both men defended the view that the whole universe of nonliving and living creatures is made up of quantitatively distinct particles. Theirs was a thoroughgoing materialistic point of view. While Democritus did not deny the distinction of man's soul from his body, yet he declared the human psyche to be atomic in structure like all other matter, its distinction arising from the fineness, smoothness, and roundness of its atoms. The knowledge which comes from the senses is conditioned by the emanation of material particles cast off by sensible objects. It does not differ fundamentally from thought, since both are results of changes in the soul-substance generated by material impressions. To save himself from an absolute identification of sensing and thinking, Democritus held that the processes of intellectual cognition reveal the existence of invisible atoms and thus show forth the true nature of things. He discussed the functions of the five senses and considered touch to be the most primitive and basic of man's sensitive powers.

The psychology of this group of philosophers offered several vulnerable openings to the thinkers who were to succeed them. It was definitely a materialistic outlook and ended where the problem of man's true nature begins. In maintaining a division between sense and intellect it was forced into an untenable position. Its distinction between the grosser and finer forms of matter, which represented the dividing line between sensitive and intellectual knowledge, was in reality a distinction without a difference. Moreover, its grounds for the distrust of the senses could be put forward as like reason for the fallaciousness of the intellect.

8

Psychologists of the Sophist School

After the end of the Persian wars around 480 B.C., the center of Greek culture shifted from the Ionian colonies to Athens. Here philosophy became firmly entrenched, and the study of man was given a place of first importance. An attitude of critical doubt grew up about the pronouncements of the earlier atomists who, more frequently than not, argued from personal viewpoints rather than from conviction about the universal and objective source of truth. Now the pendulum turned in the other direction. Individual consciousness became paramount; and private opinion, instead of public experience, was made the final court of appeal.

Gradually the attitude prevailed that there really is no objective truth but only subjective interpretation according to one's ever-changing background. This was the position of the Sophists. *Protagoras*, one of their most vigorous leaders, declared that knowledge depends on the knower. Man, in fact, is the measure of all things. Since each person's experience is a miniature of reality, everything in the human mind is equally true. It is strictly a matter of relativity. The qualities that we observe in things are the permanent possession of neither the object perceived nor the subject perceiving. *Gorgias* very logically concluded that if knowledge is relative, all things are equally false and equally true.

9

Socrates

Socrates represents a transition in Greek thinking from naïvely objective and subjective extremes to a position that would evaluate the world and our knowledge of it in terms of a critical realism. He agreed with the Sophists that knowledge has its subjective aspects; but he disagreed with the conclusion that truth does not exist except as a form of personal opinion. Thus, if people are properly questioned by a dialectical method of inquiry, they can be led to acknowledge the existence of unalterable natures and of first principles that are independent of the individual thinker. This is particularly the case with moral truths, about which a universal consent can be found to exist, even though these truths are derived from inner experience. To know oneself, therefore, is a primary duty.

The pre-Socratic philosophers had set up a distinction of sorts between the knowledges of sense and intellect. Socrates first showed that sense impressions must be tested and controlled by critical judgment. The role of intellect is to elaborate the images of sense into concepts which show the immutable essence of things that fall under experience. This ability of intellect to rise above the contingencies of matter must surely have convinced Socrates of the immortality of the human soul, even though he thought that the dialectical proof of this deathlessness was beyond the capacity of the human mind.

Socrates, as a psychologist, is important for several reasons. First, he was the teacher of Plato and Aristotle. Second, he laid the foundations of a genuinely inductive method in the study of human nature. Third, he made pioneer inquiries into the conditions necessary for a correct appraisal of human knowledge, approaching the problem of truth through its psychological antecedents. Finally, he sought to convince his students that a higher and nobler life may be achieved by a systematic analysis of the human mind. Thus, a new impulse was given to the pursuit of wisdom, both theoretic and practical, which was to bear its most precious fruit in the achievements of the great thinkers who immediately succeeded Socrates, when philosophy reached its highest development.

10

The Tradition of Plato

Plato was one of the greatest thinkers on record. From Socrates came his interest in morals; from the Pythagoreans, his love of wisdom. In psychology, he was a dualist, though not a temperate one. He was the first of the Greeks to deal, in anything like a satisfactory manner, with the notion of immaterial existences. By the world of immaterial existences is meant the world of ideas. The important doctrine of ideas was a historical development in Plato's philosophy. It derived from the failure of Heraclitus and Parmenides to explain being and becoming. These men were right in what they affirmed about reality, but wrong in what they denied. Heraclitus rightly taught that becoming exists, but wrongly asserted that being does not exist. Parmenides rightly taught that being exists, but wrongly asserted that becoming does not exist. The truth is that both being and becoming are realities. The solution of the problem depends upon our recognizing the fact that becoming is made up of both being and nonbeing or of something actual and something potential.

In the changing world around us, according to Plato, that alone is real which is unchangeable, absolute, and one, namely, the idea. He not only distinguished in things the permanent element which is their being and the object of our knowledge; but he further sought to draw out and hypostatize this element from its conditions of manifoldness and changeability and to locate it in a world entirely apart from our own, where it exists in all its oneness and immutability. According to the testimony of Aristotle, who very likely debated the issue with Plato in person, the world of Platonic ideas is a universe by itself, a prototype of the universe that we see, even though Augustine later on declared that in Plato's theory such ideas are simply exemplary forms in the mind of God, or, more simply, the divine mind itself, contemplating all the actual and possible modes of reality.

The soul of man, according to Plato, is of divine origin. It is a self-moving principle and related to the body merely as an extrinsic cause. It exists before its union with matter. The doctrine of recollection is a development of this theory of preexistence. Before it is enclosed in the prison of the body, the soul enjoys a clear vision of the ideas which we have just described. On earth it still retains an indistinct memory of its heavenly intuitions. Our ideas, then, are born with us; and to learn is to recollect what we have forgotten. The human soul is immortal; and the arguments brought forward in support of its deathless nature represent the first serious effort on the part of any ancient thinker to establish this important attribute as fundamental to any reasoned interpretation of human nature. Not every part of the soul is immortal, however, but only the intellectual principle which is localized in the head. The irascible and concupiscible parts, residing in the heart and abdomen, perish with the destruction of the body.

Knowledge begins with sense perception. But the senses do not reach to the truth of things. They contemplate the imperfect copies of reality, shadows that are merely created participations of the uncreated ideas. The best that sense experience can do is to remind us of the ideas that we understood in a previous existence. Sensible objects, therefore, are not causes but only occasions of our intellectual knowledge.

Freedom of the human will is a capital point in the philosophy of Plato. Liberty of choice, in fact, decides our parentage, physical constitution, and early education, since these things are results of decisions that were settled freely in the soul's previous state of existence. Virtue alone is the essential ingredient of human happiness and is fourfold in character: wisdom, which is the highest though not the sole virtue, as

Socrates had taught; fortitude, temperance, and justice. Here, for the first time in the annals of philosophy, we have a complete enumeration of the cardinal virtues by means of which man can reach the goal of earthly happiness.

As an idealist in psychology, Plato set small stock on physiological data so that his explanations of the phenomena of human life are very inadequate. His attachment to forms or ideas, to the neglect of the material aspects of man's nature, resulted in a pronounced underestimation of the value of sense experience. Aristotle, by contrast, gave more attention to empirical findings, with the result that he was far more successful in explaining the psychophysical complexities of man's life.

CHAPTER 4

THE ARISTOTELIAN SYNTHESIS

I

The Founding of a New Tradition

Of all the names in the records of Greek psychology, that of *Aristotle* is surely the most important. He was an original observer of both physical and biological phenomena. He was also the first to write a history of psychology. In fact, without certain chapters of his *Treatise on the Soul*, we should know very little about the psychological theories of the earlier thinkers. He drew his plan of human nature with a firm hand, laying the foundations of his psychological analysis on the data of personal observation as well as on the empirical experience of mankind as a whole. All the parts of his organic synthesis are not equally secure; but the design as a whole has never lost its first shape and meaning. He was an encyclopedic genius. Some trace of his teaching will be found in practically every school of modern psychology. He anticipated many of today's scientific theories, even though he had only a broad form of observation to appeal to.

Aristotle stands at the head of a tradition which is as important today as it was in the days of its founding. The seeds of truth have been scattered over the face of the earth. There is no race of people, however primitive, no group of thinkers, however immature, no single mind, however seduced by false reasoning processes, that does not have some insight into the meaning of reality. Truth has grown up in the wilderness as well as in the centers of culture. Wherever found, it will be

seen to have its enduring character for mankind precisely
because it is true. What we call today the "perennial philosophy," or the truth about reality, began its existence in ancient
times and sundry places, and in surroundings that were far
removed from the Athens of Aristotle or the Paris of Thomas
Aquinas.

Before philosophy moved into Greece, where it flourished
so abundantly, it already had the outlines of a tradition upon
which the Hellenic thinkers could look in retrospect. We
speak of Aristotle today as an ancient and of ourselves as
moderns. So Aristotle could speak of his forebears in philosophy as ancients and of himself as modern. It is impossible,
of course, to know all the sources from which he drew his
inspiration. Like his medieval expositor, Aquinas, he looked
into every nook and corner so that he might learn the truth
that had already been discovered by others. He was an heir
to the thought of Plato and Socrates. He was acquainted
with the ideas of Protagoras and the Sophists; of Democritus
and the atomists; of Parmenides and the Eleatics; of Pythagoras and the astrologists who searched for wisdom in stars
and numbers. As he widened his studies he encountered the
teachings of the old Ionians, so vigorously represented by
Anaximander and Empedocles. He knew something of
Heraclitus and the theories of the early Greek physicists. It
is not unlikely that there are remnants in his system of the
culture of Persia, India, and China. He may have been
touched by the speculations of thinkers — if thinkers there
were — in ancient Egypt and Babylon. And going back even
further than this, to a point beyond which there is no point,
his mind may have been influenced by elements of the primitive Revelation that God gave to man at the start of the
human race, a Revelation which had lost its original purity
as it spread from its home in Paradise but which still retained
some germ of truth that Aristotle's genius was quick to grasp,

replant, care for tenderly, and bring to ripe fruitfulness. What he claimed for himself, in all this active pursuit, was simply the right to use the things that had been truthfully said by others in the past. With this as a basis and a point of departure, he would go on to add his own insights and deductions as the world of reality unfolded before his consciousness. We know the results. For out of the depths of his shining intelligence a new wisdom was born which set on foot a tradition that was to last for all time. When in the course of these pages I have occasion to speak of "the traditional philosophy" or "the traditional psychology," it is to this stream of Aristotelian thought, absorbed and enlarged on by Thomas Aquinas and his followers, that I am referring.

2

The Psychosomatic Approach in Psychology

The Aristotelian man, like all other corporeal substances, is composed of matter and form. In the physical order, matter is that out of which a thing is made. It is the substratum of all corporeal reality, indeterminate, but capable of determination. It is the receptacle or subject of generation and corruption. It can neither exist nor be known without form. In its condition of absolute potentiality, it is called "first matter." As such, it is entirely without form. With form it constitutes second matter. Form, on the other hand, is that which places corporeal substance in a definite species. It is the principle of determination which overcomes, so to speak, the indeterminate character of first matter. Without it matter cannot exist. We very properly refer to it, then, as the "first actuality" or the "first perfection" of corporeal substance, in contrast to first matter which is pure potentiality.

Form is an object of lower or higher knowledge according to

its degree of remotion from matter. For sense, it is an object in its concrete and sensible being, detached from matter intentionally, and received into a material faculty. For intellect, it is an object in its abstracted and intelligible being, detached from matter intentionally, and received into an immaterial faculty. In this latter state, it represents the unalterable essence of things, which remains the same under the constantly fluctuating conditions of phenomenal existence.

Like the Platonic idea, form confers the plenitude of being; for, while matter is a real constituent of corporeal substance, its reality is something potential. But there is this major difference between the form of Aristotle and the idea of Plato: the Aristotelian form exists in individual things, whereas the Platonic idea exists in a world apart. The distinction of matter and form is a distinction that need involve no separation. While they can be thought of as divorced from each other, in reality they are united to produce a given corporeal substance.

3
The Body-Soul Problem

In all living creatures, man included, the soul is the form of the organism. It is the actuality or realization of the potential excellence of the body. The connection between the soul and the body is more exactly expressed as a connection between form and matter. The concrete whole, which is a compounding of the two elements, results in one substance. Thus the metaphysical formula of actuality and potentiality is first expressed as the doctrine of form and matter, and proposed by Aristotle as the only solution of the most critical problem in psychology, the problem that has vexed the philosophers down the ages: the relation between soul and body. The hylomorphic doctrine stands midway between two great traditions which were established before Aristotle and revived at regular intervals after his time: the tradition of Democritus, which is materialistic; and the tradition of Plato, which is formalistic. Here is an interpretation that uses the truth and discards the falsehood found in both points of view.

The materialist who regards mind as nothing more than another and subtler aspect of matter, and mental processes as the outcome and development of physical phenomena, is not more emphatic than Aristotle in maintaining that man has an essentially material aspect to his nature. On the other hand, the idealist who regards matter as nothing more than a projection of mind, and physical processes as aspects of mental phenomena, is not more emphatic than Aristotle in maintaining that man exhibits a formal or intellectual side to his nature. Just as the form gives essential meaning to matter when it confers specific being on it, so the soul gives essential meaning to the body when it constitutes it a human organism.

4

The Dynamic Picture of Life

For Aristotle, the term "soul" covers the whole range of biological life, manifesting itself at vegetative, sensitive, and human levels. The entire series is to be regarded as a continuous development from lower to higher: starting at the inorganic level, pushing its way up through all the manifold exhibitions of vital phenomena, and crowned at its highest cosmic level by human existence. Beyond this, there is the distinct possibility of forms entirely separated from matter, having a degree of intelligence more perfect than man possesses. Thus Aristotle viewed the universe in a sweeping vision that could range, by the power of his insight, from formless matter to matterless form.

Here, too, was a clear grasp of the dynamic principle with which the modern evolutionists are so preoccupied. I do not think it too bold to say that the Darwinian hypothesis was fairly well projected by Aristotle in the fourth century before Christ. Neither was it entirely new with Aristotle. Empedocles and Anaximander had the idea in embryonic shape; and the philosophy of Heraclitus, with its constant stress of change, contained it implicitly. Strange that the evolutionary theory, set out by Aristotle in principle, should lie dormant for over two thousand years. More strange that, at the beginning of the modern scientific age, the new philosophy enunciated by Francis Bacon, rising in rebellion against the Stagirite, should end in a restatement of a doctrine which Aristotle was one of the first to propound. Note, however, that the modern theory, though its results in the actual order of nature are the same, differs in one essential respect from the Stagirite's: namely, in either denying or studiously avoiding the principle of finality which, for Aristotle, was more important than the actual fact of dynamism in nature.

5

Vital Phenomena

The lowest species of soul is to be found in plants. Nutrition, growth, and reproduction are its characteristic functions. The acquisition of sense experience marks the transition from the vegetative to the sensitive levels of life. Add the sensitive appetites and the power of locomotion, and one has a picture of all the animal's basic capacities. The final manifestation, in which the faculties of intellect and will are added to the rest, is found in man. The increment of experience, which is at once implied by the acquisition of rational insight, marks the transition from the sensitive to the intellectual grade of cosmic being. The assimilative process is universal in all the orders of life. While the plant assimilates matter, the animal assimilates sensible forms in the act of sense knowledge, and man assimilates intelligible forms in the act of intellectual knowledge.

6

The Life of Sense

Sensation is the dividing line, as it were, between the plant and animal kingdoms. It is a vital operation in which the animal is moved in a special way. The object of sensation as a concrete whole, that is to say, as a substance composed of matter and form, does not come into play. Rather it is the form alone which is involved, since the process of sensation consists in the separation of form from matter. But it is not the physical form which is thus detached, since this would leave the object without existence; so it must be a counterpart of the physical form. We may call it an "intentional species" because it determines the subject to know. The meaning may be made clear by an illustration: the sensitive power receives its impulsion to know in much the same way as a piece of wax receives the impression of a metal seal. The impression is conveyed without any portion of the seal's being left in the wax.

In enumerating the special senses, Aristotle does not depart from the popular conception. Men commonly think of themselves as having five wits, and this is exactly what the psychologist says too. Touch is the most universal sense because it is present in every part of the body. The other senses are aspects of touch or rooted in it. In addition to the special senses, there is a common sense which is able to organize the data of sensation into higher patterns of perception, making the animal conscious of external stimuli, comparing sensations, distinguishing them, and unifying them into whole-making experiences that altogether exceed the capacities of the exterior senses.

Imagination, on the physical side, carries on the sensational process after the object has been withdrawn. It differs from sensation in its power to picture objects without their actual presence. But it is capricious in its exercise and liable to error. Memory carries with it a distinct cognizance of its objects as facts of the past. It involves a consciousness of time and depends very closely on the functioning of common sense in its apprehension of the temporal aspect of things, particularly the aspect of duration. Finally, there is the faculty of animal prudence whose office is to distinguish the useful and harmful elements of experience.

The three last-named powers all have a double function to perform in the life of man; first, the purely esthetic or sensitive activities which characterize them precisely as animal functions; second, the dianoetic or rational activities which mark them as peculiarly human, not because they are intellectual in themselves, but because they operate under the immediate influence of reason and will. Dianoetic memory is particularly helpful to man because it enables him to recollect — a function that proceeds along well-established lines of association wherein images are grouped together by virtue of their likenesses, unlikenesses, and near likenesses. Thus far, the psychology of Aristotle coincides with the general tendency of the moderns to approach the problem of man's conscious life from the side of sense perception. Without an image or sensory datum, according to the Stagirite, it is impossible to proceed to the higher processes of mind, wherein thought and volition are involved.

The sensitive appetites of man are two in number: concupiscent, which is occupied with the pleasures of sense; and irascible, which fights to remove the obstacles in the way to the enjoyment of the pleasure of sense. The locomotive faculty is diversified by the numerous organs of locomotion that we find among animals. In man it is chiefly concerned with prehensile movements, walking and running about, and the formation of vocalized sounds.

7

The Life of Reason

Intellect is the power by which man penetrates to the essence and core of reality. In this respect it differs radically from the senses. For whereas the senses deal only with concrete and individual objects, intellect has the universal and abstract nature of things as its proper diet. In Aristotle's psychology, there is a basis for the distinction of two separate powers which the schoolmen were to refer to later on as agent intellect and possible intellect. Thus the Stagirite speaks quite plainly of one faculty whose office is "to make everything," that is, to make everything intelligible; and of another faculty whose function is "to become everything," that is, to become everything intelligible. It is the power of becoming everything intelligible or possible intellect which is the faculty proper of understanding. We may refer to it descriptively as a *topos eidon* or storehouse of intelligible species. In the beginning, it is completely devoid of ideas, like a tablet on which nothing is written.

The process by which intellect rises from the particular to the universal or from the concrete to the abstract is a process of development. It postulates the essential objective dependence of reason on the senses. The material on which intellect immediately operates is the synthesized product of the internal senses or the phantasm. The task of making everything intelligible belongs to poietic or agent intellect. It is accomplished by abstracting the nude nature of the object which is represented in the phantasm. The mind of man, however, does not create the world which it understands. It merely causes the object, which is potentially intelligible, to become actually intelligible, in the same way as the light of the sun causes the color of a thing, potentially visible without that light, to become actually visible.

Although we refer to the work of agent intellect as one of developing or unfolding or illuminating the phantasm, we must remember that such expressions are only metaphorical. What the mind actually does is to abstract or separate the universal nature of its object from the concrete conditions of sense in which it is embedded. It is a process of induction, so to speak; that is, a process of bringing together several individuals under a single universal concept, like the stand of a single soldier who, in the rout of an army, becomes the center around which a new group may form. But the ideogenetic procedure does not stop with the work of agent intellect. Once the object has been made intelligible, it impresses itself on possible intellect, that is, on the faculty of becoming everything. This is brought about in precisely the same way as the sensible object impresses its species on the organs of sense. From his account it is abundantly clear that there are no innate ideas in the psychological system of Aristotle. What we do find in intellect, however, is the native power of discovering the abstract and universal elements of intelligibility in the world of matter.

8

Nature of the Intellectual Faculties

Agent intellect is a faculty separate and unmixed, which means that it is not intrinsically dependent upon any material organ. The same holds true of possible intellect. Because it houses the intellectual powers and, like them, is separable from matter, the soul of man would appear to be eternal and immortal, coming into existence from without, not generated by any material force. As to the will of man, we may describe it in two ways: either as a faculty of intellectual desire; or as a power of appetitive reason. In any event, it is essentially different from the sensitive appetites which it resembles.

Because its functions are preceded by a rational apprehension of good, it is free. This characteristic of freedom is borne out by the recognized voluntariness of virtuous habits and by the equally well-recognized fact that a man is held accountable for his actions. Intellect, precisely as it contemplates truth for its own sake, is called "speculative." As it considers the relation of truth to moral or artistic action, it is called "practical."

9

Meaning of Aristotle's Synthesis

It is hard to form a true estimate of the value of Aristotle's psychology. The difficulty arises, in the main, from our constant familiarity with the notions that he introduced into the study of human nature. The terms that he coined, one of his chief titles to eminence, are largely current in the literature of psychology today. His is the glorious title of Father of Psychology. He laid his foundations on the rock bottom of experience; and although subsequent discoveries and the invention of scientific techniques have corrected many of his mistakes, yet his brilliant guesses at truth throw his errors into shade. His dynamic approach to the study of man accords perfectly with the outlook of present-day investigation. His hypothesis of a common sense, to give an example, harmonizes with one of the most important lines of modern research: the Gestalt interpretation of perceptual data. The same may be said of his whole concept of faculties which is now being reestablished on a scientific basis. The relationship that he discovers between soul and body, as well as his insistence on a definite purposive meaning in the facts of human life, prepared the way for a satisfactory statement of the theology of human nature.

10

Philosophy Separated from Superstition

With the completion of the Aristotelian synthesis, the first great stage in the development of human knowledge, the separation of wisdom from superstition, was accomplished. In the Stagirite, we find the culmination of all the learning of the early philosophers. His doctrine of causes, to explain the nature of reality, is an epitome of everything that the Greek thinkers had achieved up to that time. But it is especially by his additions to and refinements of the Platonic teaching that his genius is to be judged. Out of the ruins of pre-Socratic thought, Plato had raised up a mansion of philosophy according to definite plan: a mansion that was beautiful and poetic in its outlines, perfect in its symmetry, but insecure and unstable because of its idealistic foundations. Aristotle, by contrast, built his philosophic synthesis on hardheaded common sense and the experience of reality as he saw it; and he evolved a structure that was not only lovely to behold and most carefully designed, but also, in its essential features, destined to last for all ages.

CHAPTER 5

DECLINE OF THE ANCIENT WISDOM

I

Eclectic Psychologists

The empirical type of investigation which Aristotle advocated almost disappeared in the century that followed his death. Later psychologists became mere samplers. They did little or no thinking on their own. They were eclectic, in the sense that they preferred to choose among the doctrines of the ancients rather than search for new methods and new truths. *Epicurus* was interested in the moral aspects of man's life. He accepted the Democritean idea that the soul is composed of smooth atoms whose balanced movement brought peace and composure, the true goal of human living. Pain and passion must be avoided at all costs, and the simplest expedient is to develop a state of complete emotionlessness. In order to free man of all concern about his ultimate destiny, Epicurus declared that the atoms which compose the human soul are scattered at death.

Zeno of Cittium founded the Stoic school. He counseled indifference, rather than tranquillity, as the end to be sought in human affairs, since all things, including man, are subject to a law of ineluctable necessity imposed by the will of the gods. The soul is a kind of fiery breath spread throughout the body and, like the latter, doomed to final destruction. Both the Stoics and the Epicureans were concerned with one of human nature's eternal problems: the reconciliation of man's higher and lower natures, the solving of the conflict between passion and reason. One school would extinguish the passions, oddly enough, by giving them so much free rein that they would become entirely inactive. The other school would ignore the passions completely, as though they had no existence or reason of being in the life of man. Unconsciously, both schools were dealing with the problem of original sin; and, as history proved, both were unsuccessful, in theory as well as in practice, in settling the struggle between the desires of the flesh and the higher impulses of the spirit. The problem some twenty centuries later was to form a point of departure for the Freudian psychology.

Pyrrho, the skeptic, distrusted all facts and principles. The only safe rule of conduct for human beings is to suspend judgment and restrain all emotions. *Cicero* was something of a professional doubter; yet he entertained a strong conviction about the natural dignity of man. The human soul is of divine origin and is distinguishable from matter. This, however, does not prevent its having a firelike element in its make-up. It is free, by nature, and immortal, as inner consciousness and universal consent demonstrate. *Lucretius*, in his didactic poem *De Rerum Natura*, gives us the first Latin account of the philosophy of Epicureanism. His outlook represents a completely materialistic interpretation of the nature of man, his origin, and the destiny of his soul.

2

An Early Medical Psychologist

Galen, the Greek physician, was also an eclectic in philosophy, but with a strong Aristotelian bias. In him we find a new peak in the culture of ancient medicine. He is interesting to the psychologist because he transformed the crude theory of the four humors into a doctrine of observable symptoms that determine a man's temperament. This theory had been put

forward originally by *Hippocrates* who was the first among the
Greek physicians to connect conscious life with the brain.
Galen worked over the idea of humors and gave it a popular
form. Dependent upon the balance of his internal secretions,
a person is sanguine, phlegmatic, choleric, or melancholic.
The work of Galen was important as a first step toward a
psychology of temperament. In modern times it has been put
on a more scientific footing by the discovery of the endocrine
glands and their relation to human personality.

3
Philo the Jew

Before closing this section, a word must be said about two
great thinkers whose influence was perhaps more theological
than psychological. *Philo* the Jew, who lived in the first
century of the Christian era, attempted to reconcile the religion
of the Old Testament with the philosophy of the Greeks. He
distinguished the ideal man, made to the image and likeness
of God, from the man of our ordinary experience, who exhibits
several different natures. He defended the Pythagorean
doctrine of transmigration and the Platonic teaching in regard
to the soul's preexistence. The spiritual nature of man is not
essentially different from that of the angels. The faculties of
human knowledge are threefold: sense, which has the concrete as its proper object; logos or word, which is the reasoning
power; and nous or intellect, which immediately contemplates
eternal truths. The contemplative efforts of man are the
result of a light that God alone can give. Body is not substantially united with soul. The former is the source of
human evil. The latter is the principle of human good.

4
Plotinus the Mystic

Plotinus was a pagan who attempted a task analogous to that of Philo, namely, to bring the spiritual elements of religion into harmony with the teaching of the older philosophers, and more particularly with the thought of the Platonists. He is acclaimed as the subtlest and most influential scholar of the neo-Platonic school. In psychology, he maintained that man is a compound of matter and an immaterial soul. The soul exists before its union with the body and survives the disintegration of the organism. But it is liable to be sent back into the material universe, incorporated under the form of an animal or plant, dependent on the strength of its attachment to carnal things while on earth. This doctrine of a future retribution implies a freedom on the part of the soul to control its destiny. Plotinus constantly preached the charms of a purely contemplative life. The depth and brilliancy of his writings, and the earnestness of his speech, moved many of his followers to give up their worldly goods in order to devote themselves more whole-heartedly to study, meditation, and ascetic practices.

5
The Great Transition

For those who hold that divine Providence is behind the unfolding of human events, it is easy to see that the great philosophies of the ancients, in which truth was preserved and developed, were preparatory stages for the acceptance of the gospel of Christ. The Church was not founded as a school for philosophizing, much less as the exponent of a particular set of psychological doctrines. Yet, there is a strong and deep-set bond that links the Christian interpretation of human life with the best psychological teaching of the ancients.

The fact is, of course, that much of the speculation which the Greeks had carried on in the name of psychological research was to be interpreted anew in the light of Christian principles. More than this! Revelation gave new insights and fresh developments to what the human mind, unaided by divine light, was able to discover about the intrinsic nature of man. In the systematic growth of her teaching regarding the supernatural character of human life, or the theology of man, the Church was able to avail herself of the truths of pagan philosophy and even to couch her religious beliefs in terms that had already been crystallized by long pagan usage. Such is her divine power of adaptation.

6

In the Year of Our Lord

The coming of Christ marks a new era and a fresh starting point in the story of psychology, just as it divides the story of philosophy and the history of the world. From this time on, there will be the supernatural as well as the natural approach to the study of human nature. Psychology profited enormously by the doctrines of Revelation which enlarged its horizons and added to its content by establishing new contacts with the deposit of faith. Doctrines of the utmost importance, such as the personalistic nature of man, the creation of his soul, the eternity of intellectual life, truths that the greatest minds of antiquity either failed to understand or discerned in shadow rather than in substance, now were to become the commonplace knowledge of all humanity.

The problems of psychology, from this point on, will have a religious as well as a rational aspect. The spirit of faith and the spirit of reason will pervade the whole course of human thinking, though not in equal proportion or equal strength. The first fifteen centuries may be characterized in a broad way as essentially religious in outlook. The last five centuries are preponderantly rational. The first period includes the patristic writers and the schoolmen. The second embraces the great pioneers in scientific investigation as well as the founders of modern philosophy and modern psychology.

CHAPTER 6

AUGUSTINE AND THE FATHERS

I

Pauline Psychology

Some of the letters of *St. Paul* are masterpieces of self-analysis. They are concerned primarily with moral problems; yet, there is an abundance of psychological information in them about our inner experiences, particularly as these experiences relate to the harmonizing of man's primitive instincts with the dictates of his conscience, with the teachings of faith, and with the ideals of a supernatural life. St. Paul was very much interested in the question of human freedom. It is a two-level system, with a reigning will on top and strong animal impulses on the bottom. Because nature has been wounded by sin, conflict is inevitable. Passion refuses to be counseled by reason. The law of the members, which ties us to the things of earth, is locked in battle with the law of the spirit, with the result that the desired good is unaccomplished and the undesired evil is sought after.

St. Paul recognized clearly the fact that human impulses, when denied, continue to exist as motives of conduct. These, in one form or another, appeal to the will. And will has to make the final decision. A unique situation, indeed, and a very difficult one, when carnal appetite is will's solicitor; and will is appetite's controller! As experience teaches, what we covet with the one is usually rejected by the other. Confusion and defeat are the common bread of humanity. Yet it is true of the ancient Pauline psychology as it is true of the modern Freudian doctrine, that the happiness of mankind, in the final analysis, depends on the way that we resolve this conflict, whether by methods of natural control or by the immeasurably more powerful assistance of divine grace.

2

The Genius of Augustine

Augustine was the first of the early Christian psychologists to employ introspection as a systematic way of investigating man's nature. The question of consciousness was one with which he was vitally concerned. This phenomenon is the most certain event in one's experience, because the very act of doubting it indicates its existence. It includes marginal areas of which we are partly aware as well as deeper levels that escape introspective analysis but which, like a hidden and suppurating wound, can exercise a profound influence on our thinking and living.

Augustine went within himself to discover a world of truth and then to return to the world of reality. Descartes, later on, was to make the same journey but without a return to the objective world. Augustine traveled inward to mind as the center of man, where he rejoiced in the vision of truth. It was an idealistic vision, as we know, with Plotinus as his guide. And if he escaped the extremities of his dream of grandeur, it was because St. Paul stood between the pagan Platonism which he courted and the Christian faith which he had embraced. With Christ came true insight into the value of wisdom and love. Any knowledge that does not advance the progress of the soul toward God is useless. Any knowledge which cannot be brought to bear on the supreme duty of loving God with all one's heart and soul is also unprofitable. This is the sort of learning that "puffeth up" because it is not informed by charity.

3
The Nature of the Soul

The soul of man is something substantial and its proper
human power is the ability to think.   It knows it is a thinking
being.   It grasps its own reality.   It fulfills its own life.   It
is immortal because imperishable truth dwells within it.   By
its nature it is living; so that to say that it is mortal is to
utter a contradiction.   Adam's soul came into existence at
the beginning and was afterwards united to his body.   The
souls of his descendants come into existence at the moment
of their union with matter.   Whether they are created or
brought into being by the act of generation is a hard matter
to decide, the difficulty here arising from the doctrine of
original sin.

The problem of capital importance is not so much what
the soul is in itself as what it is in its destiny.   Yet its very
destiny — to rest in God — is our surest clue to its nature
which is one, immaterial, and simple.   It is devoid of quantitative parts.   It has no extension in space even though it is
wholly in the body and wholly in every part of the body.
Indeed, this fact is another proof of its immaterial nature.
For if it were composed of material particles, it could not be
whole and entire, in all parts of the body at the same time.
Yet, it is; for whenever an impression is made on the body,
the soul is aware of it; and it is not part of the soul that per-
ceives the impression, but the whole soul.   The spirit of man
is essentially unique and individual.   The notion of a universal
soul is absurd.

4
The Augustinian Man

The human soul is independent of the body and its sensations.   Yet man is composed of body and soul.   How are

they united? Surely not by a hylomorphic bond, in the Aristotelian sense of the term. Man is what is best and most noble in his nature; and so man is his soul. As for the body, Augustine was much too near Plotinus and much too aware of his own sinfulness to see any intellectual good in the material part of our nature. The point is, not that the soul needs the body, but that the Creator intended their union. The body never acts on the soul. Even in sensation, it is the continuous act of the soul which makes sensation a continuous act.

Sensation is a special state of attending. It is accomplished by the soul, in the body which is animated by it. When the soul senses, it does not receive the affections of the body but simply puts forth its own acts that correspond to these affections. The sensations of the body are disordered, and the soul must learn to transcend them. "Who shall deliver me from the body of this death?" In all this, obviously, Augustine is not seeking a philosophic definition of man but only a deliverance of his moral nature from inquietude so that he may contemplate God in peace.

5

The Doctrine of Recollection

How is sensation, as a continuous process, made possible to the soul? By remembering, by experiencing together stimuli that we do not perceive together. Thus sensible experience is a kind of intellectual experience. To hear things is to judge of their truth; and knowledge is nothing more or less than a conversation between the soul and the things that exist in the world of truth. The real wonders of memory are the realities which do not come through the senses, such as the principles and laws of science, the desire to be happy and to possess truth and the Author of truth. We remember God, not as though we knew Him before and now recall Him, but in the sense that He made us, that in the search to know ourselves we are searching to know the Source of our being. It is not in ourselves but in God that we seek God.

For Augustine, then, man is to be defined in terms of his Maker — a moral rather than a metaphysical aim; just as the knowledges of man, his wisdom which contemplates eternal truth and the sciences that direct his temporal affairs, are to be understood in terms of a moral or religious organization. Hence, the study of man is a study in the ordering of the active and contemplative forms of existence. As the soul is the life of the body, so God is the life of the soul. The soul that is not spiritually happy is dead. Man is a pilgrim whose soul is where his heart is. "Thou has created us for Thyself alone, O God, and our hearts shall not rest until they rest in Thee."

6

Human Freedom

To the extent that things are, they are good; so that physical evil is not a substance but a privation of being. To be good is to be formed and ordered and properly disposed. This is true of all created things; it is true of the will of man. Moral evil is a privation of a good that ought to be present. The mystery of the human will is not its intrinsic freedom. Of that Augustine is assured. Rather, how can will be free and yet so impotent to do good? The situation would seem hopeless, were it not for the fact that God has not left man to lie helpless in his infirmities. Grace is added to nature, to accomplish what nature cannot do. A wheel does not run well in order to become round, but because it is round. So a will does not work and accomplish in order to receive divine help, but because it has received that help.

7

The Practical Man

The disciple of Plato and Plotinus was, first and last, a
moralist and a student of the Christian way of life. If he
considered the problem of truth, it was to enjoy it and to see
in it the guarantee of an everlasting vision. If he talked of
sensation, it was to show how much man's soul needs to turn
away from the things of the flesh if it is to rejoice in the things
of the spirit. If he discussed the nature of man it was not to
define him in an abstract way, but to portray the ideal of a
well-ordered human life. What he drew from Plato and
Plotinus is subordinated to what he learned from Paul.

For Plato and Plotinus, "know thyself" meant: "know that
thou art wholly a spirit" — a spirit which, for Plato, was once
in heaven but now somehow is not there; a spirit which, for
Plotinus, is always in heaven though it is not always aware
of this fact. Such a philosophy of the interior vision produced
in Augustine, not a philosopher, but a Christian mystic,
whose thought has the economy of divine love rather than the
ambitiousness of human understanding.

8

The Doctrine of Illumination

God is the source of all intellectual truth and intellectual
light. The mind of man always needs the light of God, its
sun, in order to understand. This divine illumination, without which the soul could not attain to truth, is not an objective
revelation but a subjective production of forms within the
mind that determine man to know. It is a *lumen sui generis*,
a light which is not God, yet is emitted by God. As the
senses perceive by the light of the cosmic sun, so intellect
understands by the light of the divine countenance. But

illumination, for Augustine, is not merely a question of knowledge; it is also a principle of the soul's very being. For God to illumine the soul is part of the very existence which He communicates to it.

The illumination theory of Augustine exercised a profound influence on the philosophers of the Middle Ages. Aquinas, later on, was to maintain that a supernatural light is unnecessary to our understanding. With the deepest respect for the teaching of Augustine, the Angelic Doctor still insists that the natural intelligibility of an object, the result of the abstractive power of mind, is sufficient for the grasping of the object. Nor does this gainsay the fact that the power of abstraction, with its native light, is a gift of the Creator.

9
The Influence of Augustine

Because he was not a philosopher in the technical sense, Augustine was free of the Platonic errors to which his lesser disciples were later exposed. The Greek world of Plotinus, which was an instrument of love in the hands of the Doctor of Grace, became an intellectual realm for his followers, wherein the spiritual realism of a pagan was confused with the way of life of a Christian soul. Under these circumstances, Greek idealism became a sort of barrier to a Christian heaven at the same time that it appeared to lead most directly to this goal. And so we witness the origin of a neo-Platonic crisis that began when the age of the Fathers was over.

Aquinas settled the major issues involved; but the crisis came to life again in Occam, fighting to rid Christianity of Plato and succeeding only in leaving Christianity without a sound metaphysics; in Descartes, who sought his salvation in mathematics; in Leibnitz, Kant and Bergson, all idealists and Plotinian men who lost themselves in the vision of the sun that shines out of the Platonic heaven. This was one result. But there were other men and other results. Anselm of Canterbury and Bonaventure, for example, were also neo-Platonists in their respective ways. For these scholars, however, mystical wisdom meant something more than human philosophy, even the philosophy of a spiritualized interior vision; and so their knowledge and learning and philosophic habits of thought were subordinated to the higher purposes of Christian love and Christian devotion.

10
The Trend of Patristic Psychology

The Fathers, in general, sought to take whatever psychological doctrines they considered sound in the old pagan systems and to make them part of their own teaching. But even in this early age of Christianity, the rationalizing spirit asserted itself in a tendency on the part of some of the Christian writers to subordinate revealed truth to the teaching of the ancient philosophers. From this tendency certain heresies arose that had a definite bearing on the status of psychology.

The *Gnostics*, for example, were dissatisfied with the explanations which Christian scholars were giving of the nature of man. Their tenets represent a sort of mixture of the philosophies of Philo and Plotinus with certain elements of revealed religion. As a central part of their teaching they held for an irresolvable conflict between matter and spirit. This led inevitably to a wrong idea of man's essence and properties.

Similarly, the *Manicheans* sought to introduce the old Zoroastrian doctrine of the basic antagonism of God to all material creation. With the principle of good, they contrasted an equally powerful principle of evil. In man they distinguished two souls: one that animates the body; the other a soul of light and part of the world-soul which is Christ.

The former is brought into being by the principle of evil; the latter by the principle of good. Human nature, then, is a battlefield on which the powers of darkness and of light are gripped in deadly conflict. Human action depends upon the outcome of this struggle and not upon any faculty of choice which is proper to man.

It was notions such as these that Augustine and the other Christian thinkers of the patristic age had to contend with. But this was not their sole contribution to psychology. The revelation of a trinity of persons in the Godhead brought into focus a problem that the Greeks had failed entirely to develop: the meaning of man as a human person. The critical character of the problem may be discerned in another direction by noting the large number of heresies that arose in regard to the hypostatic union, heresies that sharpened and refined the philosophical discussions of the nature of person, both human and divine. It is significant that in St. John's account of the Incarnation, the emphasis is laid explicitly on the union of the second divine Person with matter: *et Verbum caro factum est.* May we not see here an indirect reference to something that is essential in the nature of man: his body? In taking on a human form, the Word was made flesh. Surely this is no Platonic flight from reality, where a man hates to be a man because he hates to have a body.

The accretions of knowledge that came from the patristic defense of the hypostatic union were brought together by *Boethius* in his classical definition of person as *an individual substance of a rational nature.* But patristic psychology on the whole was fragmentary and lacking in unity, as were most of the philosophic efforts of the Fathers. It belonged to an era when everything except religion was decadent, and when the best thinkers were concerned in trying to provide some kind of an intellectual basis for the revealed teaching of the Church rather than in establishing a system of Christian philosophy.

CHAPTER 7

THE SCHOOLMEN

I

Renewal of Learning

The centuries that elapsed between the death of Augustine and the founding of the Carolingian schools by Charlemagne toward the close of the eighth century were arid in scholarship. It was a question of holding on and preserving, rather than of spreading out and developing anew. At this time, we note great shifts of European populations, following upon the inroads of barbarians from the North and East. There was also the continued painful struggle which the Church had to undergo in order to maintain herself and widen her membership. In the field of psychology we do not find much to record until the time of the Crusades. This was the period that witnessed the birth of scholastic philosophy.

John Scotus Erigena declared that the soul of man creates his body, employing certain incorporeal qualities for this purpose. *Anselm* held that our ideas are formed from things by the abstractive power of intellect. His account of the birth of our ideas is founded on the doctrine of intentional species, a doctrine that was to become later on a crucial aspect of the Thomistic theory of knowledge. The soul is immortal because otherwise it could not love God for all eternity. Freedom of will is exhibited essentially in the power to do good and not in the ability to sin. For *Abelard* the soul of man is spiritual and yet, because it is included in a body, corporeal. He speaks of human liberty in terms of a *liberum arbitrium* or free judgment wherein intellect and will both have a part to play. This was Augustine's mode of approach to the problem.

2

The Meeting of East and West

The position which Jewish and Arabian scholars occupied in the development of scholastic psychology was noteworthy, since it was they who gave the first impulse to the revival of the physical investigations and methods of Aristotle. The work of the Arabians helped to shape the course of Western medicine and physiology and was more significant in its scientific aspects, perhaps, than in its influence on the field of philosophy proper. The Jews of Moorish Spain, on the other hand, enjoyed a greater measure of liberty among the Christians, and philosophical studies found a congenial home in their midst. Jewish scholars aided in Latin translations of both Greek and Arabian texts. In the course of time, second-hand versions were replaced by translations from firsthand sources; so that with the revival of interest in Aristotle, which grew to such large proportions through the efforts of Albert the Great and Thomas Aquinas, it was possible to know from the original texts just what the Stagirite had taught. This had its repercussions in psychology, as elsewhere.

Arabian philosophy flourished both in Asia and in Europe. Among the great psychologists of the Eastern group the most important name is that of *Avicenna*, who held that the human soul is a spiritual substance, devoid of all matter, the receptacle of intelligible species. It is united to the body, not as a substantial form, but as a friendly collaborator. From it flows a wide diversity of powers, among which we may distinguish: (*a*) intellect in potency which is the barest aptitude to know; (*b*) intellect in effect, as endowed with first notions which will enable it to acquire science; (*c*) intellect in habit, that is,

intellect made able and ready to turn toward its intelligible
object; (d) intellect adept which actually contemplates its
intelligible object. All these intellects are simply diverse
tendencies on the part of passive understanding and must be
carefully distinguished from active intellect which is a separated power and unique for all men.

How is the contemplative act brought to perfection? Chiefly
under the impulse of active intellect. Preparation for this
contemplative process is first made in the soul itself. Here
Avicenna speaks at length of the role of the senses, especially
the interior faculties, of which he makes a very acute analysis.
The doctrine of cogitative power, the highest of the interior
senses, is well developed in his writings, and is one of the best
contributions, made by the Arabians, to the content of
medieval psychology.

In the West, the name of highest importance is that of
Averroes who held that the human mind is really separate
from the individual members of the race, an immaterial and
eternal form, endowed with numerical unity. This mind or
intellect is both active and passive. It is strictly impersonal
and objective, a torch which lights up the individual souls of
men, a perfection shared by all humanity, enabling every man
to participate in eternal truth.

How do people think? By the action of the separated
mind on the sense-images of the individual. Here, again, we
may note the skillful analysis which is given to the phenomena
of sense-psychology, so much admired and respected by
Aquinas, even though he did not agree with it in all details.
From the doctrine of a separated intelligence, Averroes was
led to infer to the impersonality of life after death. Everything in man dies except his intelligence, which is not an
individual substance but the mind of humanity, common to all
members of the race.

Avencebrol was the best known of the Jewish philosophers

in Spain. His psychology represented a combination of Aristotle with neo-Platonic teaching. In pure spirits, there is both matter and form. In corporeal substances, there are forms corresponding to the degrees of perfection that each being enjoys. Man, for example, has several such entelechies, since he is a body, a plant, and an animal, as well as a human being. His body is a microcosmic sum of all the excellences of the universe and the place of habitation for his numerous forms which derive from the world soul or cosmic spirit. This latter spirit, together with everything that stems from it, moves toward God who is the absolute and unique Good.

Maimonides also exerted a wide influence over the schoolmen, though his importance in the history of psychology is slight. His analysis of the nature of man was in the Aristotelian tradition. Here, as elsewhere, his chief concern was to show how the philosophy of the Stagirite may be reconciled with the doctrines of the Jewish religion. Maimonides had a most unusual view of the immortality of the human soul. In treating the problem, he cites many passages from the Old Testament and quotes the opinions of the commentators. He then distinguishes between the soul, which is inborn, and intellect, which is acquired. Finally he reaches the startling conclusion that only the souls of the just are immortal. This doctrine became very popular with the Jewish philosophers.

3

The Flowering of the Scholastic Movement

Alexander of Hales was the first schoolman to discuss problems of a psychological nature after the entire works of Aristotle had become known in the West. Although his teaching is Peripatetic in its general trend, it still bears the marks of a strong Augustinian and Platonic bias. While admitting that the soul is the substantial form of the body, Alexander taught that it is itself composed of a spiritual matter. Its cognitive powers are divided into reason, which deals with the external world; intellect, whose object is created spiritual being; and intelligence, which is concerned with first principles. Knowledge of the world above sense is dependent on a divine illumination.

Bonaventure repeated Augustine's division of the faculties of the soul into intellect, memory, and will. The last-named power is more noble in nature than intellect. Yet the study of intellectual functions has, for Bonaventure, a fascination and a place of eminence that one would not expect in Augustinian quarters. His theory of ideogenesis takes a rather odd turn. Possible intellect turns toward the species present in the phantasm, and by this act of conversion receives from agent intellect the power to abstract. Not all our intellectual knowledge is from the senses but only that which deals with the corporeal universe. As for objects above matter, such as the soul and God, our knowledge is achieved without the mediation of the senses. The spirit of man beholds itself immediately, and in this vision, it comes to a cognitive union with God.

How are intellect, will, and memory related to the soul? In answering the question, Bonaventure seems to have sought a position between the old Augustinian theory of a real identity and the new doctrine, which Thomas Aquinas was defending, of a real distinction. The soul and its powers form one and the same substance, within which they represent different essences.

Besides its corporeal form, the human body has a number of other forms which account for the perfection of its life. The highest and noblest of these, the intellectual soul, is itself composed of matter and form. Although he engaged in no polemic with Aquinas on the problem, Bonaventure was opposed to the teaching that there is only one substantial form in man. The rational soul comes to a body already existent by its own form. This secures to the soul a certain independence which, according to Bonaventure, is strengthened by the fact that there are elements of a substantial wholeness — matter and form — in its make-up. Hence, when the time comes for its departure from the body, there is no difficulty in the withdrawal since the relation of body to soul is like that of "Brother Ass to his rider."

4

Forerunners of Modern Science

Roger Bacon is regarded as the precursor of his namesake Francis Bacon. Along with Albert the Great, he shares the honor of being the leading scientific light of the thirteenth century. A true investigator, he advocated an inductive method of research and an objective approach to physical reality. This was the sort of attitude that would despise no man's observations, but would light its torch at every man's candle. Bacon's lack of prudence, however, largely spoiled the benefits that would have otherwise accrued to philosophy from his scientific insights and proposed methods of reform.

The psychology of *Albert the Great* is in the main identical with that of his illustrious pupil Thomas Aquinas. It is as a student of physical nature that Albert displayed the universality of his genius. His researches in botany, zoology, and physiology, among other things, were done in the temper of true scientific investigation. His was not a slavish adherence to Aristotle. In fact, he was quite ready to admit the value of the work done by the Jews and Arabians. He further acknowledged the debt that Christian philosophers owe to Plato and his followers. In psychology, he held that the soul of man is an immaterial principle, the form of the body. Intellect, as a faculty proper to the soul, is not affixed to any organ; yet through the organism it receives the material of thought. It is not intellect, then, but the body with its senses, which becomes fatigued by constant stimulation.

Albert, however, lacked the power of synthesis which was such an outstanding feature of Aquinas's work. Though both men agreed on major issues in psychology, they were not completely one in their views. Their differences arose for the most part from the way in which they approached their subject matter. Albert had a natural bent for looking at things from a physiological standpoint. Thomas was just as naturally inclined to interpret his experiences in psychological terms. One loved the particular and concrete and was analytic in his expression of truth. The other was interested in the general and abstract and tended to be synthetic in his outlook. It remained for Aquinas to weave the diverse elements of his master's knowledge and experience into a compact philosophy of human nature.

CHAPTER 8

THE THOMISTIC SYNTHESIS

I

Sources of Inspiration

Building the truths expressed by preceding thinkers into an organic whole is really as much an advance in philosophy as the introduction of new factors. The synthesis of *Thomas Aquinas* is remarkable on both scores. He not only linked together all the scattered and often fragmentary insights into reality that had been brought to light by the wise men who went before him; he also was able to add to the actual content of philosophic knowledge by his own profound analyses. He was a debtor to the Greeks, Jews, and Arabians. He drew from the patristic lore that had gathered in both the East and the West with the growth of Christianity. He availed himself of the best thoughts of all the schoolmen ahead of him. He was able, moreover, to perfect the method of the schools, by consecrating to the service of truth the dialectical skill which the rationalists so highly praised and which the mystics so roundly condemned.

Aquinas gave the final touches to the problem of universals, proposing a theory which did not neglect the good points of his opponents — a moderate realism founded on the principle that universals are formally in the mind but fundamentally in things. Here was a doctrine that reconciled the extreme positions of the nominalists who declared that universals are only names; of the conceptualists with their theory that universals are only in the mind; and of the ultrarealists who said that universals are really things. Thomas was the first to give Aristotle and his philosophy a real Christian perspective. By a stroke of genius, he was able to turn to the advantage of Christian belief the very metaphysic that the gentiles had used to defeat the purposes of Christianity. With a comprehensiveness of vision which, even in this day of broad world views, seems nothing short of miraculous, he dug deep the foundations for his vast synthetic philosophy. His thinking had a force and a sureness of touch that is hard for the moderns to understand. It detracts neither from those who contributed to his achievement, nor from the originality of Aquinas himself, to say that he crowned the labors of the thinkers who went before him by building his edifice out of the materials which they supplied.

2

Core of the Thomistic Psychology

What Aquinas did for philosophy in general he did for psychology in particular. Here the thing that characterizes his work is the new spirit with which he addressed himself to the task of analyzing the nature of man in the light of Aristotle's hylomorphic doctrine. His sense of completeness demanded that he leave nothing imperfect or unfinished; and to this end he bent all the energies of his huge body, all the inventiveness of his highly gifted mind. In his psychology we can discover Platonic elements as well as the substantial features that were Aristotelian. With a like sense of impartiality, he sought to discover the possible uses of the Augustinian doctrines that were common in his day. Nor did he disdain to consult the Jewish and Arabian commentators for the solution of his problems. He worked on the principle that all knowledge and all truth, whatever its source, is capable of harmonious adjustment.

For Aquinas, the question of capital importance in psychology is the relation of soul to body. It is of far more importance for Aquinas, in fact, than for Aristotle. By this I mean to say that the solution of the major issues of psychology, in Aquinas's day, demanded that the body-soul problem be given first place. Aristotle had merely declared that the true solution was so obvious as to make clarification superfluous, beyond a mere statement of the fact of the substantial union of these two basic principles of human nature. Not so Aquinas! He insists on a demonstration; and his emphasis on the necessity of proving this central assumption in the Aristotelian psychology, shows, I should say, that he was much closer to the temper of modern psychology and more appreciative of its needs than was Aristotle himself. The question here, to be sure, is merely one of focus.

3

The True Nature of Man

Soul and body, or, more properly, soul and a material substrate are the coprinciples of the substantial unit which is man. They are joined together precisely as form and matter, in the hylomorphic meaning of these terms. Complete substantial nature, then, belongs neither to soul alone nor to body alone, but only to the synolon or compound which is made out of both. Man is first a substance or being; then, a substance with a nature that, by virtue of its possession of a wide range of faculties — vegetative, sensitive, and rational — is able to act. The entitative nature is presupposed to the operational nature. Because he has a rational soul, man is an intelligent creature. Since this rational soul is a substantial form, and the only substantial form in his make-up, man is at once a human, an animal, a plant, a corporeal substance, a being. By taking the first and last elements of this analysis, we can shorten our description of him by saying simply that he is a human being.

The truth of the substantial union between man's soul and body is demonstrable from several points of view: (a) the very notion of soul as substantial form and the ultimate principle of vegetative, sensitive, and rational life means that there is an essential relation between soul and body, both of which, in one way or another, are required for all man's vital functions; (b) the ultimate reference of every act that man performs, his sleeping and walking, his eating and drinking, his sensing and feeling, his thinking and willing, to a single supposit which is his ego, clearly establishes the same truth of a hylomorphic union; (c) the physiological as well as the psychological nature of such unified phenomena as sensations and emotions points to the same conclusion; (d) the fact of the mutual influx of higher and lower species of operations; for example, the restraint which mind can put on bodily activities and the impediments that passion can lay in the path of reason, are also indications of the uniquely substantial character of the body-soul union; (e) the fear of sickness and injury and the natural abhorrence of death are inexplicable except on the premise that there is the most intimate relationship between mind and matter in man.

Just as the body of man requires the soul in order to be a human body, so the soul requires the body in order to have its natural perfection. Only by being and working together can body and soul achieve the goals of human activity. It is true that the soul is superior to the matter with which it is united, that in its highest functions, which are thinking and willing, it is intrinsically independent of bodily organs, and, further, that it is capable of surviving the disintegration of the body. Nevertheless, it is also true that there is no operation of the soul, however abstract and remote from matter, in which the body does not have a share. So much so that after its separation from the body, the soul is, as it were, in an unnatural state and will remain thus till its reunion with matter in the general resurrection.

4
What Is the Soul?

A thing is properly said to live when it contains within itself the principle of its movement or operation. Now the ultimate source of vital phenomena is the soul. This is the case with every species of organism: plant, animal, and man. Although we may refer to the heart, brain, sense organs, and so forth, as principles of vital functions, they are only proximate sources of life. That by which we ultimately move and have our being is the soul. There is an essential contrast, therefore, between the soul, as substantial form, and the body, as the material substrate of life.

The soul is the very life of the body. If things were otherwise, then we should have to say that bodies, qua bodies, are capable of life; and there would be no reason why all matter should not be living matter. Aristotle established this fundamental distinction between soul and body when he defined the soul as the first actuality or the first perfection of physically organized matter which is potentially alive; that is to say, which is not determined, as yet, to be living matter. Analyzing these two principles in relation to each other, we find that soul is the perfectant, since it confers life; and that matter is the perfectible, since it receives life.

5
The Ladder of Life

Since life is the power of self-movement, living things may be ranged in a scale of excellence which corresponds with the ascendant gradients of self-movement. The criterion, here, is the degree of immanence, that is, the degree of remotion from material conditions of operation. Lowest on the scale is plant life which is wholly circumscribed by matter. Next is animal life, in which there is partial remotion from matter. Finally, we find human life in which, so far as its intellectual functions are concerned, there is complete remotion from matter. Life, accordingly, may be described as an effort to overcome the essential inertia of matter. It is triumphant precisely to the extent that it is able to beat down and overcome this all-pervading inertia.

The grades of life are actually exhibited in the powers or properties that living matter displays in operation. Plant life is concerned with metabolic and reproductive functions; and the properties by which it accomplishes its purposes are three: nutritive, augmentative, and generative. Animal life has further interests. It is able to know and desire and move about; and the powers here involved are the senses, the appetites, and the locomotive faculty. Finally, human life, which is the top rung on the ladder of cosmic perfection, adds to the foregoing vegetative and sensitive properties, the further powers of intellectual cognition, and intellectual appetition.

6

How Our Knowledge Arises

In its general features, knowledge is a vital process in which subject and object are united in an intentional way. Metaphorically, it is an act of assimilation. Really, it is an act of information. Aristotle, we remember, likened the process to the impression of a seal on wax. The object of knowledge may be twofold: something composed of matter and form; or something which is pure form. In both instances, it is the form that makes the object to be what it is. Knowledge is a vital act wherein form impresses itself on the cognitive agent, producing an intentional species which, dependent on the nature of the subject that receives it, is either sensible or intelligible. In either case, note that it is an intentional form and not the natural form, which accomplishes the union of subject and object. The intimacy of the union determines the perfection or excellence of the knowledge. In sense cognition, the intentional form is received into a material faculty. It is still concrete and individual in character, since it is only partially removed from matter. In intellectual cognition, the intentional form is received into an immaterial faculty. It is abstract and universal in character, since it is completely removed from matter.

Sense knowledge is always concerned with the sensible qualities or accidental features of corporeal substance. Its objects may be grouped in three ways: (a) proper sensibles, such as the colors, sounds, odors, flavors, and tangible qualities of bodies; (b) common sensibles, such as the extension, shape, distance, size, movement, and temporal aspects of stimuli; (c) incidental sensibles which fall under sense cognition by accident, that is to say, in the course of their being sensed directly. For instance, a white object, which is sensed directly as white, is sensed indirectly as the son of Diares; in which case, the son of Diares is an incidental sensible.

7

What the Senses Know

Just as first matter is pure potency in the physical order, so the faculty of understanding is pure potency in the intellectual order. There is this difference, however: that first matter is passive potency to be; whereas, the power of understanding is active potency to learn. Intellect already possesses the seeds, as it were, of the first principles of knowledge. But at the beginning it is completely devoid of ideas; and there is nothing in it that was not previously in the senses. The cognitions of sense, therefore, are of prime importance in the growth of our intellectual life.

Sensation is an act by which the sensible object produces a modification in the sensitive power. The senses are essentially passive, which means that they have to be activated by a stimulus. But they are not merely passive, since they react, in a vital manner, to the impinging of objects. Sensation, in a general way, describes the operation of every sensitive power. But particularly, it is employed to indicate the operation of the exterior senses. It has two aspects, as we have indicated; first, the aspect of sufferance or passion which refers to its reception of the sensible species impressed by the object; second, the aspect of response or operation, which refers to the act that follows upon its being perfected by the sensible species.

What is the nature of the sufferance wrought in the sense organ by the object? It is a change which is neither wholly material nor wholly immaterial. It is not wholly material since it consists in the impression of an intentional form, that is, a form which has been separated from matter. It is not wholly immaterial, because the sensible species, impressed on the organ of sense, is received into a material power and is limited by the contingencies of matter. The sensible species, accordingly, is not a substantial entity but a living movement. Knowledge is vital and, to the extent of its remotion from matter, immanent. The action of the object, as it is brought to bear on the sense, and the action of the sense, as it responds to the impression of the object, are really one and the same action. In short: the sensible in act is identical with the sense in act.

The sensible species is the determinant of sensitive knowledge. It actuates the sense to apprehend its proper object. It is not the object in miniature. Neither is it something that we first know and then, by means of it, know the object. It is simply the living medium of communication between object and subject, functioning in a vicarious capacity for the object, and enabling the knowing subject to unite itself, intentionally, with the object known. It is called an "eidos" or a "species" because by means of it, the object is present somehow to the subject. Although there is no expression without impression, note that, in the case of the exterior senses and common sense, there is impression without expression. By this Aquinas means that for the presentative senses, the action of the stimulus and the formation of the impressed sensible species suffice for knowledge, since the object is actually present to the organs of sense. But in the case of the re-presentative senses — imagination, memory, and estimate or cogitative power — there is also the formation of expressed sensible species. These latter are called "phantasms." From them intellect derives its ideas.

It is obvious, then, that in the Thomistic economy of knowledge, the senses are highly diversified. Thus: (a) to apprehend sensible objects actually present, there are the five exterior senses and common sense which is the root and principle of all sense perception; (b) to apprehend sensible objects in their absence, there is imagination; (c) to apprehend them as past, there is memory; (d) to apprehend the biological significance or the instinctive value of sensible objects, there is estimate or cogitative power. The unique function of the re-presentative senses is to prepare that highly synthesized sensory datum which Aquinas, after Aristotle, calls the "phantasm" — bringing the product of sensitive cognition to the very doors of intellect.

8
The Birth of Our Ideas

Now let us see how we rise from the knowledge supplied by the senses to intellectual cognition. The problem here is the derivation of the universal from the particular, of the abstract from the concrete, of the immaterial from the material. In setting the stage for the solution, Aquinas recalls the Aristotelian distinction between the power that "makes all things" intelligible and the power that "is made all things" intelligible. The former is agent intellect; the latter, possible intellect. They are distinct faculties. The object, as it presents itself to the senses and is pictured in the phantasm, is indeed a concrete and contingent thing. But beneath its cloak of accidents which confine it within the limits of the here and now, lies its unalterable essence which is universal and necessary. Agent intellect at once proceeds to separate what is concrete and contingent from what is universal and necessary in the object, causing the nude nature to stand forth stripped of all the appendages of sense. This it does by the abstractive force of its light which now transforms what was only potentially intelligible in the phantasm into something that is actually intelligible.

Thus the impressed intelligible species comes into existence and plays its part by actuating possible intellect to form an expressed intelligible species which is the mental image of the object. The idea so conceived in the bosom of possible intellect has a twofold aspect. Entitatively considered, it is an accident of the mind; eidetically considered, it is a picture or image which functions as a medium by which subject and object are intentionally united in the moment of understanding. And so, what intellect first apprehends is the thing. To hold otherwise, to make the idea that which is first known or even that in which we know, would be to throw open the door to subjectivism and all the idealistic errors that follow in its wake.

To generate the idea, however, is not to grasp the perfect truth of reality. For perfect truth is found only in the act of judgment. It is possible to speak of truth, in an embryonic or partially formed way, as existing in the senses and in the simple apprehensions of the intellect. But this sort of knowledge is a mere preparation for the perfect enunciation of truth achieved when we judge and reason about things. We are speaking now of the natural order of knowledge and development. The movement toward truth is due to an innate impulsion, on the part of intellect, to react to the light of intrinsic evidence. By such a procedure we come to grasp the meaning of first principles and of the conclusions that form the pith and core of our scientific and philosophic knowledges.

9

The Order of Human Knowledge

The first notion that enters into man's mind is that of being. To be sure, it is not a clear-cut idea, such as the metaphysician's notion of being. Perhaps we might say that it is rather the idea of *something* than the idea of *being*. It is only after a long education in the use of ideas, and by reflection on its own acts, that intellect arrives at a knowledge of itself. We start with the most immediate and tangible aspect of reality, the world of sense; and from the information thus gained we form our first vague and indefinite idea of being. Since this is the natural order of events, it is manifest that God is not the first thing we know, as some have declared.

Our primitive notion of being is simply an abstraction from sensitive experience, existing, as such, only in the mind. God, on the other hand, is the first and greatest of objective realities. When we say that we see all and judge all in God, the meaning is that we apprehend everything in the light of the understanding which He has conferred upon us. Just as in corporeal vision it is unnecessary that we see the substance of the sun, so in intellectual vision there is no need to say that we see the substance of God.

10

The Life of Desire and Action

All of man's desires are somehow connected with apprehended goods and evils. In common with the animal he has sensitive appetites. These give birth to passions of two sorts: (a) concupiscible, concerned with material goods to be possessed (love, desire, and joy) and material evils to be avoided (hatred, aversion, and sorrow); (b) irascible, occupied with difficult material goods (hope and despair) and difficult material evils (courage, cowardice, and anger). What the modern psychologist calls "feelings" and "emotions" are species of appetitive movement, arising from biological needs.

In the broad meaning of the term, passion is a change. Strictly speaking, it is a change from a more perfect to a less perfect state of being. Hence, such passions as hatred, disgust, and sorrow, where evil is involved, are more truly passions than love, desire, and joy, where the movement is toward a good. To be sure, the soul has no contrary states, since it is immaterial in nature. Yet it may be said to pass from a greater to a lesser state of perfection — for example, from love to hatred — by reason of its intimate union with the body.

Every passion involves corporeal change. Like man himself, who is the subject of the passion and who is a creature made of matter and form, passion may be said to have a material and a formal element in its structure. It is at once a physiological and a psychological phenomenon. The somatic factor represents the material aspect of the passion;

the psychic factor, its formal aspect. Both are requisite in the production of the appetitive movement. We may speak of the passions of the will, but this is only by a figure of speech, since such movements do not contain any material element in their essence.

Immediately connected with the sensitive appetites and serving their commands is the locomotor faculty with which man and beast alike are endowed. Out of passion action is born. Outer behavior exhibits a definite mold and involves all the animal powers, in one way or another. The knowledge of danger, for instance, generates fear; and fear, in turn, leads to flight. The cognitive power makes known the situation; the sensitive appetite gives the orders; and the locomotor faculty executes the outer movement. The animal has no choice but to give blind obedience to the demands of its sensuous appetites. Man, too, is largely guided by the current of his feelings and emotions. But his muscles, nerves, and sinews receive a rational stamp which is impossible to the animal. Hands, feet, and tongue, in man, can be made to provide a basis for skills that are completely out of the brute's range of accomplishments.

Will has for its object the good that is apprehended by reason. The immediate goal of all appetitive movement is good. Evil enters in only indirectly, either as something that is falsely judged to be good or as something that stands in the road to the enjoyment of a good. Thus, good is the object of appetite in the same way as truth is the object of intellect. Knowledge precedes the acts of the appetites and determines their nature by serving as a motive of conduct. The good of will is twofold: general, which exhausts the intellectual concept of good; and particular, which is good only in a limited way. As intellect cannot refuse its assent to first principles, so will cannot but desire the general good when it is present. Choice is possible only in respect to particular goods; just as a diversity of opinions is possible only in respect to conclusions from first principles.

When intellect presents a particular good to will, it does so in a manner that leaves will at liberty to choose or reject it as something which does not completely fulfill the notion of good. The roots of freedom, therefore, are in our intellectual apprehensions. The *liberum arbitrium* is as much a matter of intellect as of will. After a comparison of the two powers, Aquinas decides that, absolutely speaking, intellect is superior to will. However, in view of the fact that the object of will, under certain circumstances, is more perfect than the object of intellect, the former power may be relatively superior to the latter. From this point of view, will in loving God is more excellent than intellect in knowing corporeal things.

II

How We Perfect Our Powers

The numerous abilities of man, and more particularly his intellectual powers, are like seeds that must be brought to flower and fruition by use. Exercise is the pathway that leads to perfection; and when properly employed, results in the easy, graceful, and pleasurable functioning of the faculties. Such, of course, is habit, which according to the Thomistic teaching is rightfully an excellence of reason and will. If the lower powers of man are also habituated, if they become accustomed to act in certain ways, this is because of their subjection to the influences of rational insight and volitional control. Habit is a developed faculty. It is a mean between the power to operate and actual operation.

In the strict sense of the term, a habit is always operational in character. What is called "entitative habit" is nothing more than a disposition affecting the substance of a thing — for example, beauty or health of body — rather than its powers or faculties. Every habit may be strengthened or weakened in two ways: (a) by its own acts; (b) by the acts of other habits. The only habit that cannot deteriorate is that of first principles. From the psychological point of view, a habit is good or bad insofar as it is convenient or nonconvenient to the nature of man. From the moral point of view, a habit is good or bad to the extent that it leads man to or away from his last end.

12
The Person of Man

To say that man is a person is to place him at the peak of the scale of cosmic perfection. He is the most excellent of all corporeal creatures. The reason of this excellence lies in his possession of an intellect that can penetrate into the meaning of things and a will that can direct all his actions toward a goal of human happiness. Man, so to speak, can take himself in hand. No other creature can do this. He is the master of his own destiny. He can weave his habits into a pattern with eternal designs. As a person he is a substance, an autonomous being, undivided in himself, yet divided from every other creature: an individual, a thinker, a doer.

As a person man is a complete substance, able to stand on his own, subsisting in and by himself, separate from the rest of creation, responsible for his own conduct; an entity incommunicable and incapable of being assumed by another being; a supposit belonging to the order of reason and liberty and spirit, with a bill of rights in his soul and a declaration of independence on his lips. No other creature in the visible universe can claim such distinctions.

13
The Spirit of Man

The soul of man is immaterial. From this fact we also infer to its essential simplicity, since it can have neither entitative nor quantitative parts. As a substantial form, it is present in the whole body and in every part of the body. The exterior senses are obviously operative in the material organs that nature has designed for their special functions. The soul's visual power, for example, is not mediated by the ear. All the faculties of man are in his soul, as in their principle; but only intellect and will are in his soul, as in their proper subject. To show, then, that the soul is inextended and immaterial, it is sufficient to demonstrate the incorporeal nature of man's intellect. This is done by appeal to certain indisputable facts: (*a*) intellect can know all bodies and therefore cannot itself be a body; (*b*) intellect can reflect on itself and so cannot be extended; (*c*) intellect can think of universal and incorruptible things.

The immaterial nature of intellect, however, does not prevent its being dependent for its objects on the data of sense. The phenomenon of mental fatigue is accounted for by this dependence on powers that have their definite saturation points. The essential corelationship between intellect and sense, so stoutly maintained by Aquinas, is a crucial point in his psychology, for three reasons: first, it denies the idealistic doctrine that intellect is not even objectively influenced by the administrations of sense; second, it denies the materialistic doctrine that intellect is subjectively determined by the character of organic processes; third, it gives full scope and meaning to the empirical analysis of conscious phenomena by holding for an essential connection between mind and matter.

If the soul of man is immaterial, it is also immortal. Aquinas argues as follows. A compound can be corrupted by the separation of its matter and form. A form, on the other hand, can be corrupted only if it is dependent on matter for its existence. Reflect on the human soul. It is neither directly corruptible, like the compound; nor indirectly corruptible, like those forms that are dependent on matter for their being. Moreover, the soul of man is perfected by intellectual knowledge and moral virtue. Now, intellectual knowledge and moral virtue are conditioned by a certain degree of separation from matter. Every idea we acquire and every good moral act we perform lifts us above the material and instinctive levels of life and empties our souls of the accretions of sense. Indeed, all our thinking and willing gives evidence of an absolute truth and an absolute good toward which we are working and which we can properly enjoy only by an eternity of knowledge and love.

From its immaterial nature, we conclude that the soul is created. It cannot be evolved out of the potencies of matter. Neither can it be produced by the division of another soul. Nor is it an emanation from the divine substance. Hence, it must be brought into being out of nothingness. Since it is naturally destined for union with matter, it does not antedate its union with the body, as the Platonists held. In the next life, reunion with matter will be a demand of its nature.

14

Appeal to Experience

It is obvious, from the foregoing study of Aquinas, that his psychology is based squarely on experience in all its initial data. The central doctrine of the substantial union of spirit and matter in man is inferred from several facts of observation, facts that can be verified in the daily lives of all men. The biological unity of human activities, from the lowliest types of vegetation to the highest achievements of reason, is also proof of the essential oneness of man's form. Further, from analysis of what goes on in human consciousness, it is possible to arrive at a knowledge of the true nature of our ideas. Then, from the universal and necessary character of our ideas, we can conclude to the immaterial nature of intellect and its proper subject, the human soul. This, in turn, leads us to the conclusion of the soul's immortality, as the goal of its existence; and of its entrance into being at the hand of the Creator. Here is empirical psychology in the best and only correct sense of the word, a psychology which conforms strictly to the formula that the operations of a thing furnish a legitimate clue to its nature. It is by such a principle that all generalizations, whether in the scientific or the philosophic dimension, are inductively established.

15

Philosophy Separated from Revelation

We cannot close this chapter without citing again the significant contribution which Aquinas made to human knowledge when he determined the true relation between faith and reason. In a sense, this was a problem for the psychologist, since it involved a correct appraisal of the thinking faculty and its ability to solve the great questions of life and being, nature and supernature. To concede too much to human reason would be to fall into the arms of the rationalists. To concede too little would be a surrender to the claims of the false mystics. The work of Thomas was accomplished not so much by inventing something new as by assimilating and transforming what had already been discovered.

Some truths belong to faith alone, for example, the mystery of the Trinity. Other truths belong to reason alone, for instance, the fact that man is essentially distinct from the animal. Still other truths belong to both faith and reason, such as the existence of God. But faith views truth in the light of divine Revelation, whereas reason views it in the light of intrinsic evidence. Thus while it is a fact that theology and philosophy are distinct forms of knowledge, it is also true that they are, objectively, in complete agreement with each other. The author of the revealed mysteries of faith is also the author of the first principles of natural knowledge.

Moreover, faith strengthens and supplements reason, widening its horizons at the same time that it shows the limits of human thought, beginning, as it were, where reason leaves off. Reason, on the other hand, aids faith, furnishing motives for credibility, supplying analogies for the expression of truths in the supernatural order, solving objections that unbelievers urge against the deposit of Revelation. All this teaching had existed in solution from the earliest days of Christianity. Aquinas crystallized it and gave it a form that was to be final. Aristotle, once and for all, distinguished philosophy from superstition at the same time that he showed the basic continuity of every man's experience with the reflective observations of the metaphysician. In an analogous way, Aquinas distinguished human from divine wisdom at the same time that he showed the basic continuity of philosophic and theological experience in the total content of man's knowledge.

CHAPTER 9

THE DECLINE OF MEDIEVAL WISDOM

I

At Loggerheads with Aquinas

The Angelic Doctor was the first to give a complete account of Aristotle from a Christian point of view. As we explained in our last chapter, he fixed for all time the true relation that must exist between reason and Revelation. In point of detail, he contributed the doctrines that eventually came to distinguish the Thomist psychologists from the non-Thomists or better, from the anti-Thomists. These were, chiefly: the stout defense of the oneness of the substantial form in every individual; the doctrine of subsistent forms, that is to say, forms that have no matter in their essence; the doctrine of the individuation of informing forms by matter; the affirming of a real distinction between the soul and its faculties; the denial of innate ideas, and the assertion that all human knowledge, precisely as human, begins with the cognitions of sense; the defense of the essential superiority of intellect over all other human faculties.

Following closely on Aquinas and generally considered as the most gifted opponent of the Thomistic theses was *Duns Scotus* who taught that the substantial form of man is not essentially one; and that the principle of individuation is neither matter nor form nor quantity but a "thisness" or individual property added to human nature. The psychology of Scotus is voluntaristic in its outlook. In contradiction to Aquinas, he taught that will is superior to intellect. He also maintained that the immortality of the human soul cannot be proved by reason; and here again his position is in contrast to that of St. Thomas. Scotus further claimed that the essence of final beatitude consists in the love, not the vision, of God; and that the natural law depends on the divine will and not on the divine intellect. On all these points, his teaching was at loggerheads with the Angelic Doctor. In justice to both men, however, it should be said that their differences arose not so much from "the wish on the part of Brother John to gainsay everything that Brother Thomas had taught" as from a basic opponency in the temperaments and outlooks of the two scholars.

2

A Little Learning

Durandus, born toward the end of the thirteenth century, was an independent thinker who sought to simplify the Thomistic psychology but who accomplished his aims at the expense of thoroughness. His shallowness is so marked that he obviously had no real acquaintance with the doctrines which he criticized. Thus he contended that the theory of "species" was first introduced into psychology to explain sense perception and that it was later illegitimately made to account for intellectual knowledge. In the end he rejected all notion of intentional forms, failing to realize that in the teaching of Aquinas the species or cognitional determinant is simply a medium of union and communication by which the object of knowledge becomes present to the subject of knowledge. A similar misunderstanding obtains among many of our present-day writers who regard the theory of species as untenable, but for reasons that were never entertained by St. Thomas.

Durandus also abandoned the agent intellect of the Thomists as a superfluous faculty, on the ground that there is no more need of an active reason than of an active sense. Here again he simply failed to grasp the Thomistic doctrine. As Aquinas clearly taught, while the object of sense is actually sensible, the object of intellect, which is the universal nature of things, exists under material conditions of which it must be divested before it can become actually understandable. The task of abstracting the nude nature from these conditions of contingency is the function of agent intellect.

3
The Psychology of Occam

Occam, too, denied the need of intentional species in the cognitive process, contending that knowledge takes place by the immediate and intuitive contact of subject with object. In ridding his psychology of the distinction between agent and possible intellects, he declared that causes are not to be multiplied without need. This is the well-known principle of parsimony, more commonly called "Occam's razor." It means that one must be as economic as possible in giving the reasons of things. Occam also distinguished between a rational and a sensitive soul in man. While the former is immaterial, the latter is extended and corruptible. Only the sensitive soul is immediately united to the body. With regard to the rational soul, neither reason nor experience can prove either that it is the substantial form of the body or that it is spiritual and immortal. On the last-named point, Aristotle's authority cannot be invoked because the Stagirite himself does not appear to be sure; hence we are obliged to accept the soul's immortality on faith.

By implication, Occam was a skeptic in his outlook on reality. The trend of his thought pointed the way to the revival of the pagan humanism of the Quatrocento. His attempt to simplify the traditional teaching was a praise-

worthy thing, meant to offset the ultrarealistic tendencies of
the Scotists; but it fell short of the mark when it degenerated
into an extreme form of conceptualism if not an out-and-out
terminism. The errors that it brought in its wake were
greater than the evils it tried to remedy. Occam's philosophy
was alive with the ghosts of the neo-Platonists. His followers
neglected the serious study of the masters of the schools, and
thereby contributed to the ignorance of the genuine tradition
which, during the fourteenth-century Renaissance and the
transition to modern philosophy, made it impossible for the
adherents of the old wisdom and the advocates of the new
science to reach an alliance. These observations are true for
psychological knowledge as well as for the other parts of the
philosophy of nature, though to lesser degree in the former
case since science developed along cosmological lines at first.

4
The Fruits of Misunderstanding

When the Renaissance finally came, the antagonism between the philosophers and the scientists had taken on the
aspect of an open warfare. This was due in no small measure
to the inability of the latter to distinguish between the methods
of the earlier schoolmen, like Albert the Great, and the practices of the degenerate scholastics who had fallen into the
habit of testing all philosophic truth by appeal to the authority
of a master. What Aquinas and the great Thomists had done
was to establish the independent value of philosophy, by appeal
to reason, and of theology, by appeal to authority; and to
show that the two forms of human knowledge, when genuine,
can never contradict each other. In this manner they established between the natural and the supernatural principles of
knowledge the same sort of relation which Aristotle had set
up between matter and spirit, namely, an order of distinction

without opposition. The period extending from the middle of the fifteenth century to the beginning of the seventeenth was one of intellectual ferment in which the philosophy of the schools gradually disappeared, modern experimental science laid its foundations, and the influence of the religious reformations in Germany, England, and elsewhere began to be felt.

If, with all these changes, a development of the tradition did not follow, if the philosophy of the golden age of the tradition was unable to adapt itself to the changing mode of existence, the fault lay, not in the traditional wisdom itself, whose intrinsic principles were surely capable of such progressive movement, but in the men who represented the philosophy of the schools at this crucial period, men who failed to put the ancient and medieval wisdom in its true light when it most demanded such an intelligent exposition. Scholars who could have spent their time and talents on more serious things now busied themselves with foolish trifles, abusing the syllogism and fighting out their debates in a tongue that made some observers wonder if it was the language of the Romans they were using, or a dialect of barbaric origin.

It was an age when too much importance was attached to unimportant things. Logic chopping and quibbling were the fashion in academic circles. Problems were created that had no relevance to practical life; and good abilities were often shunted into channels that ran far afield of the demands of the new science and its followers. The attitude which many of the Christian philosophers of the sixteenth century assumed toward the discoveries of Galileo and Kepler is well known. The antagonisms of the old to the new were the fruit of profound misunderstandings. There is no inherent contradiction between the broad principles of the Aristotelian and Thomistic cosmology or psychology, on the one hand, and the authentic discoveries of the new physics or the new psychology on the other. Aristotle advocated the investigation of nature; and

THE FRUITS OF MISUNDERSTANDING

Albert the Great, Thomas Aquinas, and all the best minds of the tradition similarly insisted on the necessity of building our knowledge of man and the cosmos on the sound basis of empirical observation. The schoolmen who attacked the genuine investigators of scientific reality were therefore false to the principles of their philosophy.

Had the scholastics of the sixteenth century fully grasped the spirit of Aristotle and Aquinas, they surely would have put an end to their fruitless discussions, shaken off the false methodologies with which they were encumbered, and gone forth shoulder to shoulder with the students of the new physics to investigate nature together. Instead, they antagonized the scientists and produced a condition that made the deepening of the true philosophic spirit impossible. Men who were sympathetic with inductive research and who wished to arrive at some settled philosophic position in regard to their new discoveries could not be blamed if they failed to see that in the principles of the Aristotelian wisdom they had the one ultimate analysis of nature that best accorded with the growing sciences.

CHAPTER 10

THE DEVELOPMENT OF MODERN PHILOSOPHY

I

A Turning Point

Towards the middle of the seventeenth century, *René Descartes* offered the world its first systematic expression of modern philosophy. His ideas have dominated the course of men's thinking ever since. In the field of psychology he is important, not for what he did, but for what he undid, as we shall show in a moment. Voltaire once remaked that Descartes was born to discover the mistakes of the ancients and to replace them with his own. Humor here has encompassed a profound truth.

After Descartes came such men as Spinoza, Leibnitz, Locke, Berkeley, and Hume, all of whom, in one way or another, shaped the destinies of modern psychological thinking. During this period, empiricism and a sceptical outlook characterized the non-Catholic philosophers. It was a time when intellectual activity within the Church was confined more or less to the domain of theology; and battles that involved some of the most vital principles of religion were fought outside the Church in the field of a highly secularized philosophy which was no longer the handmaid of revealed truth. And so it came about that one of the great ideals for which Aquinas had so valiantly struggled was lost, when philosophy sank to a position of being no man's helper — neither the theologian's with his doctrinal problems nor the scientist's with his vision of new worlds to be conquered.

2

The Cartesian Philosophy of Human Nature

In its general features, Descartes' psychology may be summed up as a doctrine of two substances: mind and matter, the world of extension and the world of inextension, dwelling side by side yet independent of each other, holding no commerce with each other, unable to influence each other. The essence of mind is to think. The essence of matter is to occupy space. Mind and matter, then, are at opposite poles of reality. They have nothing in common. Their union in man is a purely accidental affair. The human body is a machine, built in such a way that it can be extrinsically propelled into motion by the soul.

The Cartesian "mind," it should be noted at once, is narrower than the Thomistic "soul" and wider than the Thomistic "intellect." The shades of meaning here implied are very important. Thus Descartes uses the word "mind" in its operational sense when he makes it synonymous with "thinking substance"; whereas Aquinas employs it in its entitative sense when he makes it the equivalent of "rational soul." The difference, of course, is the difference between a principle of action and a principle of being. On the other hand, Descartes extends his notion of "mind" to include certain sensitive acts that are common to man and animal; whereas Aquinas confines its operational meaning to phenomena of a strictly human or rational nature, such as thinking and willing. At this point in its history, psychology may be said to have lost its soul and gained a mind. At a later stage in our story, it will lose its mind too when consciousness, which is supposed by the Cartesians to be the very pith and core of mind, is thrown into the discard as an unscientific relic of the past.

In accounting for man's purely organic functions, including the physiology of his senses, Descartes made appeal to his famous theory of animal spirits. These are described as principles of body heat and body movement. In brutes, there is no awareness of pleasurable or painful stimuli but only a mechanical reaction to the objects of their environment. Man's ideas are either (a) occasioned by sensations, making their appearance in mind by a kind of opportunism which enables us to capitalize on external events; or (b) the result of volitional combinations of elements of thought and therefore built up by the mind itself. Besides these two classes, there are also innate dispositions to develop certain ideas.

Will is superior to intellect because it is unlimited. Its freedom is revealed by our direct and immediate consciousness of the power to perform or omit certain actions. It is the source of error when it commands assent to what we do not understand. Man's passions, like his cognitive states of consciousness, are forms of thinking. They are not, therefore, bodily states, even though the body is the occasion of emotional phenomena. When an impression, calculated to arouse the passions, is conveyed to the brain, the animal spirits are set in motion; and the thought of this movement is the emotion. Here we see the suggestion of an ideomotor theory that was to find favor with later scientific investigators. Because it is a form of thinking, emotion is impossible to the brute. The primitive passions of man are admiration or wonder, love, hatred, desire, joy, and sorrow.

3
The Beginning of Chaos

Unfortunately for the later history of psychology Descartes did not found his doctrines on experience. A generation before him, *Francis Bacon* had sought to reform the sciences by the introduction of the inductive method in lieu of the syllogistic process. Descartes would secure the same reforms by the use of mathematical, in place of inductive, techniques. His whole approach to the study of man is vitiated by his theory of an absolute antithesis of mind and matter. He created a chasm between subject and object which made null and void all that Aristotle, Aquinas, and the great school-men had done to explain the nature of man and his knowledge. How to bridge this imaginary chasm is a problem that all psychologists, outside the tradition, have sought in vain to solve since the days of Descartes.

Failure to understand the relationship between mind and matter or between body and soul, is really a failure to grasp the purposes of philosophic inquiry. Thus for Descartes, psychology was reduced to a study of individual consciousness, or to a series of mathematical deductions from internal experi-ence. The objective study of man was abandoned, with nothing to take its place except a pale and often imaginary analysis of states of awareness. Like Augustine, Descartes went within himself to discover the world of truth. Unlike Augustine, he was caught in his own subjectivism. He meant to return to the world of reality, he tried to extricate himself, but he never actually succeeded.

The inversion of the natural approach to psychology was the cause, among other things, of the heavy impregnation with idealistic tendencies from which our notions about human nature have suffered for the past three centuries. For the hylomorphic approach of the Aristotelian, we see substituted the extreme dualism of the Platonist, thereby developing, at the very beginning of modern philosophy, an altogether un-necessary antagonism between spiritual realities and values in human life, on the one hand, and the data of empirical research, on the other. It was this unwarranted antagonism that drove many psychologists to adopt a mechanical concept of the soul and eventually to glory in the fact that they had cast it out from psychological study. Moreover, the same dualism, absolute and uncompromising, made it impossible to hope for any satisfactory results from the attempted correlation of psychological phenomena with physiological processes.

4
Like Father Like Son

The elements of a mystical psychology, latent in the doctrines of Descartes, were soon brought to the surface by some of his disciples. For *Blaise Pascal* faith alone can answer the questions which reason proposes, love alone can solve the meaning of human life. The heart, rather than the head, is the supreme criterion of truth in the speculative order as well as the supreme norm of virtue in the moral order. On the principle that matter is essentially inert, *Arnold Geulincx* declared that sensations do not arise from the body, but, like the higher forms of knowledge, are caused by God Himself. The function of the body and bodily stimuli is simply to supply the occasion of conscious phenomena. *Nicholas de Malebranche* held that the exterior senses deceive us in presenting things as colored, odorous, audible, and so forth, since extension is the sole quality that material objects possess. Similarly, the impressions of imagination are erroneous. Whence, then, our ideas? Not, surely, from the external world! Only God can act as an efficacious cause; only He, therefore, is the true source of our knowledge. In Him we see everything. The soul is thought. Thinking, in fact, is its very life and essence.

5
The Gentle Pantheist

Baruch Spinoza's psychology was colored by his doctrine of substance. It was also influenced by the strict geometrical method of analysis which he employed throughout his whole philosophic system. Substance is one and infinite. It is, in fact, nothing less than God. Thought is an attribute of the divine substance under the aspect of inextension, just as the human body is a mode of the divine substance under the aspect of extension. The order and connection of thought-modes is determined by the order and connection of extension-modes. Hence, everything thinks: animals, plants, and matter, as well as man. The human mind is a mode of the divine substance. It is the idea of the body. Soul and body are one and the same reality hiding behind the mask of thought and extension, respectively.

To say that the soul is the idea of the body is to say that it is the consciousness of the body. But it is more than this. It is the idea of the idea of the body, that is to say, it is self-consciousness or the awareness which we have of ourselves through our bodily states. Man's knowledge develops from inadequate to adequate levels by the stages of reasoning and intuition, advancing from a limited individual point of view to a state wherein it sees all in God and God in all. Will determines whether or not a man shall reach the intuitive level of cognition. Will, therefore, and not intellect, is the source of all error.

6

British and French Empiricists

Another side of the Cartesian heritage soon made its appearance in England. From the beginning, the trend of British philosophy was positivistic rather than speculative. It was the outstanding trait of *Thomas Hobbes*, first of a long line of sensists. All that exists is matter, all that occurs is motion. The soul, as a spiritual substance, can neither exist nor be conceived. Neither is there anything in human knowledge superior to sense. Ideas are associated sensations. "Substance," "body," "imagination," and "intellect" are really synonymous terms. Hobbes was intrigued with the problem of emotional life which he linked up with his theory of politics. Man's passions are of the very essence of human nature. On them he has built the edifice of civil society. Around them he has thrown a bulwark of human laws. They are the main-springs of his earliest efforts at culture and contribute to the shaping of his language. Proof of this is found in the fact that man's speech is the result of his desire to exhibit what he is thinking and planning.

There is all the single-mindedness of the ancient Greek materialism in the teaching of Hobbes. He tried to avoid the dicotomy which Descartes had set up between matter and spirit, but succeeded only in producing a sixteenth-century version of Democritus and Lucretius. Like the earlier atom-ism of the Greeks and the later brain-mechanics of the associa-tion psychologists, the sensistic theories of Hobbes are self-refuting. The epistemology of materialism is shot through and through with contradictions. It claims to know how we know; yet the very conditions that it places on knowing make that knowledge impossible when it explains the processes of reasoning in terms of the shape, size, and motion of atoms, or the juxtaposition of sense elements, or the linking together of ideas that are nothing more than the pulverized contents of mind.

The positivism of Hobbes' psychology was given fresh life and impulse in the writings of *John Locke*. All knowledge comes from experience. It is wholly empirical. It is born out of the womb of time and space and never really gets above the limitations set by our sensible nature. Experience is twofold: (*a*) sensation, or the perception of external phe-nomena by means of the senses; (*b*) reflection, or the percep-tion of the activity of the intellect itself. The qualities of bodies are primary and secondary. But the secondary quali-ties, such as colors, sounds, odors, flavors, pressury attributes—

the proper sensibles of Aristotle and Aquinas — do not really
exist in bodies. To establish this fact all we need do is chill
one hand and warm the other, then plunge both into a vessel
of lukewarm water. The heated hand now feels cool and the
cold hand feels warm. Only the primary qualities of objects,
such as bulk, figure, movement, and so forth — the common
sensibles of Aristotle and Aquinas — have real existence outside the mind. Their function is to produce in us ideas of
secondary qualities. The distinction between the physical
and psychological aspects of secondary qualities is overlooked
or ignored by Locke.

Ideas were defined by Locke as the objects of understanding
when we think. The definition was passed on to his followers
and had the most unfortunate consequences. For by making
ideas, rather than things, the objects of understanding, it
gave rise to the subjective idealism of Berkeley and the
sceptical philosophy of Hume. In opposition to Descartes,
Locke denied the innateness of our ideas. But he so explained
the product of our thinking that what was left was not, in
fact, an idea but an image; just as Descartes explained
imagery in such a way that what was left was not an image
but an idea. While the association of ideas is discussed in
terms of natural correspondence, chance, and custom, the full
development of this doctrine, in its atomistic aspects, came
at a later period in the history of English empiricism.

The cardinal principle of the Cartesian psychology, the
antithesis of mind and matter, appears as a tacit postulate in
Locke's inquiry into human understanding and underlies
everything that he wrote about man's knowledge. His contribution to psychology lies chiefly in his critical spirit. The
method he used in analyzing the human modes of knowing
was empirical rather than rational. His aim was to found
all his psychological teaching on experience. Any other
method is both unprofitable and unreal. Locke attempted

to apply to the study of mind the technique which Francis Bacon advocated in the study of the physical universe. As a result, he built up a system which laid too much stress on the senses and not enough on the abstractive functions of the intellect. His premises led to a materialistic outlook on human nature; yet, with apparent inconsistency, he stoutly maintained the spirituality of man's soul.

While in England, *François Arouet de Voltaire* became an enthusiastic admirer of Locke, and on his return to France introduced the leading ideas of English empiric philosophy. From the principle that mind and knowledge in man are completely encompassed by matter, it was an easy advance to hedonism in ethics and unbelief in religion. The first to formulate a thoroughgoing psychology of sensism was the *Abbé Condillac*. All knowledge is reduced to experience and all experience to sensation. The so-called higher forms of consciousness are nothing more than aspects of the life of sense. Personality, too, is the sum total of our sensations. If man is distinct from the brute, it is solely by virtue of the superiority of his sense of touch. The desires of man spring from his remembrance of pleasant sensations. What we call the good and the beautiful are so only because of their pleasure-giving qualities.

Julien de la Mettrie, too, was a materialist for whom everything beyond the ken of sense was a delusion and physical enjoyment the highest goal of life. The soul is simply a name — unless by the term we mean the brain, which is the organ of thought. The last representative of psychological materialism in the eighteenth century was *Pierre Cabanis* who taught that mind and matter are identical and that thought is a secretional function of the brain.

7
Phrenological Interlude

Franz Gall gave the first impetus to the study of phrenology. He claimed that different kinds of mental activity cause enlargements of the cerebral cortex. The results are bumps on the cranium. According to Gall, there are twenty-seven inner senses, representing the sum total of man's abilities. Although such teaching was bound to meet with scientific scorn, it had the effect of stimulating research on the problem of cerebral localization. Gall is sometimes described as the grandfather of neurology. He referred to himself as a craniologist rather than a phrenologist. He was urged on by a true scientific spirit, even though his work led to the most bizarre sort of theorizing about men's faculties. The neurosurgeon today really owes a great deal to Gall for the interest in brain anatomy which his researches set on foot. Surely he had no idea that his determination to get some meaning out of the shape of peoples' skulls would advance the frontiers of medical science. Under *Johann Spurzheim*, the fashion of examining cranial bumps for special abilities went into a decline. The shift in emphasis from strict anatomy to the plotting of character charts and diagrams of morality was too much for the philosophers and medical men alike.

8
The Idealists

Psychology, after Descartes, may be described as busying itself, unsuccessfully, with the central problem of the relation of mind and matter. Spinoza attempted a solution by merging the two in the unity of the infinite substance. The empiricists sought another answer by reducing mind to matter. But neither pantheism nor materialism succeeded since each labored with the hopeless task of reconciling what was, by the very terms of the case, irreconcilable. The idealistic movement represents still another approach to the enigma of man's nature, a movement that essayed to explain the antithesis between mind and matter by reducing matter to mind. Of course the intentions of the idealists went beyond the solution of the Cartesian problem, since they also included a reaction against the purely positivistic concept of philosophy as well as an attempt to restore the esthetic and religious ideals that had been blighted by the forces of empiricism.

Gottfried von Leibnitz was somewhat hesitant in his profession of idealism; yet the drift of his thinking was surely in that direction. His goal in philosophy was to reconcile all the systems of his predecessors: Plato with Democritus; Aristotle with Descartes; Aquinas with the moderns. In psychology, he applied his cosmic principle of preestablished harmony in order to show the perfect correspondence of mind with matter. The universe is composed of monads: individual substances, simple, incapable of being divided or destroyed. Each monad is a microcosm, a mirror of all reality, endowed with a power of representation which varies from one monad to another. Each contains a passive element which is matter and an active element which is form. Each is therefore partly material and partly immaterial. Here is Aristotelian terminology without Aristotelian meaning. From the lowest monad, which represents unconsciously, to the highest created monad, which represents consciously and is the human soul, there is continuity. By a divine arrangement, monads from the beginning have been so adapted to one another that changes in one are paralleled by changes in all the others.

The doctrine of preestablished harmony, already hinted at in the teaching of Descartes, is perhaps best and most easily seen in the psychology of Leibnitz. The body and soul of man are causally unrelated. Like two timepieces working together they act in perfect unison even though one has no influence on the other. As a result, every physical movement of the body has its exact counterpart in a psychic movement of the soul. This is not hard to understand when one reflects that every monad in the universe is partly material and partly immaterial; or, stated differently, that there are no bodiless souls and no soulless bodies. Such being the case, the distinction between intellectual knowledge and sense knowledge is simply one of degree.

But if mind is unconnected with matter and if the soul has no windows that open on the outside world, what is the origin of our ideas? There is only one possible reply: our knowledge must be developed from germs of thought that are innate. Do our ideas, then, have any objective value? Yes, because the evolution of the soul from potential to actual knowledge is paralleled by the evolution of the cosmic monads in the outer world. Here, as elsewhere, the harmony of the universe, which was planned by God at the beginning, is preserved. The immortality of the human soul follows from its very nature as a self-active and self-sufficient monad.

It cannot be said that Leibnitz neglected to attempt a solution of the critical problems of psychology. But his approach was Platonic, in spirit and tone, rather than Aristotelian. It was inspired by idealistic and poetic purposes, rather than grounded on the facts of experience. It was unreal. Leibnitz was a paradox in philosophy, in many respects. He was as fully alive as any of his contemporaries to the value of scientific study and experimental investigation. Yet when he came to construct his psychological system, he based it entirely on aprioristic definitions and assumed principles. His merit lies in the staunch opposition which he displayed to the currents of materialism that had undermined practically every important doctrine of the traditional psychologists.

In the philosophy of *George Berkeley* we find the idealistic trend carried to the point of an absolute denial of the reality of matter. Locke had announced the principle that our knowledge extends only to ideas; then, as Berkeley observes he contradicted himself when he maintained that the primary qualities of bodies have a reality that can be cognized by a sensitive experience which is the foundation of intellectual knowledge. Berkeley aimed to start where Locke left off, by establishing the fact that all things are ideas. Thus all the qualities of matter, primary as well as secondary, resolve themselves into mental phenomena. *Esse est percipi:* to exist is to be perceived. Matter simply has no being. Only spirit is real. Berkeley's study of Plato convinced him of the uncertain, ever-fleeting, and changing nature of sensible things and of the consequent low character of sense knowledge which is properly no knowledge at all but only a kind of opinion. If we have ideas they must come from God. If these ideas are preserved during our states of unconsciousness, it is because they are kept alive for us in the mind of God.

9
In Praise of Process

David Hume advocated close study of the phenomena of physical nature. He was a reactionary to most of the things that Berkeley stood for. The mind of man is synonymous with its contents, just as perception is synonymous with consciousness. Perceptual experience gives rise to two kinds of data: impressions and ideas. Impressions, which are innate, have a clear and lively character. They include emotions as well as sensations. Ideas are images of our impressions. They are contrasted with the latter, first, because they are not inborn but acquired; second, because they have a faint and elusive quality which makes it hard for us to analyze them. All knowledge can be explained as a combination of what we sense and feel with what we imagine. Mind is just a series of successive perceptions. Its substantiality has no rational grounds, any more than the relation between cause and effect has a basis in experience and reason. Hence, there is no way of proving that the soul is a substance. In fact, if Berkeley is right in ruling out the existence of a material world, his arguments should be just as valid in the other direction, that is, in negating the existence of a spiritual world. There is no way of knowing the truth of any of these things.

Thus the work of the Cartesian psychology is complete: first, the separation by Descartes of matter and spirit; next the denial, by Locke, of the reality of everything substantial in matter except its primary qualities; after this, the negation, by Berkeley, of even these primary qualities; finally, the same solvent applied by Hume, to spiritual substance, the soul or mind, leaving nothing but consciousness and its phenomena. If the ego of man is not substantial, then the soul's immortality is not a datum of reason. Such is Hume's conclusion. Only divine revelation has brought this fact of immortality to light. In psychology, as in every other field of speculation, Hume is a phenomenalist and a sceptic. Not only are mind and matter mere phenomena, but there is no ontological connection between cause and effect. Accordingly, there is no way of proving human freedom. Nothing is permanent in the world of experience; nothing can justify our surmises about the nature of things that do not fall under the senses. It was this final destruction and throwing overboard of the universal and necessary content of human knowledge that roused Kant to action.

10

A Résumé and a Transition

The period from Descartes to Hume is a perfect exhibition of the disastrous consequences wrought by the doctrine of the absolute dualism of mind and matter. It was the attempt to solve this problem that was largely responsible for (*a*) the pantheistic monism of Spinoza; (*b*) the material monism of the Hobbes, Locke, Condillac, la Mettrie; (*c*) the partially idealistic monadism of Leibnitz; (*d*) the wholly idealistic monism of Berkeley; (*e*) the out-and-out phenomenalism of Hume. The term of all this speculation was the denial of the substantial nature of both mind and matter. Immanuel Kant now appears on the scene. Among other things, he will attempt to reestablish the spirituality of the human soul and the essential freedom of man.

But before discussing Kant, we must mention *Christian von Wolff*, who is important because of the influence which he exercised on Kant's early training. Wolff sought to restore the Leibnitzian philosophy. In doing so, however, he modified some of the essential features of his precedessor. He restricted the doctrine of preestablished harmony to an explanation of the relations of soul and body. Here was a return to the original position of Descartes and the restatement of a soluble problem in insoluble terms. Wolff is really the father of the so-called faculty theory, that is, the pigeonhole concept which was so roundly rebuked by later psychologists. Small wonder that the men of science could not swallow the Wolffian doctrine of mental compartments, which had got so far afield from the teaching of Aristotle and Aquinas!

Wolff devoted much of his attention to philosophic method, but again with unfortunate results. Psychology was completely removed from the philosophy of nature and placed among the branches of metaphysics, and this despite the fact that it is both "empirical" and "rational" according to the Wolffian misconstruction of these terms. Such a division of psychological subject matters has been the source of a great deal of misunderstanding, even among the followers of the tradition. In fact, it is only within recent years that scholars have come to recognize that this is not the authentic Aristotelian and Thomistic approach. Certainly "empirical" and "rational" are not synonymous with "scientific" and "philosophic" since the latter is also empirical in the sense of being founded on experience. Neither do these words have the same meaning as "psychology of sensory processes" and "psychology of intellectual processes" since, again, the latter type of psychology is also empirical in character. Far better if terms of this sort were dropped altogether from the language of psychology! Wolff's whole methodology is a sample of the excessive formalism which has led some of our best scholastic minds to the point of actually inverting the natural order of philosophic inquiry.

II

The Sage of Königsberg

For *Immanuel Kant* there are three forms of syllogistic reasoning corresponding to three ideas: of the soul or thinking subject; of matter or the world of phenomena; of God or the supreme condition of all possibility. Man's reason has no direct relation to these three objects which may be described as psychological, cosmological, and theological respectively. In fact, to attempt by purely rational means to establish them as existing outside the mind must necessarily lead to all sorts of contradictions. The Wolffian psychology, which speaks of the oneness, subsistence, and immortality of the human soul as conclusions from rational consciousness, is wrong. Reason can neither affirm nor deny the truth of such propositions. Their proof rests, not on rational premises, but on moral consciousness.

Kant rejected the rational psychology of his master which he considered to be false in its starting point, namely, that we have an intuitive knowledge of the meaning of human understanding. The principle of consciousness is devoid of all empirical content. It is a noumenon, that is to say, an unknown factor. When the Cartesian says "I think," there is really no meaning to the term "I." It is the emptiest of all forms, a psychological subject which can never become a logical subject. Only empirical psychology can tell us anything about our mental life; and its scope is definitely limited to the range of phenomena. It gives no information about the ego. This is not to deny that man is a person with a soul which is one, subsistent, and immortal. But such truths, as we remarked a moment ago, must be demonstrated on a basis of man's moral consciousness. Kant endeavored to correct what he considered as impractical aspects of the Wolffian psychology by showing (a) that its rational elements can never be known, such elements being nothing more than a logical manipulation of concepts; (b) that its empirical contents are much too narrow to provide a satisfactory theory since they lead to the assumption that there is nothing beyond the range of experiential data.

The fundamental character of intellectual consciousness is its tendency to combine our experiences into unity. This synthetic function occurs in space and time which are innate factors in experience and not derived from sensation. The judgments of theoretic intellect are either contingent and particular, or necessary and universal. In the latter case they are aprioristic; that is to say, they are based on innate forms or categories which are anterior to experience. In fact, they render empirical knowledge possible. In themselves they are void and empty; yet they alone can give intellectual meaning to the knowledge that is derived from experience.

When the synthetic activity of knowing is directed toward a goal of human living it is called practical reason. This is the transition from the field of psychological experience to the field of moral experience, from the analysis of thought to the analysis of action. Here we discover the existence of God, the freedom of the will, and the immortality of the soul, for all of which realities there is no justification in pure speculation. The moral law is imperative and not merely persuading or advising. Its commands are categorical. On it are based the important truths just mentioned: (*a*) the existence of God, since the moral law demands the reality of a good which is supreme and complete; (*b*) the freedom of the human will, since the *ought* and *ought not* of the moral law imply an ability to do or not to do; (*c*) the immortality of the human soul, since its perpetual existence is alone sufficient for the fulfillment of the moral law. Thus, while theoretic reason refuses to admit or deny any substantial reality to the subject of our conscious states, moral reason declares that such a substantial carrier ought to exist.

Feeling is a distinct state which arises when the synthetic activity of intellect has attained unity between the heterogeneous elements of experience. It is the determinant of pleasure and is distinct from knowledge, on the one hand, since it contributes nothing to cognition; and from the activity of the will on the other, since it is not directed to a rational goal. Although Kant treated knowing, feeling, and willing as states rather than as faculties, it is easy to see how the modern tripartite division of mental phenomena into cognition, appetition, and conation is foreshadowed in his psychology. It is noteworthy that since the content of empirical consciousness, for Kant, is in a constant state of flux, there is no possibility of founding a real science of psychology.

12

The Light That Failed

Kant's influence on the development of modern psychology cannot be overestimated. His principles form a watershed from which the torrents of modern idealistic, agnostic, and materialistic trends in mental science are derived. His psychology of man's moral consciousness and his insistence on the supremacy of the moral law had the further effect of making Christianity appear rather as a natural ethical system than as a body of revealed truths. Had he understood the genuine tradition of philosophy, represented by Aquinas and the other great schoolmen, he might have corrected the errors of Leibnitz, Spinoza, and Descartes. At least he would have regained the wisdom of the ancients and the solid cultural contributions of the medieval thinkers.

Kant, in a sense, stands for the modern man, with his ignorance of the tradition, his rejection of authority, and his emphasis on the value of individual accomplishment. Still, he was a good man, rightly motivated, and honest in his expression of reality as he saw it. His tragedy is all the more pitiful because he came so near to being a sound philosopher as well as a brilliant one. His greatest psychological error was on the nature of ideas, which he completely failed to understand as products of abstraction. He did not see that the intuitive faculties of sense provide the materials for the nonintuitive knowledges of intellect. As a result, he denied that there could be any acquaintance with noumenal or intelligible reality. He failed to establish a sound metaphysics simply because he could not conceive properly of substance. This had its fatal repercussions in psychology, since it meant the inability of those who were to follow in the Kantian tradition to appreciate the true nature of man as a being composed essentially of matter and form. It is not difficult to see how, with the dissolution of the concept of substance, psychology could be divided between completely idealistic and completely materialistic notions of human nature.

13
After Kant

Johann Fichte was the first post-Kantian who attempted to reduce the cumbersome synthesis of his master to a single all-embracing formula. His was a philosophy of panegoism, understanding ego here to mean not merely consciousness of self but also consciousness of duty. *Friedrich von Schelling* was an idealistic monist, *Georg Hegel* a dynamic idealist. Both tried to achieve a more complete unity of Kantian thought. The latter has reached farthest and deepest, perhaps, into modern philosophy, because of his principle of development or idealistic dynamism, a principle that has dominated scientific as well as philosophic thinking for the last two centuries. It is to be observed that the goal set by these men, to bring all reality under a single law of explication, was indeed a praiseworthy one. But we should recognize that it is an unattainable one in practice. The highest synthesis which the human mind can accomplish must necessarily fall short of absolute unity. To presume that such a goal can be reached is to be guilty of a pride that may be more irreligious and more destructive of genuine knowledge than any philosophy of agnosticism.

Johann Herbart is commonly alluded to as the founder of our modern science of teaching. In psychology he was the first of a long list of opponents to the faculty theory, that is, to the doctrine of faculties in the Wolffian meaning. The soul is a simple substance. It does not have multiple powers but only one basic urge or tendency which is to preserve itself in its indestructible first nature. Perception arises from the conflict of this self-preservative tendency with the same tendency in other beings. Mental states represent an equilibrium of conflicting forces. The aim of the investigator should be to reduce psychic life to a mechanical level where the laws of mind will be operative in the same way as the laws of matter operate on the purely physical levels of activity.

In line with his refusal to accept a faculty theory and with his assumption of a knowable mechanics of mind, Herbart identified willing with thinking, and taught that human liberty is the assured supremacy of the strongest idea or mass of ideas in consciousness. Unfortunately, his throwing out of all faculty analysis meant the removal of man as the object of psychology. It is as though we were to try teaching a class in physics without ever saying a word about the properties of matter. For the study of human nature Herbart substituted the study of states of awareness. He may be described as a kind of vital associationist. He developed the theory of apperceptive mass which determines how one shall select among and interpret new experiences. He applied this principle to education by emphasizing the importance of proper attitude on the part of the pupil toward the things he is supposed to learn. He further advised that education be allowed to proceed along a plan of natural interest. His discussion of unconscious activities led to further research on this important side of human nature.

Arthur Schopenhauer developed a theory of panthelism in which will is identified with all reality. His teaching reflects an age grown weary of the excessive claims of the rationalists and idealists. His insistence on the nonrational character of reality, as well as the pessimistic tone of his philosophy, represent the efforts of a thinker to escape from the highly unnatural atmosphere of transcendental metaphysics. His disciple, *Eduard von Hartmann* attempted to reconcile the world-as-will theory of his teacher with the evolutionary idealism of Hegel. The result was a philosophy of the unconscious which held that the absolute ground of reality is not an unthinking and irresponsible will, but a will acting as though it were intelligent. The individual is freed from the misery of life by attaining to a negation of Schopenhauer's will-to-live. The whole world, in fact, is moving toward redemption by means of a universal denial of will.

In Germany, a reaction against the idealistic movement set in with the proclaiming of the evolutionary hypothesis and the establishment of the law of conservation. The demand for a new philosophy of nature, particularly for a new philosophy of human nature, seemed urgent in view of the results of scientific investigation. The answer to this demand was a rising wave of materialism that attempted to include all mental phenomena, psychic as well as psychosomatic, within the closed system of physical energizing. This deterministic point of view is found in the writings of men like *Karl Vogt, Jacob Moleschott, Ludwig Büchner*, and *Ernst Haeckel*, all of whom, in one way or another, influenced the course of psychological thought among the scholars of their age.

14
Psychologists of the Scottish School

Transcendental philosophy was the answer of the German thinkers to the scepticism of Hume. The doctrine of common sense, developed by the Scottish school, represents another answer to the same sceptical outlook on reality. *Thomas Reid* was the first to formulate the doctrine. All knowledge must be built on principles that are self-evident. Of these principles, every man who has common sense is a competent judge. What is the meaning of common sense? It is twofold, according to Reid: (*a*) the combination of qualities that make up the faculty of sound judgment; (*b*) the aggregate of original principles planted in the minds of all men.

Reid also developed a theory of perception that is interesting because of the terminology in which it is couched. He rightly traced the idealism of Berkeley and the scepticism of Hume to the Cartesian principle that what we directly and immediately perceive is not the external object but a subjective modification or image of the object. But knowledge is not re-presentative in this way. To counteract such a view, Reid proposed his own presentative theory: our knowledge of external objects is immediate. He concluded, however, that we are not conscious of such perception.

Thomas Brown defended the existence of indemonstrable first principles. But he sought to restrict the number of these primitive principles and to allow more scope to the factor of association in accounting for the origin of our universal and necessary judgments. In his analysis of the process of sensation, he attached a great deal of importance to the muscular sense.

William Hamilton made psychology synonymous with metaphysics. Its task is threefold: first, the observation of facts and phenomena; second, a study of the laws that regulate these facts and phenomena; third, an analysis of the real results that may be inferred from the facts and phenomena. The activities of the human mind are grouped together under the main headings of cognition, appetition, and conation. The faculties of cognition include: (*a*) a highly diversified group of senses; (*b*) an elaborative faculty, known among the ancients as "theoretic intellect," whose task is to judge, reason, and generalize; (*c*) a regulative faculty which Aristotle and his school called "practical intellect" and which Reid refers to as "common sense." The data of this last-named faculty are not matters of experience but rather the native cognitions of mind that lie at the roots of all our knowledge.

At this point it may be well to recall the two ways in which the traditional psychologist uses "common sense" when he gives it an intellectual meaning: first, as the common consent or the universal witness of mankind to the truth of certain propositions; second, as the immediate apprehension of self-evident first principles of thinking. It is only in this second meaning that common sense can be regarded as the basis of philosophy or the beginning of wisdom. And certainly common sense, as primitive knowledge of the first principles of speculation, is not what Aristotle and his followers have in mind when they talk about "practical intellect."

With regard to self and nonself, Hamilton declared that these things are simply unknowable in their substance. Our consciousness, however, reveals self as a unity amid successive changes. Moreover, the experience we have of the external world warrants us in representing it as a reality which is permanent as to the quantum of experience, even though its cosmic forms are always changing. In any case, our knowledge of both mind and matter is only relative. Agnosticism is the only logical issue from our efforts to solve such problems!

Hamilton's division of the data of psychology into cognitive, appetitive, and conative is still to be found in many of our textbooks. It is wrong on two scores: first, because it is redundant, since appetition and conation, or desire and volition, are both appetitive phenomena; second, because it lacks balance, since, on the hypothesis that appetition and conation are sensitive and intellectual forms of orexis, there should be a corresponding division of knowledge into sensitive and intellectual cognition.

On the whole, however, the common sense school was a good influence. It came into being as an honest effort to break the deadlock that had appeared in philosophy as a result of the doctrines of Berkeley and Hume — one denying the existence of matter, the other questioning the reality of spirit. It is psychologically significant because it was largely responsible for the revival of interest in the problem of man's ego. The doctrine of unity of self had waned in philosophic circles. Indeed, it had been practically ruled out of court by the empiricists. The common sense school brought it back and made it once more a respectable topic of discussion.

15

French Psychology in the Nineteenth Century

The period of reconstruction in France at the beginning of the nineteenth century witnessed a reaction to the sensistic ideas that were rampant during the revolutionary crisis. *Louis de Bonald* is remembered as a traditionalist who taught that language was not an invention of man but a gift of God; and moreover, that knowledge of all essential truths in the psychological, moral, and religious domains was given to primitive man with language. *Félicité de Lamennais* held that the human mind is incapable of arriving at a knowledge of truth. The only safe criterion is collective reason or the universal consent of mankind. Such attempts to discredit the value and function of individual reason resulted finally in a loss of respect for religion and called for a denouncement of traditionalism by the Church.

Pierre Maine de Biran worked in another direction to stem the flood tides of scepticism and sensism that engulfed French thought. Now the appeal was to psychological introspection, rather than to tradition, as the supreme test of philosophic truth. By reflection we become aware of voluntary effort which distinguishes external from internal experience. In this way we come to know the ego as distinct from the nonego, and to understand the true nature of mental phenomena. For the metaphysician who is too abstract, as well as for the sensist who interprets internal phenomena in terms of external causes, the soul must always remain an unknown factor. Only the psychologist who introspects can grasp the meaning of man's spirit and its activities. *Victor Cousin* seems to have eventually reduced philosophy to a matter of historical interest. All systems can be included under four headings: sensism, idealism, scepticism, and mysticism. There is some truth in all, said Cousin; but the whole truth can be found only in a synthesis of those doctrines which common sense judges to be true. *Théodore Jouffroy* held that physiology and psychology are knowledges between which there is no relation whatever. *Paul Janet* was an eclectic who sought to make a spiritual reconstruction of human nature. His philosophic outlook combined the points of view of two of his predecessors, Cousin and Jouffroy.

Auguste Comte is often referred to as the father of modern positivism. Briefly, this philosophic heresy holds that there is no such thing as an ultimate cause or an absolute, and hence no such thing as valid metaphysical knowledge. All human cognition is confined to facts that fall under the senses, and the relations of these facts. Human thinking has successively passed through three stages in its development: (*a*) the theological, which corresponds to its infantile level; (*b*) the metaphysical, which represents its adolescent stage; and (*c*) the positive, which is the level of maturity. In his classification of our positive knowledges, Comte made psychology a part of biology, spurning the data of introspection as matters that can never be scientifically tested.

Comte's stages of human thinking are false for several reasons. First, they are wrong historically, because metaphysics reached maturity before theology. Second, they are wrong genetically when they presume that metaphysics developed from theology, and science from metaphysics. Actually these are distinct forms of human knowledge; neither did one cease to exist when the other came into being, as the infant ceases to exist when the adolescent comes into being. Third, they are wrong epistemologically since they are grounded on the premise that there can be no knowledge of ultimate causes. The fact is that without the reality of such causes, and especially without the reality of substance and the philosophic principle of causality, science simply could not exist as a body of generalizations. For, the goal of scientific inventiveness is the formulation of laws; and laws are generalized statements that describe the unvarying operational relation between causes and effects.

Henri Bergson represented a healthy even if somewhat extreme reaction to the cult of science and positivism which threatened the very existence of philosophy in France at the turn of the present century. He defended the view that reality is dynamic and always becoming. The whole universe is the creation and expression of an *élan vital:* a living impulse, an idealistic tendency, whose nature is continuously to change and evolve. This is especially true of the human ego which is a substratum of change uniting our diverse psychological states. It was the error of the atomists, said Bergson, to have separated these states as though they were static. They are continuous. The materialists in psychology regard mind either as the sum total of neural correlates which make up the brain; or as a highly attenuated material substance surrounding the brain, like the halo around the head of a saint. They are wrong. The brain is not consciousness, nor does it hold the secret of conscious processes. It is simply an organ, the point at which consciousness enters matter. It has been evolved by consciousness for purposes that are bound up with the necessity of action. And what is this consciousness? It is the *élan vital,* the creative force, of which we spoke a moment ago.

16

Champions of Associationism

The theory of the associationists, in its rigid form, holds that sensations, images, and their linkage together in consciousness under different patterns, are sufficient to explain all the data of human experience. The doctrine was put forward by Hobbes and discussed in a general way in the writings of Locke. Hume also treated its principles; but it was the physician *David Hartley* who gave it the most concrete expression. All mental phenomena may be reduced to sensations and associated vibrations of the white medullary substance of the brain and spinal cord. When our sensations are repeated, they leave traces which are simple ideas. These, in turn, are patterned together to form complex ideas. While all our senses supply us with ideas, the visual and auditory fields yield the most abundant crops. Despite the materialistic expression of his theories, Hartley protested against the identification of the soul with the body. Though there is a correspondence between the psychic activities of the former and the physiological functions of the latter, each species is irreducible to the other.

Joseph Priestley enlarged upon the materialistic features of Hartley's teaching. He contended that the soul is a kind of matter, that thought is merely a function of cerebral tissue, and that psychology can be reduced to a physics of the nervous system. Inconsistently with these views, he maintained that psychological materialism does not negate the immortality of the soul or the existence of a Creator. *Erasmus Darwin* held that ideas are configurations of the fibers which make up the organs of sense. *James Mill* combined the doctrines of Hartley with those of Hume. He taught that sensations are types of feeling, while ideas are residual effects after the sensations have disappeared. The phenomena of emotional and volitional life are explained by the same types of associations.

John Stuart Mill made experience the sole source of knowledge. Body is reduced to the permanent possibility of sensations, mind to the series of actual and possible conscious states. But how can mind, which is a series, be aware of itself as a series? The only reasonable answer would seem to be an admission that there is some sort of linkage among the series, some bedrock that constitutes the ego. This acknowledgment of an underlying factor which ties together the loose ends of our conscious states was like a trap door set down in the middle of Mill's phenomenalistic psychology.

Alexander Bain sought to avail himself of all the advances in physiological knowledge in his studies of mental phenomena. He is commonly reckoned as an associationist, though he appears to have abandoned its materialistic implications as he deepened his researches into the intricacies of mind. It is to Bain, chiefly, that we owe the reintroduction of the concept of habit into modern psychological theory; but his analysis was only a vestige of the traditional account which places habit in its proper context as a medium between faculty and action. Bain's explanation of it as an effect of "happy hits" among the first random movements of the nervous system was an anticipation of Lloyd Morgan's principle of trial and error in learning. In 1874 Bain founded a journal called *Mind* which was the first periodical devoted primarily to matters of psychological research.

17

Evolution and Psychology

About this time *Charles Darwin* proclaimed his doctrine of organic descent and applied it to man. The principle of genetic development was incorporated in the writings of

Herbert Spencer who distinguished three stages in our learning: (*a*) common experience, which is nonunified knowledge; (*b*) science, which is partially unified knowledge; and (*c*) philosophy, which is completely unified knowledge. One of the important facts of psychology is the distinction of self from nonself. The former is constituted by the current of faint manifestations of the unknowable power, the latter by vivid manifestations. Among mental phenomena there are no organic differences. Accordingly, reflexes, sensations, instincts, and intelligence are mere stages or degrees in the development from the simple to the complex or from the homogeneous to the heterogeneous.

The first units of consciousness are tiny "nervous shocks." These, in time, become related by a law of unity of composition. Just as, in physical evolution, the conjoining of two elements produces a new compound, so in mental evolution, new factors are constantly being brought into being through the association of conscious elements. The chief principle of association, for our ideas, is contiguity in time. Consciousness flows along in temporal succession and is measured in much the same way as physical objects; but the latter also vary by spatial dimensions. As in biological evolution we find atavism or reversion to primitive types, so in psychological evolution. Instinct, in the animal, is a form of lapsed intelligence.

Behind the changing shapes and forms of our awareness we must grant the reality of a substance of some kind; but this substance is unknowable. In regard to the origin of our ideas, Spencer held a middle position between the theory of the empiricist who refers all the elements of knowledge to the experience of the individual; and the theory of the idealist, who regards the universal and necessary elements of thought as forms of intuition. In accordance with his general principle of evolution, he explained human thought by organized and

semiorganized arrangements that first appear in the cerebral
nerves of the infant and sum up the experience of its ancestors.
From these inherited dispositions, we derive our inability to
contradict first principles.

18

In Retrospect

Looking back over the story of psychology from Descartes'
time on, I believe it is possible to evaluate the leading thinkers
by reference to a single criterion: the idea of substance. By
this I mean that the psychological systems of the moderns
have been right or wrong precisely to the extent that their
views about substance have been right or wrong. The problem of substance lies at the very roots of metaphysics and
determines the nature of one's whole philosophical outlook.
Descartes, it may be said at once, held for the notion of substance; yet, by his exaggerated dualism, he prepared the way
for its disappearance. Thus, if there be a complete division
between body and soul, if, moreover, extension constitute
corporeal substance, and thought be the essence of mind,
then sooner or later someone will infer that the knowledge of
senses, which is in the realm of body, can never reach the
mind. This would mean that our knowledge of physical
reality must be limited to sensible impressions.

According to Descartes, substance is "a thing which exists
in such a manner as to require no other thing for its existence."
This definition was accepted and improved upon by Spinoza
who declared: "Substance is that which is in itself and is
conceived by itself; in other words, it is that whose concept
does not need the concept of anything else from which it
should be formed." Locke, too, admitted that substance is a
reality, but his notion of it is hardly that of St. Thomas.
According to Locke, when we get an idea of a substance, for

example, a horse or a stone, our knowledge consists in "a collection of those several simple ideas of sensible qualities which we are accustomed to finding united in the thing called a horse or a stone." This would amount to a unification, in the sense faculty, of such qualities as colored, extended, hard, round, and so forth. Hume went further and called into doubt the objectivity of substance. If it exists, we should be able to reach it directly by the senses since sense perception is the only kind of knowledge that reaches the essence of things.

Kant's theory of substance is the outcome of his subjectivist theory of knowledge. The correspondence of thought with reality can never be ascertained, and so we never know whether or not our thought is true. This must be said even of the consciousness which the thinking subject has of himself, of his own substance. The Kantian refutation of substance agrees with the Angelic Doctor's statement that we cannot strictly prove the objectivity of substance. In trying to establish what is obvious, namely, the objective character of our knowledge, Kant succeeds in proving that we cannot prove it and concludes erroneously that perhaps there is no such thing. From this error, he is able to proceed with logical force to a series of other wrong conclusions. The simplest way of refuting the Kantian system is to say that it led to a complete bankruptcy of the human mind. For surely such a liquidation of philosophic thought is exemplified in all the followers of the Sage of Königsberg.

As we cast our glance back over the course of philosophic psychology in the nineteenth century, three further things are seen that have immediate reference to our historical study: (a) the associationistic trend of thought which was uppermost at the time that psychology set out to be a science under the direction of investigators like Weber, Fechner, and Wundt; (b) the evolutionary doctrine which, from the very beginning, had a profound influence on the development of psychological thought and on the course of experimental and clinical research; (c) the sharp definition of the positivistic attitude toward philosophic knowledge in general and psychological data in particular.

It may be pointed out, at this juncture, that the mistakes of the association psychologists continued down to our contemporary men of science. Their errors may be expressed as an attempt to reduce all operations of intellect to the mechanical association of ideas, that is, of sensations or sense images. It is easy to see here the prototype of the behaviorist's attempt to reduce thinking to a tie-up of reflexes; and of the structuralist's explication of ideas as faint images combined in atomistic patterns. The paradox of the associationist is in thinking that he does not think. He is like all other sensationalists who, in blotting out the distinction between sense and intellect, or between the contents of these powers, are producing a psychology that is suicidal in its terms.

As to the genetic approach to the problems of human nature, the important point is not how much scientific truth there is in any of the propositions that have been formulated by the biologist, but rather how these propositions apply to man. Facts cannot be gainsaid; but we must be careful to determine their proper locus. Thus it may be true that the body of man has been the subject of an evolutionary process. But it can never be true that the soul of man has undergone such a genetic development. The critical problem here is drawing the line of demarcation between the material and the immaterial aspects of man's nature. In respect to the former, scientific evidence may establish or reject the hypothesis that the body of man has evolved. In respect to the latter, it is futile to expect that evidence of an evolution of the human soul from a lower species of vital principle will ever be discovered.

The history of positivism, which goes back to Democritus

and his tradition, is the story of the persistent attempt to degrade philosophy to the status of sense knowledge and nothing more. It is an old story, expressed today in the effort to make philosophic wisdom the handmaid of science. It is the result of a development which was set in motion by Bacon's plan to check unchecked speculation through an appeal to strict inductive methods. This, in itself, is a praiseworthy ambition. But, in the hands of material-minded scientists, it has resulted in the complete surrender of all problems of human knowledge into the hands of the investigator, who alone, by his technical procedure, is supposed to be able to supply the answers. If this were true, no self-respecting man, surely, would want to be a philosopher. The failure, here, is due to the philosophers as well as to the scientists, since both groups have been unable to see that philosophy and science are habits of mind that differ in their respective goals and methods; that is to say, in the problems and techniques that are proper to each.

CHAPTER 11

THE RISE OF SCIENTIFIC PSYCHOLOGY

I

Psychology and the Other Natural Sciences

Psychology, as a science of human nature, has been largely influenced by the demands of the other empirical sciences. Thus physics, chemistry, astronomy, and physiology, to mention a few, are dependent in great measure on the precision with which human judgments are formed. Such judgments, in turn, are founded on careful sensory discrimination between objective events and the resultant changes in the consciousness of the observer. Oddly enough, it was the insistence of the physical investigators on the need of more exact use of the senses and more stringent standards of judgment of natural phenomena, rather than a desire to deepen their knowledge of man, that turned psychologists away from philosophy and into the avenues of experimental research. For this reason it is important that we know some of the discoveries in the field of the nonpsychological sciences which led to the development of a scientific approach in the study of human nature.

2

Facts and Findings

Albrecht von Haller pioneered in the field of modern physiology by furnishing experimental demonstration of certain truths that had been treated previously as mere theoretic propositions. From more than five hundred pieces of research on nerve muscle, he established the fact that irritability is a property of nerve tissue and of muscle supplied by nerves. In trying to get some concept of the nature of nerve impulses, he concluded that such impulses have no perceptible volume since a ligatured nerve shows no swelling on the side toward the brain. Still, its material character is shown by the fact that it is nourished by food and can be restrained within limits.

Antoine Lavoisier was interested in the problem of respiration. His work showed that animal heat is a product of combustion due to the action of oxygen. In this way the revolutionary discovery was made that oxygen, and not the Cartesian animal spirits, is responsible for body heat and other vital phenomena of the organism. *Robert Whytt* disproved the notion that all nerve impulses originate in the brain by showing that reflexes may be mediated by isolated segments of the spinal cord. His work was later confirmed by *Marshall Hall* who established the point that the simple reflex arc, as a unit of action, is independent of consciousness or volitional control. *Luigi Galvani* produced spasms in excised muscle tissue by using electrical discharges from Leyden jars. He attributed this reaction to the presence of animal electricity. *Alessandro Volta* disputed the point and held that the spasms are due to the contact of the muscle with dissimilar metals which create a current.

The notion of animal magnetism was exploited by *Franz Mesmer* and had a long popular appeal until the myth was dissipated by competent medical investigations. It was Mesmer's idea that magnetic energy, borrowed from the stars and planets, could be used to heal the ills of mankind. To be sure, the force which Mesmer had unwittingly let loose on his patients was as old as humanity itself: the power of mental suggestion. The trancelike state that he was able to produce in his subjects was known by his name for some time. *James Braid* introduced the term "hypnotism" to describe the same phenomena and the new name was generally accepted. His work was done in a true scientific spirit, without the hocus-pocus which Mesmer used. He explained the hypnotic trance as a result of physical conditions in his subjects, brought on by a fixed stare, repose of body, concentration, and suppressed respiration. Later on, in the hands of men like Charcot, Janet, Breuer, and Freud, the technique of hypnosis led to some remarkable discoveries in the field of psychology.

Charles Bell found that when he cut nerves leading from the dorsal side of an animal's spinal cord no contractions in muscles resulted; but when he touched the nerves from the ventral side of the cord the muscles of the trunk immediately twitched. He drew a distinction between nerves that carry impulses to the brain and those that carry impulses away from the brain. The incoming lines of conduction became known as sensory nerves: the outgoing lines were called motor nerves. Bell devised several interesting experiments in the field of sensation. In visual experience, he noted that the colors of the spectrum are not equally bright. In accounting for the phenomena of audition he suggested that the inner ear is like a musical instrument with fibers of varying length attuned to different pitches. In matters of taste he showed that no sensations occur unless the taste buds are stimulated. In the case of smell, he pointed out that only excitation of the olfactory nerve causes sensations; for, if the nerve is severed, olfactory stimuli produce only tactual sensations. *François Magendie* confirmed the anatomical work of Bell by establishing more exactly the difference between sensory and motor nerves. The findings of these two men were justification for the insight of Aristotle that sensations of strain and fatigue which result from intellectual effort are really not due to the exercise of intellect but to the energizing of the nervous and musculoskeletal systems.

Pierre Flourens gave the first reliable account of the effects produced by the removal of parts of the brain of animals. He found that birds and dogs whose cerebellum has been cut off from the rest of the nervous system are very disturbed in their ability to coordinate muscular movements. Injury to the central part of the medulla results in asphyxiation; destruction of the semicircular canals causes loss of balance. Flourens' interest in neurophysiology convinced him that there is a basic unity of action throughout the whole nervous system, even though its separate parts have different functions to perform. His work anticipated the presentday Gestalt outlook. He was the first to establish the fact of nerve regeneration.

Paul Broca introduced the modern method of brain surgery. He is also noted for having discovered a way of determining the ratio between the size of the brain and the size of the skull. But he is best known for the area of the cortex which is named after him. This area mediates speech and was defined by Broca after a post-mortem examination of a patient who had practically lost his speech and whose brain exhibited a definite lesion in the left frontal convolution of the cerebrum. In contrast to the unverified statements of the phrenologists, here was real scientific evidence of cerebral localization. In 1870 *Gustav Fritsch* and *Eduard Hitzig* applied electric stimuli to various spots on the cerebral cortex and found that certain restricted regions in front of the fissure of Rolando were associated with specific movements in different parts of the body. These observations indicated that there are motor areas on the cerebral surface in addition to the speech area discovered by Broca.

Friedrich Bessel, whose main interest was in astronomy, noted the differences between people in the speed of reaction to stimuli and especially in the estimates of small time values. He called the difference, in each case, the "personal equation." There was a famous case on record of an assistant at the

Greenwich observatory who was dismissed because his calculation of the time it took the reflection of a star to cross the hairline in a telescope varied by eight-tenths of a second from the estimate of the director. Bessel knew of this case; and for years he gathered evidence to show how individual differences arose and what variations might be expected from one person to another.

3

Start of the Experimental Period

Ernst Weber made the first experimental study of sensation. He measured the limits of variability within certain types of sense reaction. In touch, he found that an object pressed on the skin must be increased by about one-thirtieth of its total weight before a change of pressure can be noted. But if the object is picked up with the fingers, a change of about one-fortieth of its total weight can be detected. The weight of any object has to be varied by these same fractions before a difference is discernible. He found, moreover, that in other kinds of sensory discrimination, such as differences of brightness in vision or differences of tone in hearing, the stimulus must be varied by a constant fraction for each noticeable difference in sensation. His generalization became known as "Weber's law," and may be stated by saying that the observed difference between two objects is not absolutely independent of the objects but is relative to the stimulus and is a constant.

The ability to judge the spatial characteristics of touch sensations also interested him. He devised two methods for getting information on the matter. One consisted in the application of two points to the skin in order to ascertain the minimal distance at which they could be distinguished as separate. The finest discrimination occurred on the tongue; the grossest in the middle of the back. On the limbs, the separations are greater along their length than crosswise.

The other method was to apply a single point stimulus to the skin of a blindfolded subject who then, himself, tried to locate this spot with a stylus. The distance between the two spots thus involved was a measure of sensitivity. Here, again, the lengthwise discriminations were wider of the mark than the transverse ones.

Weber referred to the ability to localize as "place sense." Its acuity, he said, depends on the anatomical arrangement of the nerve ends of touch. This view was supported by his experiments on a twelve-year-old boy who gave finer reactions than an adult. The results, according to Weber, were due to the fact that on the boy's smaller skin area the distance between nerve ends was less than on that of the adult. He also held that temperature sense is related to the sense of touch, since a cold coin feels heavier than two warm ones when resting on the skin. In the visual field, he sought to determine the relation between the anatomical structure of the eye and the acuity of visual sensations. To establish this relation, he measured the distance between the nerve ends of the retina and the distance between two visual stimuli which could just be seen as separate. He found, for example, that two parallel lines can just be distinguished as separate when the distance between them is sufficient to stimulate alternate nerve ends on the retina.

In smell, Weber observed that when the nostrils are filled with a highly scented substance, such as eau de Cologne, no odor is sensed. He concluded that stimuli for smell must be in a gaseous state before they can arouse olfactory sensations. Weber was a careful and industrious worker. Within two years' time he performed something like sixty-seven thousand experiments in annotating and comparing sensations and their stimuli.

Johannes Müller gave final form to the principle that each sensory nerve has its peculiar energy which physiologically determines the character of our sensations. This doctrine is found in germinal form in the writings of Aristotle: but Müller established it on a scientific footing. According to Müller, the individual quality of a sensation is independent of the nature of the stimulus that arouses an impulse. Rather, it must be traced to a specific energy in the nervous system. Thus, physical pressure, electric shock, or light, impinging on the optic nerve, will produce a visual sensation. This would indicate that when nerve fibers are aroused by a stimulus, they give only one kind of reaction irrespective of the nature of the stimulus. The principle of specific nerve energies was proclaimed as a death blow to the old emanation theory of Democritus which, under one form or another, had exerted an influence on psychological research from the beginning. Müller, however, did not say exactly where the nerve energy is specified: in the sense organ, along the neural track, or in the brain.

Müller's work on the problem of visual space perception was anatomical in approach. In explaining the fact that we see a single field of vision with two eyes, he formulated his theory of identical retinal points. Single nerve fibers, coming from the cortex, split at the chiasma into two parts, each part exhibiting the same specific nerve energies. There is a corresponding arrangement of fibers in the brain. Hence the experience of space is innate. This was Müller's famous nativistic theory which he introduced in 1826. It was almost immediately called into question. The invention of Wheatstone's stereoscope in 1833 showed that a disparity of retinal images is important for depth perception.

In treating the phenomena of color vision, Müller criticized the idea that colors result from mixtures of black and white. The notion had been defended by *Johann von Goethe* who appealed to the fact that the positive afterimage of the sun gradually goes through a series of color changes, from yellow

to orange, to red, to violet, to blue, to black. Müller accepted
the observation but argued that it proved nothing since the
sensation of black is only a state of repose of the retina. He
opposed Newton's seven primary colors, reducing them to
three: red, yellow, and blue. But he accepted Newton's
erroneous claim that spectral mixtures of yellow and blue
produce green.

In the sphere of auditory sensations, Müller held that the
semicircular canals as well as the cochlea are involved. The
function of the canals is to reinforce the sound waves. He
agreed with Weber that the bony shelf of the cochlea serves to
spread out the auditory nerve fibers, thus affording the greatest
possible exposure to the vibrations set up by the fluids of the
ear and by the bones of the head. In hearing and vision,
Müller did not attempt to explain the exact manner in which
the nerves involved are actuated. He assumed that it was
sufficient to bring the physical stimulus into contact with
the nerve and that the principle of specific nerve energies
would do the rest.

Rudolf Lotze applied the theory of muscular tensions to
account for space perception. For example, when the retina
is stimulated peripherally, there is a tendency to move the
eyes in such a way as to focus the image on the center of the
retina, which is the point of greatest sensitivity. As a result,
each part of the retinal surface becomes associated with a
definite sensation of the amount of effort necessary to move
the eyes so that the image will be thrown on the central fovea.
These sensations, which arise even when the eyes remain
unmoved, are different for each point on the retina. They
are called "local signs."

As the eyes move, there is an orderly stimulation of all
intermediate retinal points along the arc of ocular movement.
This excitement of a regular sequence of local signs produces
a percept of adjacency and gives us information as to the

size of the object at which we are looking. The local signs of the skin depend mostly on differences in touch sensations due to variations in the thickness of the skin or of the underlying tissue and bone. Movements of stimuli across the skin also give rise to a percept of extension or size. Lotze concluded that local signs are not innate, but develop through the improved use of the sensitive powers. The empirical and genetic character of this idea brought about more fertile research than the nativistic theory of Johannes Müller.

Hermann Helmholtz proposed the theory that our discrimination of material qualities in objects may be based on the anatomical structure of the sense organs themselves. In the auditory field, he thought that the principle of sympathetic vibration could explain the manner in which the ear is stimulated. Does the organ of hearing contain a sufficient number of selective units to respond sympathetically to the range of audible tones? After much investigation Helmholtz fixed on the basilar membrane as the answer to this query, because of the large number of its anatomical units and because its fibers vary in length, mass, and tension, like the strings of a harp. He further decided that the semicircular canals have no auditory functions since they do not possess organs suitable for sympathetic vibration. Dissonance in sounds is explained by the presence of beats among their overtones. Harmony, on the other hand, is an effect of simple ratios between overtones, as, for example, in the two to one ratio of octaves.

In the field of vision, Helmholtz brought back the neglected color theory of *Thomas Young*, who had reduced the kinds of nerve substance in the retina to three. These retinal elements are sufficient to account for the perception of all colors: singly, for red, green, and violet; and mixed in the proper proportions, for any other color. Helmholtz pointed out that the selection of red, green, and violet was arbitrary since, as far as he knew, the only way of determining the fundamental

colors would be by a study of the phenomena of color blindness — discovered by *John Dalton* in 1798. Helmholtz followed the Müllerian doctrine of specific nerve energies, contending that light was no more natural a stimulus for vision
than pressure or electricity. The fact that light initiates a
definite photochemical reaction in the retina, it should be
noted, was not brought out until 1876 by *Franz Boll.*

As a result of his experimental work on the visual perception
of space, Helmholtz was able to give the first correct explanation of the change in the curvature of the crystalline lens.
This effect is due to a contraction of its surrounding ciliary
muscles. Helmholtz was also the first to attempt a measurement of the nerve impulse. He noted the time it took a
muscle in the toe to contract after its nerve was stimulated
close to the muscle; and then the time it took the same muscle
to contract when its nerve was stimulated in the area of the
thigh. He placed the rate of transmission somewhere between
50 and 100 meters a second. This rate for human nerve
currents is somewhat under the later determinations that
place the velocity around 123 meters per second. Previously,
it had been supposed that the speed was as fast as that of
electricity. Helmholtz showed that, although there are
certain magnetic phenomena in the nerve impulse, it cannot
be identified with an electric current as such. His work in
the fields of hearing and vision was made easier by his invention of the resonator and the ophthalmoscope.

Gustav Fechner, who coined the term "psychophysics,"
investigated ways for measuring the range and extent of the
phenomena of consciousness. Three types of psychophysical
approach were employed: (*a*) "the method of just noticeable
differences" in which a stimulus is gradually varied until the
observer can detect a change in sensation; (*b*) "the method
of right and wrong cases" in which a score is kept of the per-
cent of correct judgments made by an observer upon some

slight difference of two stimuli; (c) "the method of average error," according to which the observer himself makes the changes in one stimulus until it is like another stimulus. The first type studies threshold values and was originally employed by Weber in his comparison of weights and pressures. It is also called the "method of minimal change." The second type is used when a gradual series of changes in stimuli cannot be arranged. It was improved on by Georg Müller and is now known as the "method of constant stimuli." The third type measures the fineness of the observer's powers of discrimination.

Fechner gave a new version of Weber's law. In its revised form it states that the intensity of a sensation increases arithmetically as the intensity of the stimulus increases geometrically. Fechner's use of the term "arithmetic" implied that each noticeable difference in sensation is to be regarded as a "sense unit" equal in value to every other just noticeable difference. This treatment of sensations as "units" aroused a great deal of remonstrance from other psychologists who looked upon changes in the intensity of a sensation as a continuously adaptive process. For example, is it true that the perceived difference between the light of one and two candles is the same as the perceived difference between the light of eight and sixteen candles?

The basic issue here involved would seem to be a more satisfactory determination of the concept of quantity as applicable to data that fall outside the realm of physics. In any event, recent investigations show that the Weber-Fechner law holds good only within certain sensoria, and that even here it has a limited range. It is not so important today. Rather its value lies in the new impetus which it gave to psychophysical researches when scientific psychology was in the throes of being born.

The possibility of stating Weber's law in a mathematical

way was of particular interest to Fechner because he thought it might lead to a scientific expression of the relationship between mind and matter. While Fechner's goal was commendable in itself, we must not forget that his philosophic outlook was definitely warped by the parallelistic views which he entertained regarding the nature of man's spiritual and material activities. The most he could hope to do was to show how mind and matter operate side by side without being substantially related. Yet the very presumption on which he worked as a scientist, namely, that physical intensities of stimulation can be a clue to psychological intensities of consciousness, is a presumption that demands a substantial relationship between mind and matter before it can have any meaning for the scientist or the philosopher. The psychophysical parallelism of Fechner, like that of Wundt and his followers, was based on a totally false premise, namely, that strictly immaterial energies, such as ideation and volition, must be kept apart from the system of material energies which is closed and made impregnable by the law of conservation. Their implicit acceptance of a dichotomy of mind and matter made it impossible, of course, to account for psychophysical relationships in any terms except those of parallelism.

Ewald Hering proposed a theory of color vision which rivaled that of Helmholtz. If the latter approached the problem from the physical and anatomical side, the former may be said to have developed a distinctly physiological and psychological attitude. It is based on the data of introspection and the principle of biological adaptation. Hering insisted that there are six basic color experiences: red, yellow, green, blue, black, and white. Moreover, in these color experiences, two prominent tendencies are always present: (*a*) the appearance in consciousness of complementary colors, as in afterimages and in the phenomena of simultaneous contrast; (*b*) the pairing off of colors in twos, namely, green with red, blue with yellow, and white with black, as in the varying sensitivity of the retina to color reaction and in the different types of color blindness. The fact that both these tendencies are constantly present is made the basis of a new color theory.

Hering claimed that in the retina there are three distinct biochemical processes, one for green-red color vision, one for blue-yellow, and one for black-white. Each process has its building up and breaking down phases. Green, blue, and black stimuli cause anabolism; red, yellow, and white induce catabolism. Further, these processes exhibit a biological adaptability by spontaneously reversing themselves toward a neutral state which gives to visual consciousness the grey value that results from a mixture of complementaries.

Hering also ascribed the functions of anabolism and catabolism to the thermal sensitivity of the skin, declaring that the type of change in the nerve endings determines whether warmth or coldness is experienced. He observed the existence of what he called a "physiological zero," that is, a variable point of adaptation at which neither warmth nor coldness is felt. Thus, while Helmholtz emphasized the importance of physical and anatomical facts in explaining the data of psychology, Hering laid stress on introspective and biological phenomena. The significance of their work lies in the new standpoints which they introduced into the experimental analysis of sensation.

4

The Genetic Approach

Reference has already been made to the work of *Charles Darwin* and the change of outlook which it brought about in the biological sciences. Natural selection, which he proclaimed as the efficient cause of evolution, represents two processes: (a) environmental selection, wherein plants and animals either become adapted to their surroundings or die off; (b) sexual selection, wherein the males that have the greatest powers of competition succeed in mating with the females. Darwin sought to use his genetic concepts in the solution of psychological problems. He suggested, for example, that many of our human emotions are continuations of responses found in animal life. Thus the sneer is the human counterpart of the animal's preparation to bite. He also attempted some comparison between the cognitive abilities of men and brutes. Evidences of imitation, curiosity, imagination, and even intelligence, so-called, were discovered. Most of the Darwinian citations however, were based on anthropomorphic anecdotes and lacked the objective accuracy required by the genuine scientist. Particularly was this the case in the analogous use of the terms "reason" and "intelligence" which, in the animal, do not signify a power of abstract thinking, but an instinctive ability to adapt itself to varying external and internal circumstances.

Darwin's researches focused interest on the problems of animal life and the possibilities of inheriting mental aptitudes. In his comparative studies between men and animals, and especially in his efforts to explain the meaning of emotion, he held for a purposive interpretation. His findings sent the academic psychologists scampering back to their laboratories to get the answers to the questions which he posed.

The genetic approach was soon extended into the cognate fields of animal, child, and race psychology. A veritable flood of unreliable data was reported. Then a more critical attitude appeared. *George Romanes* coined the name "comparative psychology" and wrote on the psychological evolution of animal life. *Wilhelm Preyer* made the first systematic study of child psychology and drew up a much-quoted list of reflexes and instincts. His pioneering work, which was of excellent quality, is largely responsible for the enthusiasm with which this type of research is pursued today. It is easy to see the influence of Herbart in his writings. *Edward Tylor*, who was obviously swayed by the theories of Darwin, attempted a scientific account of the primitive origins of man's beliefs. He also sought to give an interpretation of the primitive mind in terms of the modern mind. *Cesare Lombroso* offered an evolutionary hypothesis to account for habitual criminals, contending that such individuals represent atavisms or reversions to primitive types in both the psychological and the physiological dimensions.

One good feature of the genetic approach was the fresh vista it opened up of human nature as a thing capable of almost infinite development. The static view, which tried to explain man's psychological life by a cut-and-dry association of percepts, images, and ideas was now replaced by a more dynamic approach. Human nature has to be studied in its functional aspects — as modified by such factors as age, environment, degree of education — if it is to be understood in all its richness and variety. The powers of man, too, especially his intellectual abilities, are vital and expanding things that differ from individual to individual. To be grasped in their true character they must be examined in the long section; that is to say, as properties whose very nature is to unfold and develop by action and habit.

5

The Problem of Heredity

The story of the development of the genetic approach to psychology would be incomplete without some reference to the researches of *Gregor Mendel* in the field of heredity. Mendel is rightly regarded as the father of modern genetics. He discovered that the coloration of sweet peas in hybrid plants is regulated by definite laws. In the first generation of hybrids the color of one parent appears more often than that of the other. It is called the "dominant" color. That which appears less often is known as the "recessive" color. When the hybrid offspring are mated with each other, their progeny in turn exhibit the dominant color in about three-fourths of the plants and the recessive color in about one-fourth.

August Weismann also was interested in the problem of genetics. He is known chiefly for his rejection of the idea that there can be an inheritance of acquired physical characteristics. He insisted that germ cells in animal organisms have no biological connection with the parent stock except through the blood supply, and proclaimed the fact that the germ cells of any generation are direct divisions of the germ cells of all preceding generations. Thus there is a "continuity of germ plasm" which makes it physiologically immortal. Further, except for metabolic changes, this continuity is uninfluenced by the activities of succeeding generations.

6

Individual Differences

Contemporary with the work of the geneticists, we find other important developments in the psychological field which were related to the problem of physical heredity. The work of *Francis Galton* was particularly outstanding in this connection. He is sometimes referred to as the Darwin of psychology. It was he, in fact, who first attempted to apply, in a thoroughgoing way, the principles of variation, selection, and adaptation to the study of human individuals and races. In one analysis he sought to show that there is a tendency for superior intelligence or genius to run in families, as shown by the biographies of famous men. In another study he demonstrated, by a statistical measurement of height, talent, and so forth, that the characteristics of offsprings tend to go back toward the average level of the family stock. This is his law of filial regression. It is expressed by saying that a child never varies more than one third from the characteristics of its parents. In a study of heredity in animals, he tested the effects of transfused blood on succeeding generations of offspring and found no changes in stature or pigmentation. He concluded, with Weismann, that there is no inheritance of acquired characteristics. Galton also introduced the science of eugenics. One of its avowed aims was the elimination of the unfit members of the human race. In 1905 he helped found a eugenics laboratory in London.

Galton made the first attempt to perform exact quantitative experiments on the problems of mental association. He estimated the time required to make response-associations following the presentation of a stimulus word or some other signal. The initial reaction was a gesture, the next a verbal association, the final and slowest a concrete image, such as a visual picture. He further investigated the types of imagery most used by people in their recall of past events, and discovered that they differ considerably in their preferences. Galton was a man of many parts; but his most notable contribution to psychology was his proof of "individual differences." Up to his time, practically all discussions of psychology had presented simply the general analysis of the normal adult. The significance of variability was overlooked or understressed.

Galton's aim was to obtain actual standards of human abilities so as to have a basis for his eugenic principles. What he needed, most of all, was a quick and ready method by which to measure the performance of large numbers of individuals. Among his many devices, he made use of lists of words, to see what associations were made in the minds of ordinary people. Many of the past and forgotten experiences of his subjects were brought to light so that, in making these personal records, Galton was unwittingly anticipating the technique of the later psychoanalysts. His studies in verbal imagery also led him to investigate what are called nowadays "synesthetic phenomena." There are cases where the data of one sense seem to provoke images out of another sensorium. They are common enough and find expression in such phrases as "a bright tone," "a warm color," "a dark brown taste," and so on. Galton's use of mathematics in computing averages of hereditary traits and individual characteristics gave rise to the statistical method in psychology. The method had been used, among other things, to estimate the average number of wins in games of chance; but Galton was the first to employ it in anthropometric research. His workshop in London drew several interesting young men. Here, for example, the budding genius of Charles Spearman was nourished and inspired to follow the lines of psychometric research which were suggested by Galton's experiments.

While it is true that the traditional psychology, up to this time, represented an analysis of the normal and the average, it is not true that the traditional psychologists were unaware of the significance of differential factors in the structure of human nature. Thomas Aquinas was well acquainted with the fact that the powers of one individual differ from those of another; and it led him to conclude, most interestingly, to differences in the souls of men. Such differences, of course, do not refer to human nature itself which is the same for all men, but only to the properties of that nature. How do these variations arise? From the soul's union with matter, which determines the amount of perfection that a particular power will enjoy. Thus, in each body, the soul possesses an existence which is strictly conditioned by the capacities of the body. The more excellent the texture of the matter of human nature, the more excellent are the results that the soul can accomplish in the use of its powers. Intellect is a finer instrument in one individual than in another because the body is better disposed to receive and convey impressions of the external universe. Moreover, the better disposition of the body naturally makes for an easier and more effective employment of the senses. Because intellect requires the services of phantasms, it follows that those in whom the imaginative, memorial, and cogitative powers are of better quality are better disposed to understand the data presented by the senses.

CHAPTER 12

THE ESTABLISHMENT OF PSYCHOLOGY AS A SCIENCE

I

The Wundtian Tradition

Wilhelm Wundt is generally credited with being the founder of scientific psychology. He was the first to establish it as a modern science, separate from the philosophy of human nature. He perceived that the other sciences were making frequent use of psychological facts in the study of their problems and that there was a need for experimental proof of the reliability of these facts. Since every natural science is dependent ultimately upon experience, Wundt defined psychology as the science of immediate or direct experience of conscious events; whereas other sciences are concerned with mediate or indirect experience, obtained through instrumental technique and records. In psychology, the data of consciousness must be analyzed by systematic self-observation which will give a methodical account of experiences as they occur. The tool to be employed is *Selbstbeobachtung* or introspection: having an experience and then describing it.

Wundt erected the first experimental laboratory at Leipzig in 1879. In it students from many parts of the world were trained. Wundt's interest in experimental psychology grew out of his earlier physiological researches with Helmholtz and Johannes Müller. His initial investigations were concerned with perception and the meanings attached to sensation. For instance, he showed that actual localization is more accurate upon those parts of a person's body which he can see. This would indicate that associated visual images assist us in our judgments of tactual space. Wundt treated sensations in terms of their inseparable properties which he called "attributes." Of these there are four: quality, intensity, extensity, and duration. Such a treatment, of course, tended to lay a great deal of stress on sensations as units of experience and gave the Wundtian psychology a distinctly atomistic flavor.

Wundt analyzed feeling as an elementary experience similar to sensation. It has basic qualities, like sensation. It is tri-dimensional according to its characteristics of pleasantness or unpleasantness, excitement or depression, strain or relaxation. But we fail to find the careful distinction of feeling, as an appetitive event, from sensation, as a cognitive event, which is basic in the traditional psychology. Even today investigators are not clear on the distinction. This is particularly the case when they are dealing with organic sensations, where the orectic background of the cognitive event is very pronounced.

Wundt also proposed a parallelistic theory to account for the relation between the physical and psychic features of sensation and feeling. Just as the conscious aspects of sensation find a noncausal concomitant physiological activity in the sense organs, so the conscious aspects of feeling are accompanied by, though not causally related to, a definite physiological rate and intensity of breathing and pulsation. Wundt's parallelistic views, however, are not quite so radical as Fechner's since he allowed that, in the formation of apperception masses, will is able to admit one sort of stimulus while it rejects another. He discarded the substantiality of the soul and in its place substituted conscious processes. He leaned heavily on the doctrines of association in interpreting psychological data.

Wundt transformed the astronomer's problem of personal equation into an experimental study of mental functions that can be tested by the reaction-time method. He tried to determine what part of the total time involved in a reaction is occupied by each of three factors: (a) the "sensory time" needed for response to a single stimulus; (b) the "discernment time" required for reaction to the correct one of two stimuli; and (c) the "will time" necessary for proper choice between alternative responses, for example, for the right hand to react to a blue light and the left hand to a red light. Further, he tested the time it took a subject to form various ideational associations, as in thinking of a particular term like "chair" when responding to a general term like "furniture."

In studying attention, Wundt found that in the simultaneous presentation of two stimuli, one will be perceived before the other if it is expected. This "prior entry" feature was demonstrated by sounding a bell at some time during the movement of a pointer across a metronome. If attention is directed to the pointer, the pointer seems to move farther across the dial at the time the bell is heard than if attention is directed to the sound of the bell. [In the field of vision, Wundt was one of the first to use the newly acquired fact of photochemical action in the retina. He suggested that there are two such processes: the first, for brightness, since all colors pass gradually from one into another; the second, for color alone.

In the visual perception of depth, Wundt compared the influence of the convergence of the two eyes with the part played by the accommodation of the lens in each eye.] To test convergence, a vertically arranged thread was moved toward or away from an observer's line of vision as he looked with both eyes through a tube. The observer reported the least degree of movement he could discern. To test accommodation, he made the same sort of judgment using only one eye. The results showed that a finer discrimination is made for movements of approach, especially when both eyes are used. Wundt concluded that visual space perception involves sensations of convergence and accommodation, besides the visual fusion of images on corresponding points of the retina and nonfusion of images on noncorresponding points.

Wundt's experiments in audition were meant to try out the validity of the Weber-Fechner law. The results seemed to run counter to that generalization. Observers were asked to say which one of several tones seemed to be exactly midway between a given higher and lower tone. The intermediate tone fixed upon was usually one closer to the arithmetic than to the geometric mean, contrary to what the law seemed to demand. Although Wundt experimented on touch and temperature reactions, the discovery that sensations of pain, pressure, warmth, and coolness are mediated by distinct spots on the skin did not come from his laboratory. He accepted the evidence that there are four elementary experiences in the field of taste: sweet, salty, sour, and bitter. He sought to add metallic and alkaline to the list, but these were soon shown to be dependent upon the other four qualities.

Wundt's influence upon experimental psychology in general consisted largely in the impulse and orientation that he gave to the researches of his students. He was not a genius, so much as a careful director. It is significant, in view of his ambition to make psychology a science separate from philosophy, that most of the work done in his laboratory was published in the *Philosophische Studien*, the first journal of psychology in German, founded by Wundt in 1883. His chief concern was to analyze mental processes according to their conscious elements. Then he sought to explain how these elements are conjoined in everyday experience: first, by incidental combinations that result from the laws of association; second, by apperception, which was Wundt's notion of intelligence. Toward the end of his long and fruitful life, he seems to have recognized that he had not succeeded in finding the principle by which the elements of consciousness are held together; and so he sought a new basis of mental organization in the phenomena of folk psychology. On this latter subject he wrote some ten volumes.

2

Further Trends in Experimentation

Ernst Mach declared that everything in the world of conscious experience exists merely as a complex of sensations. His interpretative point of view is strongly reminiscent of the phenomenalism of Hume. Space and time, instead of being realities apart from our awareness of them, are nothing more than simple sensations. Hence they belong to the domain of psychology rather than to that of physics. They do not represent objects but only the perceived relations between objects. For example, the display of three separate dots arouses an immediate spatial sensation of triangularity. In a similar way, a group of sounds arouses an immediate temporal sensation of melody or rhythm. In the experimental field, Mach was responsible for establishing the fact that the sense of rotation is due to the movement of the fluids in the semicircular canals.

Hermann Ebbinghaus was the first to investigate seriously the functions of the interior senses in an experimental manner. His chief interest was in the sphere of memory. He devised a quantitative measurement by dividing memorial tasks into equal units, assuming that such units could be formed through the presentation of nonsense syllables. These are words made by placing a vowel between two consonants. They were used, first, because they seemed to furnish memory with material that was uniformly simple; second, because they had no association value for the learner. The measurement consisted in a tabulation of the numbers of nonsense syllables that could be remembered in a certain amount of rehearsing.

Records were also made of the number of syllables that were forgotten during given intervals of time.

Ebbinghaus employed the method of repetition because he accepted the traditional principle that those images are most readily revived which have been most frequently repeated. He used two techniques in presenting his material. One was called the "learning method," in which the reading of the syllables is repeated until the first complete recall can be made. The other was called the "saving method," in which varying intervals of time are allowed to elapse after the material has been mastered, and then a record is taken of the number of rehearsals necessary to relearn the list. The first method gave rise to the well-known learning curve which has been altered only slightly since the time of Ebbinghaus; the second method produced the equally well-known curve of forgetting. From his experiments, Ebbinghaus showed that learning occurs most rapidly at first, then gradually decreases as additional material is committed to memory. Similarly, forgetting occurs most rapidly at first, with a decrease in the rate of losses which is proportionate to the effort and time involved in learning.

Aquinas and Aristotle, as we recall, distinguished between memory which is purely sensitive and reproduces the events of the past in a passive manner; and memory which is reminiscent or creative, a power of active search for images, implying purpose and reflection and a syllogistic method of inquiry into the past. Ebbinghaus followed the same distinction when he observed that some experiences are recalled to consciousness with entire spontaneity or without any special act of volition, while others are revived only by deliberate efforts directed to this goal.

Georg Müller was second to none in the scope of his experimental program. His laboratory at Göttingen became the counterpart of Wundt's at Leipzig. He added several new

features to the studies of memories made by Ebbinghaus.
For instance, he devised a method of "right associates,"
according to which syllables are learned in pairs; then the
reaction time, taken to recall one when the other is read off
to the observer, is recorded. Müller also was the first to
report and analyze the "perseveration tendencies" of memory.
These may be described by saying that an image which has
once appeared in consciousness tends to become conscious
again very soon. Müller gave a new impulse to psychophysical investigation and devised a "method of constant
stimuli" which has been widely used ever since. It was an
elaboration of Fechner's "method of right and wrong cases"
in which only two stimuli were compared at a time. In
Müller's technique, several stimuli are laid beside one standard
stimulus in order to obtain a more accurate determination of
the probable distribution of judgments. His best work along
these lines was in the field of tactual sensation.

3
How We Learn

The tradition of experimental work on memory, established
by Ebbinghaus and Müller, has continued to grow apace.
The practical aspects of such investigations have long since
been recognized. The respective merits of learning by whole
and by parts were studied by *Lottie Steffens* and the results
were made known for the benefit of teachers and pupils alike.
Working in the same spirit, *Robert Ogden* published his researches on the effects of the rate of learning upon retention.
Then shortly after the turn of the century, *Ernst Meumann*
brought together all the literature that had been written up
to this time on the economy and technique of learning. Next,
Philip Ballard gave the first scientific description of the
phenomenon of reminiscence. This term, it should be noted,

is used by the modern experimenter in a meaning somewhat different from that employed by Aristotle and Aquinas. The usual experience, in memorial work, is to forget the things which one has learned but does not repeat. Reminiscence, in the experimental sense, is an exception to this rule because here one finds that memory actually improves without practice, due to the perseverative tendencies which Müller described.

The studies made by *John McGeoch* on the phenomena of retroactive inhibition have also been significant. Some reference, too, must be made at this point to the work of *Edward Thorndike* and his associates at Columbia University on adult learning. The problem of age and memory developed interesting results which ran flatly counter to the opinion that memorial power decreases with the advance of years. It was shown that a man of forty-five could learn as rapidly as a youth in his teens. This would indicate that an older person is not seriously handicapped in memorial tasks, especially in fields related to the one in which he is actively engaged. If he fails to learn a new trade or a new business or a new language at sixty, the failure must be chalked up to lack of time, interest, or desire, and not to lack of ability. In regard to the general trend of experimental work on memory, it may be pointed out that most of the researches have been concerned with mechanical associations, such as those that obtain with the type of material which Ebbinghaus devised. One might ask with good reason if the laws that have resulted from this kind of experimentation can be applied to ordinary learning which is occupied with the memorizing of meaningful data.

4

Interest and Apathy

Théodule Ribot introduced the study of experimental psychology into France. He made special use of the facts of neuropathology to demonstrate the influence of physiological states upon consciousness and he wrote at length on what he called the "maladies" of memory, will, and personality. He pointed out, for example, that in certain degenerative diseases there is loss of memory for recent events first, and then, by gradual stages, for earlier experiences. The same type of deterioration is observed in emotional states. The highly esthetic feelings that distinguish the person of advanced culture are the first to disappear. Unstable situations in the affective dimension, common in hysteria, were referred to by Ribot as instances of "emotional infantilism." He emphasized the role played by bodily movements and sensations of kinesthesis in the acts of attention. Further, he cited the slowdown of breathing, constriction of the blood vessels, frowning, leaning forward, tapping of the fingers, and walking about as "physical manifestations of emotions." Ribot's general tendency to explain mental states in terms of their organic accompaniments led to a motor interpretation of the facts of consciousness.

James Ward is remembered, not for any contribution that he made to scientific psychology, but rather for his significant lack of interest in experimental research, characteristic of the British at this time. He wrote the first separate article on psychology to appear in the *Encyclopedia Britannica*. Heretofore the subject had been treated under the more general topic of metaphysics — an example of the Wolffian concept of its position in the family of philosophic knowledges. Ward would replace the associational approach, to which English thinkers had been so devoted, with a more genetic and operational point of view. He conceived of psychology as a study of the relations between a purposively acting subject and a continuous medium of sensory and motor events which impinge upon the subject's consciousness.

CHAPTER 13

ACT PSYCHOLOGY

I

A New Angle of Vision

In contrast to Wundt, *Franz Brentano* emphasized the activities of consciousness instead of its contents. He sought to explain how mind comes into possession of its factual data rather than what these data are in terms of their elements. He declared that only the study of mental operations can be properly called "psychology." His point of view, therefore, has much in common with the traditional Aristotelian approach with which he was familiar. Brentano held that the main activities of mind are perceiving, apprehending, judging, and desiring. His psychology is intentional because it stresses the essential relation of our cognitive functions to appropriate objects. Using the terminology of the schoolmen, he expressed this view by saying that every act of knowledge involves the intentional inexistence of its proper object, that is to say, the presence of the object, not as existent, but simply as intended.

Carl Stumpf followed Brentano in limiting psychology to the study of mental operations. These are partly cognitive, such as perceiving, understanding, and judging; and partly appetitive, such as enjoying and sorrowing, seeking and avoiding, willing and rejecting. The acts of consciousness beget its contents; and so we speak of the percept of the object, the idea of it, the desire of it. The elementary materials used in building up our mental products are sensations and images; but these elements are never experienced in isolation. Thus redness is never seen or imagined by itself but always as a red-colored object or surface. Elementary sensations, therefore, are "preperceptual." The study of them is only a propaedeutic to psychology.

Stumpf, obviously, was not in sympathy with the Wundtian concern for sensations in themselves, as atoms of psychological life. His chief experimental interest was in the field of sound and music. On these topics his researches rank very close to those of Helmholtz. In contrast to the latter's physical theory of consonance, he maintained that the harmonious blending of tones cannot be explained merely by the objective material characteristics of successive waves, such as the blending of their overtones, but must be the result of a mental fusion of discrete stimuli into unity so that they appear in consciousness as a single experience. In short, education, as well as physical patterning, is a factor in the appreciation of musical intervals.

Christian von Ehrenfels attributed to sense elements the power of producing new conscious data which he called "form qualities." Mach's spatial sensation of triangularity and temporal sensation of rhythm were taken as examples. Melody is a higher species of form quality. Ehrenfels commented on the fact that while form qualities depend on sensations and their stimuli, they nevertheless enjoy a sort of natural and independent variability. For instance, the attribute of triangularity may persist in consciousness even though the size of the component parts of the triangle is changed; just as a particular melody may remain in consciousness despite the transposition of its notes into a different key. Ehrenfels' theory of form qualities looks backward to Kant's a priori categories and forward to the configurational experiences of the Gestalt psychologists.

2

The Failure of Content Psychology

It should be noted that the general trend of act psychology was one of revolt against Wundt's breaking down of consciousness into atomistic contents. The Wundtian picture, it was said, gives us no real insight into the operational nature of mind which is the only true picture of the essential dynamism of our human faculties. The point is worth emphasizing again that the drift of act psychology is definitely toward the traditional way of looking at the data of consciousness. Thus human nature rejoices in the possession of a set of basic abilities, some of which are cognitive, others appetitive, others motor, but all of which are designed to perfect man by actual performance of their respective tasks. The act approach was to prove a congenial one to American psychologists, as we shall see in a later chapter.

3

Higher Mental Activities

Oswald Külpe worked in the spirit of Brentano though he was influenced undoubtedly by Wundt. He is remembered for two important contributions that he made to psychology: first, his refinement of the technique of introspection; second, his development of the theory of imageless thought. He modified Wundt's definition of psychology as the analysis of immediate experience by making it a study of experience "as dependent on the experiencing individual." The processes of thinking, feeling pleasure or sorrow, and even sensing things in a simple way are peculiarly one's own. The awareness of the difference between two sensations, for example, is not something present in the stimuli of such sensations, but a fact or an achievement of the consciousness of the observer.

It is manifest that for Külpe the problem of introspection was one of critical meaning in psychology. Here is the tool of tools for digging out the data that the science of human nature is supposed to investigate. Experiment can no more take the place of introspection in psychology than it can that of observation in physics. In fact, psychology without introspection tends to become either purely physiological, so that it is no whit different from the nonconscious biological analysis of structures and organic functions; or purely mathematical, in which case it resolves itself into a mere statistical expression of quantitative relationships between human acts and human powers. In neither instance is it a psychological description of psychological data, which surely should be the goal of both the science and the philosophy of human nature.

But introspection must be careful, systematic, and controlled. In the hands of Külpe and his Würzburg school it meant a special attitude, the adoption of which enables the observer to study his experience in detail, as though under a microscope. The whole conscious period is recorded methodically and divided into sections, if that proves necessary. The same tasks are performed over and over again so that the observer's account may be corrected and amplified. Sometimes he is asked to direct his attention to special points, but more often he is left to guide his own conscious acts without any preconceived notion of what he is expected to record. The main thing is to get at the truth of mental experience.

Külpe and his colleagues made a special analysis of mental states in which an awareness of meaning or purpose was clearly manifest but was not composed of sensations or images. These nonsensory or nonimaginal aspects of consciousness were called "imageless thoughts." Their presence was studied in experiments on controlled association. Observers were instructed to be ready to think of a particular word when a general term was presented. Before the announcement of the stimulus word with which an association was to be made, the observers found that they had a definite awareness of their task, which revealed itself in a repeated whispering of the instructions of the experiment, a hasty recall of two or three instances, and so forth; but with repeated trials under the same instructions, consciousness of the task was reduced to a faint expectancy though the correct results were still forthcoming. A similar change in attitude was noted in preparing to carry out an arithmetic problem as soon as the figures were presented. During the actual solution of the problem, consciousness of the task persisted in nonsensory or nonimaginal terms, although imagery, of a sort related to the problem, was present at the same time.

Of all the work done at Würzburg under the leadership of Külpe, the experiments on imageless thought attracted the widest attention. *August Messer* and *Karl Bühler*, two of Külpe's best pupils, entered heartily into the ideas of their master and sought to confirm his findings. *Karl Marbe*, also of Würzburg, took up the problem of judgment and discovered that sensations and images did not play an important part in the estimates made by his subjects of varying weights. *Alfred Binet*, in France, was inspired to follow up these adventures into the higher levels of mind, and his researches set up a new outpost on the frontiers of psychology. In America, *Edward Titchener* violently opposed the theory of imageless thought; but his efforts were offset by the experiments of *Robert Woodworth* and *Thomas Moore* who corroborated the work of the Würzburgers.

4

Imageless Thought and the Thomistic Teaching

Does the theory of imageless thought cancel out the traditional doctrine that thinking always requires imagery, or that abstraction is always made from a sensory datum? One way of answering the question would be to distinguish between the two aspects of "meaning" which a thinking process implies: (a) the simple apprehensional aspect; (b) the propositional aspect. Now, it is clear from the teaching of the Angelic Doctor that every concept, in its apprehensional aspect, is derived from some sort of phantasm. On the other hand, Aquinas also allows that, in going over a propositional concept, previously abstracted from sensible data, intellect is not bound to revert to the particular phantasms from which the concept was first derived. It may even be argued that, in propositional thinking, where abstract relations are concerned, no phantasm can picture the essence of a judgment or an inference, as such. The judicial or inferential act, wherein relationship is grasped in a purely immaterial way, has no counterpart in sense imagery.

But this sort of argument really does not touch the point at issue in the Thomistic doctrine. For Aquinas and his followers, the necessity of converting to imagery in the act of intellection is a metaphysical one. It is simply part of the larger need that intellect has of sense, or mind has of matter, or soul has of body. It is a necessity which is in the nature of things. The Angelic Doctor does not say that the phantasms which we employ in thinking have to be conscious ones. As a matter of fact, the work of agent intellect, in the Thomistic economy of knowledge, is accomplished on an unconscious level. We are unaware of its abstractive processes. In working over a sensible datum and making it into something that can be understood, agent intellect is simply following a law of metaphysical causality. We think only on the condition that we experience; and so there must be some kind of sensible image from which our thoughts are derived. But our phantasms do not have to be conscious forms or objects of knowledge. As a matter of fact, whether or not they fall within the field of awareness is entirely irrelevant. The point is that for Aquinas they are necessary in our present state of existence where intellect is conjoined to sense and soul is immersed in matter.

Here an item of common experience may be noted: the more our thinking is directed to outward action, the less apt we are to be aware of imagery. The converse of this is also true: when our thinking is turned within, imagery is liable to be dominant in consciousness. One could point to the contemplatives whose records of high intellectual communings with the divine are full of the most intense sensible imagery. Moreover, in experimental procedures, it is obvious that consciousness of what goes on in the mind of the subject is of the first importance. The fact that he is not aware of imagery in certain types of thinking really has nothing to do with the metaphysical necessity of some sort of phantasm in every act of understanding. Since the process of abstraction falls outside the realm of consciousness, it cannot be submitted to experimental proof. So, too, in respect to sense images: their necessity for thought is not established by scientific tests but founded on an analysis of human nature. Where spirit is united with matter, as in the case of man, such a spirit requires phantasms if it is to illumine and abstract, to idealize and think. It is only on this condition that man's intellect can work at all. But whatever meaning we put on the work of the Würzburg school, its sincere interest in the psychology of thought and its wholehearted efforts to direct research toward the higher aspects of conscious life could not help but be felt as a good influence. From this point on, it will be difficult for any accredited scientist of human nature to say that sensations and images are the only things that the psychologist ought to bother his head about.

5

Studies in Volition

Mention must be made here of another of Külpe's accomplished pupils, *Narziss Ach*, whose name is linked with important studies in the field of human volition. Ach was particularly concerned with what he called the "determining tendencies" of the will-act; that is to say, the fact that when will accepts a task, there is an unconscious carrying over of its original purpose into actions that secure the intended end. The relation that exists between means and end in human decisions had been known to the scientists through their studies of attention. But Ach was the first to give this relation a scientific name. He also furthered Külpe's work by developing the technique of introspection to a high degree of accuracy.

In devising a method of investigation for the will-act, Ach arranged a series of experiments which involved the overcoming of obstacles. He made his subjects learn pairs of syllables and then asked them to name out loud the first syllable of each pair but not the second. Of course the memory trace of the second syllable created a real impediment, and required a special act of will to prevent its being spoken aloud. Many of Ach's subjects declared that, for the first time in their lives, they were really conscious of the presence and meaning of volition.

In his Louvain laboratory, *Albert Michotte* also made a number of studies of the will-act. Together with *Emile Prüm*, he arranged an experimental situation in which a choice was allowed the subject between sets of arithmetic problems. A Morse key was to be pressed just as soon as a selection was made. Here was an advantage over Ach's method, inasmuch as the will-act appeared in the main part of the demonstration and not before it had begun. The subject was not allowed to complete the task, but was interrupted the moment his choice was fixed. Despite the insignificance of the materials used, all subjects experienced a serious consciousness of alternatives and conflicts, much like the decisions that must be made in everyday life. It was only with considerable difficulty, however, that they learned to observe and describe their volitional activities.

In England, *Honoria Wells* carried out some similar experiments on choice. Now the range of alternatives was increased. Different liquids, practically colorless and odorless, were prepared. Some were pleasant to taste, others unpleasant, others indifferent. In a set of preliminary tests, the gustatory qualities of each liquid were learned to be associated with a definite nonsense syllable. When the subject had thoroughly mastered the associations, he was ready for the experiment. Two glasses of liquid were presented on a table just beneath the spot where the nonsense syllables appeared, and the subject was asked to decide, for a serious reason and as quickly as possible, between the two. Here, as in the tests of Michotte and Prüm, the choice was sometimes made simply because the subject felt an obligation to go through with the experiment. But in other cases where no differences in value could be discerned, a final settlement was reached as a result of what was called "self-determination": that is to say, by the injection of one's ego between two otherwise nonresolvable alternatives.

Otto Selz became interested in Ach's idea of measuring strength of volition by the amount of energy necessary to overcome obstacles. Attacking the problem from a new angle, he fixed his analysis on the resolve itself, rather than on its execution in outward behavior. Acceptance of a painful task, in preference to a pleasant one, was brought forward as a case in point. Is this actually so? *Johannes Lindworksy* seemed to think not. He made note of the fact that the impression of strong will power in action is often due to the characteristic outer movements that accompany volition, such as twitching of the muscles, tensions, tears, and so forth — things that do not enter at all into the essence of the will-act.   As Lindworsky observed, resolves are fortified by focusing on motives.   He compared volition, therefore, not to the stroke of a hammer, but to the closing of a switch, and concluded that the only proper way of referring to strength of will is in terms of motives, that is, of values that have become firmly entrenched in consciousness.   This would explain, first, why some individuals are strong-willed in one respect, but weak-willed in another; second, why extraordinary will power is not reserved to any particular sex or age but may reveal itself in the most unexpected quarters.

CHAPTER 14

MIND AS STRUCTURE

I

An Ardent Wundtian Disciple

Edward Titchener adhered closely to the teachings of Wundt. Altogether too much time, he declared, was being spent on the problem of functions. The main need today is for an analysis of conscious elements. The science of mind should restrict itself to a description of its structural contents, in the same way as the science of anatomy describes, part by part, the make-up of the body. Titchener held the view that if mental functions are investigated before the structure of consciousness is fully examined, psychology will never succeed in its ambition to become a strict positive science. The best it can achieve will be a naïve animistic explication of mind; much as physiology arrived at the same kind of animistic outlook before there was a sufficient knowledge of anatomy. Aristotle is a sample of this very thing. He began with a functional description of the data of consciousness, and ended in the shadows of a superstitious vitalism. Titchener openly opposed the theory of imageless thought. It seemed to him that the thinking procedure could be adequately accounted for in terms of faint images. In fact, all abstract ideas, attitudes, and meanings which appear in consciousness can be reduced to images or sensations. To the end of his days, Titchener refused to admit the evidence for "higher mental processes," that is to say, for data that could not be reduced to purely sensory products.

2

Atoms of Consciousness

The simplest units into which conscious contents can be resolved are sensations, images, and feelings. They are like the elements about which the chemist speaks. Every atom of matter has its own distinctive properties. Just so, every atom of mind has its own inseparable, though variable, attributes. These are five in number, all of a simple sensory character: quality, intensity, extensity, duration, and clearness. There is the possibility of a sixth: vividness. Titchener's belief in the elementary nature of sensations and their attributes is illustrated by his use of simple geometrical schemes to show their relationships. Thus, the connections between the hue, purity, and brightness of colors are pictured, after Ebbinghaus, in a "color pyramid" which indicates graphically at what brightness each of the four primary colors, red, yellow, green, and blue, has the greatest purity and how the purity decreases as the colors change in brightness toward black or white.

To show the connections between auditory sensations, Titchener devised his "tonal pencil," a bell-shaped figure which represents the association of large volume with low tones and of small volume with high tones. He also designed a "touch pyramid" to indicate the relations between the dozen or more distinct types of cutaneous sensations which he and others had discovered. On this pyramid, one corner represents neutral pressure, another pricking pain, while the third and fourth corners indicate qualities of ache and strain. Sensations of heat are placed at a point midway between pressure and pricking pain. They result from the simultaneous stimulation of adjacent warm and cool spots on the skin.

Titchener adopted Henning's "olfactory prism" which

shows the relations of six principal odors: fragrant, ethereal, spicy, resinous, putrid, and burned, each of which corresponds to a distinct chemical structure in the odorous substance. He also made use of Henning's "taste tetrahedron" which supposes that each of the four elementary taste qualities is stimulated by a distinct type of chemical body. Combinations of such bodies produce corresponding manifolds of tastes, represented along the edges of the tetrahedron.

3
The Problem of Attention

Titchener searched for some aspect of consciousness which might be identified with attention. Change in clearness would seem to have been the factor most frequently mentioned by previous investigators. Accordingly, for the structural psychologist, it is sufficient to say that the sensory attribute of clearness and the phenomenon of attention are one and the same thing. Titchener interpreted the statement that there is a focus and a margin of consciousness to mean that there are two levels of clearness in attending processes. The evidence to support this contention was supposed to have been discovered in the findings of *Wilhelm Wirth* who succeeded Wundt at Leipzig. Wirth measured the ability to discriminate small changes in brightness within an illuminated area, while attention was directed to other parts of the field of vision. Differences in acuity were noted when attention shifted from a point near the light to one more remote; and these were presumed to represent differences of clearness. Titchener tried to give further support to the theory by referring to the change which occurs during the inspection of picture puzzles where the outlines of hidden objects are mingled with the lines of the total picture. When the hidden objects are detected, there is a sudden narrowing down of the field of clearness from the picture as a whole to the parts newly revealed.

4
The Field of Orexis

Titchener regarded feelings of pleasantness and unpleasantness as irresolvable; that is, experiences which cannot be broken down into simpler components. Hence, pleasant and unpleasant feelings are conscious elements in the same way as sensations are conscious elements. There is a difference between these two types of phenomena. Feelings are not localizable, as are sensations. Again, feelings are always attached to sensations upon which they are dependent. Moreover, feelings are neutralized through the intermittent repetition of a given experience, whereas sensations are adapted to continuous stimulation. For example, one may always notice the same odor of chlorine every time he enters a laboratory, though he eventually ceases to dislike it. Then, too, feelings have no attribute of clearness such as we find in our sensations. If one stops to analyze his feelings, he discovers that they tend immediately to disappear. Yet they have the attribute of intensity and a further quality which appears to be most comparable to the sensory quality of pressure.

5
Bones to Pick

In objecting to Titchener's position that conscious elements and attributes are all that we need for a complete scientific account of mind, *Carl Rahn* pointed out, among other things, that sometimes one of the supposedly inseparable attributes is discerned by itself. He cited the experimental work of Külpe on abstraction, in which the subject was enabled to detect common characteristics, such as form, color, or pattern, in a succession of designs, each of which was momentarily shown to the subject. When he was watching for a given characteristic, for example, form, he often was unable to report what the color of the object had been. Hence this attribute may be missing from the consciousness of the observer. In response to Rahn's criticism, Titchener modified his position somewhat by occasionally substituting the term "dimensions" for "attributes." This implied that the observable qualities of an object under examination result from the particular experimental procedure used to investigate consciousness.

The dimensional point of view has been worked up and expanded by *Edwin Boring* who tells us that the unsatisfactory results of structuralism were due to Wundt's distinction of consciousness of the psychological world as immediate experience, from awareness of the physical world as mediate experience. Boring maintains that consciousness is not prior to the external universe, even though the knowledge of physics is derived through consciousness. He further observes that consciousness is dependent upon physical factors, such as the state of the nervous system, the cerebral cortex, and so forth. Moreover, the sensations, images, and feelings which Titchener treated as atoms of consciousness do not appear as elements in the actual everyday experience of people. Boring concludes that conscious elements are comparable to physical elements, such as electrons and protons, inasmuch as both kinds of data are inductions from experience.

6

Further Findings of the Introspectionists

John Baird greatly extended the use of the introspective method on which Titchener laid so much importance. The danger here, of course, is overrefinement; that is to say, introspection pushed to the point where one has ranged outside the bounds of ordinary human experience, or where the analysis is so subtle that only the experimenter knows what is being introspected. Baird's students investigated the higher mental processes of abstraction, recognition, and choice by means of a "complete introspection" which attempted to report every detail of consciousness. This method was considered necessary if psychology is to approach the accuracy of the other natural sciences where the investigator tries to account for all possible factors in an experimental situation. Sometimes the reports of events that occurred within a space of three or four seconds actually took forty pages of typewritten matter to describe.

Raymond Wheeler used the method of complete introspection to study the process of choice. The subjects were asked to select one of several musical compositions to which they listened. Consciousness of the task involved, it was said, seemed to consist largely in muscular strains directed toward the final goal of making a decision. The sensations of strain were accompanied by a succession of visual and verbal images. Wheeler came to the conclusion that the entire process of choosing could be described in terms of sensations and images; that there is no "unanalyzable residue" remaining in consciousness to indicate the presence of an ego that directs the choice.

In contrast to this materialistic interpretation, *Mary Calkins* cited the evidence of a unique consciousness of self in the process of volition, as well as the fact that all other psychological experiences are referred to self. Thus the testimonies of the two investigators are basically at odds and give us some idea of the controversial state in which the problem of self-awareness has remained for most of the scientific psychologists.

We have already described the work done on choice by some of the European investigators. The intimate connection between choice and the ego has been remarked by several investigators and in different lines of research. There is *Narziss Ach's* "I really will" formula; *Francis Aveling's* "adoption by the self . . . of the motive or motives for the selection of one of the alternatives"; *William McDougall's* "supporting of a conation by the cooperation of an impulse, excited within the nervous system, of the self-regarding sentiment"; even *Sigmund Freud's* "superego," which must have some connection with will since it represents his idea of natural morality. All these are so many independent sources of information, leading to the notion of self as revealed in volitional activity. The agreement here is all the more remarkable because it derives from such divergent systems of psychological thought.

CHAPTER 15

THE OUTLOOK OF FUNCTIONALISM

I

The Dean of American Psychologists

William James described mental life as a process of biological adjustment between the impression of stimuli and the expression of the organism. He was not a functionalist in the technical meaning of the term; yet his outlook on mental phenomena gave rise to the trend which we know today as "functionalism." This tendency is somewhat analogous to act psychology. Thus we find that both approaches share a mutual opposition to the concept of mind as composed of elements. In a sense it is true to say that James, with his functional outlook, occupied much the same position with regard to the structural psychology of Titchener as Brentano held in respect to the content psychology of Wundt. The contrast, here indicated, seems to run through the whole story of modern psychology: (*a*) content psychology opposed by act psychology; (*b*) structuralism opposed by functionalism; (*c*) the introspective approach opposed by the purely objective or behavioristic approach; (*d*) mechanical interpretations opposed by purposive or hormic interpretations; (*e*) the psychology of the conscious opposed by the psychology of the unconscious.

According to James, the conscious life of man always reveals a "pursuance of future ends and a choice of means." Psychological operations are always accompanied by bodily changes and show a dependence on bodily conditions. A person's age, for instance, has an effect on his ability to remember. Following the lead of Fechner and Wundt, James suggested that the most practical hypothesis regarding the relation of mind to matter is a simple parallelism. He attempted to combine the teachings of Wundt and the act psychologists with his own organismic approach. His aim was to produce a comprehensive system into which all the new discoveries of the mind explorers might be fitted—a laudable ambition, no doubt, but based on a dualism between the spiritual and material elements of human nature that made such an integration impossible.

2

The Problem of Emotion

James accepted Darwin's idea that the bodily expression of emotions represents an instinctive modification of movements which were originally useful for self-preservation. His theory of emotion, announced at the same time by the Danish psychologist *Carl Lange*, ranges the order of events as follows: (*a*) knowledge of emotional stimulus or situation; (*b*) physiological changes resultant upon such knowledge; (*c*) affective experience, wherein the object-simply-apprehended is transformed into an object-emotionally-felt. The James-Lange theory was later seriously questioned by men like *Charles Sherrington* and *Walter Cannon*. The latter places affective experience before the physiological changes, in the sequence of events. Cannon's work is notable for two insights: (*a*) emotional behavior may be present without true emotional experience; (*b*) emotions cannot be classified on a basis of physiological changes since the latter may be identical in different kinds of affective experience.

The traditional point of view, as expounded by Aquinas, is to regard physiological changes as essential to the emotional procedure, regardless of their position in scientific theory. Thus, knowledge is the efficient cause, bodily resonances the material cause, and conscious affect the formal cause, in the total explication of an emotional response. Properly speaking one cannot discover a sequence of material factor upon formal factor, or vice versa, in a phenomenon whose unified nature demands the simultaneous presence of both factors.

3

The Stream of Consciousness

James explained will-acts in terms of an "ideomotor" activity. This would mean that volition is an idea which leads to action. In making a choice between alternatives, there is always initially a conflict between the tendencies of different ideas toward realization in overt behavior. Eventually, the most intense idea, or the idea that is reinforced by the greatest number of associations, prevails over its weaker rivals and issues in outer conduct. James did not deny man's freedom of will; yet there is the definite implication in his teaching that ideomotor activity is determined by past events. Consciousness of self is a complex experience built up from many aspects of life. These aspects include awareness of external things, such as friends, home, financial condition, and so forth; and awareness of internal phenomena, such as sensations of internal bodily states, muscular stress and strain, and so on. Descriptively, the ego is identical with the stream of one's consciousness. As early as 1875, James introduced some experimental demonstration into his lectures on psychology at Harvard, though the first American laboratory was not formally opened till 1883 at Johns Hopkins.

4

The Value of Performance

James McKeen Cattell developed a system which was called "capacity psychology." In it emphasis was laid on the individual's power of performing certain tasks. The approach was objective, in contrast to most of the psychological research that was going on at the time. Cattell visited Wundt's laboratory where he conducted numerous reaction-time experiments. He tabulated the normal reaction times for common verbal associations, and thus devised a standard by which to test responses of an unusual or abnormal character. For a year, Cattell worked with Galton from whom he received his inspiration to study individual differences. Soon after, he wrote an article in which he introduced the expression "mental tests" into the language of psychology. He also presented a number of physical and mental tests in his lectures at Columbia University, employing them for the first time on large groups of persons.

Cattell collaborated with *George Fullerton* in reexamining the data of psychophysics and declared that such data reveal merely the range of error in the total response of the individual. They do not show the existence of distinct mental aptitudes, such as the sensory units which Fechner postulated. Cattell also devised a measure for rating some of the more generalized types of judgment. This measure was called the "order of merit." Various items were graded in serial order according to some criterion of worth, proceeding from one extreme of value to the other. By this technique, Cattell tested and compared the judgments of a number of people on our American scientists. It is high time, he said, that we use our psychological devices to determine just what promotes and what hinders the advance of science.

5

Interest in Adolescence

Stanley Hall enlarged upon the scope of genetic psychology. He was a thoroughgoing evolutionist and made extensive use of the theory that, in the development of the individual, both before and after birth, all the steps of organic evolution are telescoped. This was an application of Ernst Haeckel's principle of ontogenesis: the embryonic history of an individual is always a reenactment of the history of the race. To illustrate the point, Hall declared that dreams of floating are memory tokens of an early age when our protozoan ancestors glided about on the surface of the water. Similarly, the gill-like formation which appears in human embryonic life is reminiscent of the fish stage of our history, just as the action of a young infant in clinging to a horizontal support rehearses the behavior of our tree-climbing forebears.

All of Hall's theorizing was wrapped up in this sort of evolutionary covering. The doctrine of descent was expressed or implied in practically everything he wrote. Man, whose history looks back to a primitive one-celled stage of existence, went through eons of growth before his present skills of thought and speech and his moral habits were possible. If Herbert Spencer was the first to give evolution a place in modern philosophy, and Francis Galton the first to apply the genetic principle to the study of individuals and races, Stanley Hall was the first to attempt to build up a psychology of mental development in terms of a gradual organic emergence from lower forms of life. His complete surrender to the influence of Darwin paved the way for the behaviorists and their kin.

Hall particularly stressed the need of studying the adolescent age of man. Here is the crucial stage in the evolution of every individual. The rapid growth manifest during the teens, the awkwardness and embarrassment that seem to be a constant feature of these transitional years, are often the cause of a loss of mental poise. Adolescence also brings a change in the individual's social habits. The practices of childhood are cast aside before the settled ways of adulthood are acquired; and so another fertile source of difficulties is opened up. Despite the conjectural nature of much of his work, Hall's emphasis on the deep-lying sources of human motivation was an inducement to his students to extend the scope of their psychological inquiries. In 1883, he founded the first laboratory of psychology in America at Johns Hopkins. Four years later, he published the first magazine devoted to the problems of mental science: the *American Journal of Psychology*. His great organizing ability also helped in establishing the American Psychological Association in 1892, of which he was first president.

James and Hall are often compared. They were the real progenitors of psychology in America. James, with his literary grace, intrigued people into studying psychology; Hall, with his abounding energy and wide range of interests, forced them to listen. James set things in motion; Hall ounded them. James's attitude, as someone said, was paternal; Hall's was avuncular. James was at heart a philosopher; Hall was essentially an experimentalist. James loved the soft influences of the academic halls; Hall preferred the rugged highways and byways of life. Both men were explorers in their own fashions. Within the range of their magnetic orbits moved many of the youth who, in our own day, are carrying the burden of psychological research in America.

6

Naturalism in Psychology

John Dewey described mental functions as the unified organization of stimuli, sensations, and reflex arcs. The synthesis of these elements comes from their common reference to a biological end. Separately, they are mere artifacts. It is only through the process of adaptation to environment that such factors acquire significance for the psychological organism. Dewey regarded mental science as a part of biology and claimed that its problems should be the problems of successful living. His naturalistic point of view has been extended to the field of education where it has exerted an enormous influence. In particular, he recommended the study of the psychophysical organism in relation to its environmental needs. He declared that the stimulus-response bond is of interest only in respect to the end to be attained which is the achievement of a harmonious pattern of individual life and successful incorporation into society.

7

The Functional Ideal

James Angell sought to give a clear statement of the functional position in psychology. As a system, according to Angell, it emphasizes mental operations rather than mental contents, seeks to know the designs of such operations, searches for the "fundamental utilities of consciousness." The functional school, however, lost much of its prestige and usefulness as it fell back on purely organic descriptions of psychological data. The work of *George Ladd* represents a trend toward physiology which reached its peak in America with the development of the behavioristic school.

The whole functional movement in psychology is in an obvious reaction to the Wundtian atomistic method of approaching psychological data. In America, it has taken the form of a marked opposition to the psychology of Titchener which was in the strictly Wundtian tradition. The functionalists, from James on, have been interested in knowing, not what the contents or elemental factors of consciousness are, but what mental processes develop into, what purposes they serve in life. Representatives of the school have been biological-minded. They would make psychology a more practical form of knowledge. Their goal has not been so scientifically precise as that of the structuralists; yet for this very reason, perhaps, it has been closer to the experience of the average man.

The functional ideal was championed by men who had a sincere interest in the workaday world. Undoubtedly there are bigger names in academic psychology. Wundt was a martyr to facts and precise measurements. Ebbinghaus spent years in an exact study of the laws of memory. Weber performed thousands of experiments to try out his law of sensitivity. These men were indefatigable; and their rigid adherence to the methods of the laboratory has definitely forwarded the cause of scientific psychology. Yet the contributions of men like James and Cattell and Hall seem more vital and closer to the problems of daily living. The regulation of habits and emotions, the proper development of mental aptitudes, sympathetic recognition of the difficulties that accompany adolescence, are surely pressing needs for every human being. The functionalists, as mind explorers, tried to use the laboratory as a furnace for forging laws that would help the teacher and pupil, the parent and the growing child, the industrialist, the social worker, and those who are called to be leaders in the practical walks of life.

CHAPTER 16

PSYCHOLOGY AND ITS CLOSE RELATIVES

I

Connection of Psychology with Other Sciences

We have already pointed out how, at the beginning, the science of psychology was molded in large part by the demands of the physical investigators. Men in the laboratory were looking for more accurate information about the cognitive faculties, more certainty about the origin of scientific judgments. It was also true that, as psychology waxed stronger, the findings of the other sciences were conditioned by the demands of the students of mind for further knowledge of facts bearing on psychological phenomena. Such facts are important either because they show the connection between mind and matter, or because they yield comparative insights into the nature of human operations. But in employing the data of another science the psychologist ought to know something of the experimental work that brought them to light.

It is obvious, for example, that a knowledge of the physical world will help us to a better understanding of the character of sensory processes. It is even more obvious that a knowledge of physiological activities will give us a better grasp of the nature of psychological processes. Man is a creature composed of matter and spirit; and this very condition of his being would indicate that there can be no science of psychology unless the relationship between the psychic and somatic aspects of human acts and properties is properly gauged. It is not surprising, then, that most scientific psychologists have been extremely preoccupied with physiology. The danger, here, is not from physiology, but from the psychologists who have lost themselves in the wonders of the body, either forgetting that man has another side to his being which is even more important for an understanding of human nature; or refusing to admit that psychological data need any explication other than that which can be supplied by physiological analysis.

In the following sections we shall see what insights have been added to psychology by more recent discoveries in the physiology of the nervous system, by animal researches, and by the studies of the psychopathologists. Thus physiology presents certain concepts, regarding the structure and function of nerve mechanisms, which psychological theory cannot overlook. Again, exact experiments on animals are important because they provide an objective check on many aspects of human psychology. Finally, a study of exaggerated mental tendencies, or of deviations from the normal, furnishes us with a magnified view of certain facets of human nature. This kind of analysis, as we shall see, has been a most fruitful source of information for both the science and the philosophy of mind, as well as for better human living.

2

Further Contributions of the Physiologists

Some of the great advances made in the field of physiology within modern times, and of immediate interest to the scientific psychologist, have already been described. Further research along the same lines has added new clarifications of the problem of psychophysical functions and relationships. Among the findings of the physiologists, none have been of greater significance than the developments of neurological knowledge, since it is in the sphere of neurophysiology that we discover the immediate basis of psychological processes. First of all, there is the concept of the neurone which grew out of the larger notion of the cell as the physical unit of plant and animal tissue. Several types of nerve units or neurones were reported by investigators, for example, the large nerve bodies of the brain described by *Johannes Purkinje* in 1837. Evidence of the connection of the nerve bodies with nerve fibers was introduced by *Augustus Waller* in 1850. Waller also devised a method of cutting fibers near the cell body and observing their degeneration. This made it possible to trace the course of nerve pathways.

In 1873 *Camillo Golgi* discovered that nerve tissue becomes distinctly visible when stained with silver nitrate. He also showed that neurones develop from embryonic specks which enlarge into cell bodies. Each neurone sends out a single long axone from one side of the body and shorter many-branched dendrites from the other side. In 1889, *Santiago Ramón y Cajal* devised an improved type of staining that enabled him to make a more careful study of the connections between the axone of one neurone and the dendrites of another. He declared that the network, formed at this point of interconnection, represents a functional, not an anatomical, unit. The network later came to be known as a "synapse." *Charles Sherrington* defended Cajal's point of view and demonstrated that nerve currents normally travel in one direction only. He cited the further fact that the speed of a reflex is slower than the speed of a nerve impulse along an equal length of continuous nerve fiber, as confirmation of the functional activity of the synapse. The strength of the nerve impulse usually exhibits a definite intensity, regardless of the intensity of the stimulation it receives.

In 1912, *Edgar Adrian* proved that the impulse acts in an "all-or-none" way. The presumption is, therefore, that variation in the intensity of sensory and motor responses is due to the participation of a greater or lesser number of nerve fibers in the reaction. The duration of a single impulse at any given point along a nerve tract is less than a thousandth of a second. Following excitation, there is a "refractory period," first noted by *Francis Gotch* and *George Burch* in 1899. During this resting stage, the nerve is immune to excitation, after which it settles down once more to normal excitability. However, the refractory period is so short that, in a normal excitation of the sense organs, there are several hundred impulses per second passing along the nerve fibers.

In 1913, Adrian demonstrated that when the refractory phase of one series of impulses corresponds with the refractory phase of another, "inhibition" results. On the other hand, if the active phase of one series corresponds with the active phase of another, "summation" appears. Adrian also became interested in the Müllerian principle of specific nerve energies. From his studies he concluded that nerve impulses are differentiated according to the form, rate of impingement, and intensity of the stimulus. Fibers of different sense organs may also vary in their time reactions. As the theory of Müller is stated today, it usually takes account of nerves and end organs together.

3

Functions of the Autonomic Nervous System

The distinction between voluntary and involuntary muscles became clearer with the work of *John Langley* on the autonomic part of the nervous system. When the physiologist uses the term "voluntary" in reference to the musculature of the body, he means that area of movement which is controlled by the cerebrospinal sector of the nervous system. "Involuntary," on the other hand, designates the musculature which is regulated by the autonomic sector of the nervous system. This latter system consists in a series of motor nerves which leave the spinal cord at three different levels — the cranial, the thoracic-lumbar, and the sacral — and terminate in the vital organs. It is a purely motor system, interconnected by synapses outside the spinal cord, and relatively independent of the central or cerebrospinal nervous system.

It was noted, for example, that when the heartbeat is increased, digestion may become disturbed without one's being conscious of it; also, the pupils of the eyes may dilate. This physiological picture at once furnished support for the traditional description of emotional conduct, in which organic resonances play a capital part. The regulation of glandular secretions, too, is an important function of the autonomic system. Some of the glands have ducts or cavities; others are ductless, pouring their hormones directly into the blood stream. The latter have a decisive role to play in the well-being of the organism. The adrenals, for instance, cause the production of blood sugar and thus increase bodily vigor in times of emotional stress. The thyroid, in the throat, also serves to increase our kinetic energies according to the demands of bodily mobilization. The pituitary, lodged in the brain, has a profound influence on organic growth. Knowledge of how these ductless glands act as a physiological basis in shaping personality has been given effective treatment by many psychologists.

4
Brain Physiology

Interest in cerebral localization has grown far beyond the pioneer work of Flourens and Broca. The facts that have been brought to light lead to different points of view. On the one hand, numerous clinical researches have linked specific forms of sensory and motor phenomena with definite brain injuries; on the other, various experimental reports seem to indicate that functions of the brain are not so definitely confined to one area that they cannot move to another. As early as 1907, *Shepherd Franz* pointed out that the cerebrum may act as a whole, rather than by parts, in producing its effects. He cited several cases of injury to the brain which resulted in a loss of speech, followed, after a time, by a reeducation of the speech habit. He surmised, accordingly, that other parts of the cortex act in a vicarious way for an area that is injured.

In 1920, *Henry Head* described several cases of brain injury where the connection between the cerebral cortex and other lower parts of the brain centers had been destroyed. These lower parts appeared to function quite readily without their usual cerebral control. Patients, for instance, suffered excruciating pain from a gentle stroking of the palm or from the sounding of soft music. Other victims exhibited exaggerated and immoderate traits of behavior, such as contortions of the face and raucous laughter. Head concluded that cerebral control, which is relatively greater in the higher animals and greatest in man, has a tempering effect on responses which would issue in violence if they passed through the lower brain centers only. *Gordon Holmes* was associated with Head in his studies of cortical injuries. The work of both men gave direction to the researches of Cannon on thalamic degeneration and emotional upsets, mentioned in the preceding chapter. In 1929, *Karl Lashley* made some prolonged studies of the injured brains of rats and concluded that the cerebral substance is relatively equipotential in character; that is to say, there is a "non-specialized dynamic function of the tissue as a whole." The trend of his experimental work would indicate that the need of postulating localized brain centers is not absolute, even though such centers do generally exist.

The meaning for human psychology of the splendid studies of Franz, Head, and Lashley may be briefly set down. First, there is definite evidence that our sensory and motor skills cannot be explained in terms of rigid one-way tracks in the cortical system. Second, as these skills and habits increase in complexity, they involve much wider brain areas and cortical patterns than was formerly suspected. Third, the more naïve and less analytic view that the brain functions as a whole appears to be established by solid clinical findings. Fourth, although cortical centers actually exist their need is not absolute, since their functions may be taken over by other areas. On the other hand, this equipotentiality does not mean that there is a free wandering of sensory and motor activities over the entire cerebral cortex.

From the classic work of the older brain physiologists, modern explorers are bounding on to further discoveries. Another chapter has opened up with the discovery of the uses of chemicals in treating injuries to the brain. The mysteries of the cerebral cortex, with its estimated ninety-two billion nerve cells, are now being attacked with new tools and new techniques. But with all this advance, the work has hardly begun. A map of the human brain, with its lines of nerve conduction fully shown, would be incomparably more criss-crossed and netted than a chart of all the telephone and telegraph circuits in North America. The men in white, however, are not discouraged at the problem which faces them; and the future will place great reliance on what they find in the delicate chemistry of the brain. They have already devised a way of recording the electrical activity which goes on in these "master tissues" of the body when a person is engaged in mental pursuits. Just as we have cardiographs that tell us how the heart is acting, so now it is possible to get encephalographs which record the magnetic phenomena that take place in the cerebral regions of the head.

5

Experiments on Animals

Animals offer an opportunity for the employment of experimental techniques that are obviously impossible in man's case. The researches in this direction are illuminating because of the comparative insights that they reveal. In 1869 *Friedrich Goltz* removed the cerebra of frogs and noted that they continued to eat, croak, and find means of escape from enclosures, when urged along by stimulation. Excising the cerebella, he found that the frogs sat and crawled with great unsteadiness. When further deprived of their medullae, they responded with simple reflex movements if their toes were pinched.

Jacques Loeb offered an account of animal behavior which was purely mechanistic in its terms. For example, he regarded the plunging of insects into a flame as an automatic response which was determined by the irritant action of heat on different parts of the body surfaces. He called this sort of action a "tropism" and declared that the movement of the insects, under such conditions, is just as mechanical as the turning of the leaves of a plant toward the sun. He pointed to the development of unfertilized eggs of sea urchins to a larval stage — simply by immersing them first in weak acid solutions and then in increasingly stronger solutions of salts — as another instance of the mechanical nature of life. He repeated the method of separating the eggs of frogs with a needle so that several organisms were produced where only one would have grown originally.

To be sure, *Hans Driesch* had done the same thing, and his conclusions were quite different from the machine interpretations of Loeb. Driesch was firmly convinced that living phenomena cannot be explained by purely mechanistic concepts. *Herbert Jennings*, too, counseled moderation in the acceptance of the mechanistic viewpoint, because of the great variations which he observed in the behavior of protozoa. Such conduct, he declared, cannot be described wholly in terms of physical and chemical reactions. Jennings, however, could not be classified as a belligerent vitalist, in the sense in which Driesch fought for hormic or purposive concepts in biology. But the general nature of animal activity, Jennings maintained, must be put on a different level of description from that which obtains in the purely physicochemical domain. His researches gave a new impulse to the study of consciousness in animals and marked another stage in the development of comparative psychology.

Lloyd Morgan established the concept of "trial and error" which he limited to animal behavior and interpreted as a "lengthy and somewhat clumsy process" of solving difficulties. This was around 1900. Soon the significance of the method for human learning was put forward by other investigators. *Ernst Mach*, whose work has already been mentioned, made an application of it to reasoning processes. He described the results as a kind of "thought experiment." Mach denied that reason, in man, is a guiding faculty. For the traditional notion of thinking as the product of an ability to abstract and generalize, he substituted his own concept of reasoning as a state of activity aroused by the need for some kind of readjustment. As long as the need is present the state of activity will persist. John Dewey at Columbia followed through the ideas of Mach and made them part of a functional interpretation of human nature.

Ivan Pavlov observed that a response which ordinarily results from a given stimulus will follow from another stimulus provided the latter is frequently presented just before the usual stimulus. The common example is salivation at the sound of a bell. This relation was noted from several experiments performed upon dogs. Thus, the ringing of the bell would produce the same salivary effects as result from the stimuli of sight or smell. The new response was called a "conditioned reflex." *Vladimir Bekhterev*, another Russian physiologist, worked along the same lines; and there is little doubt that both investigators did much to shape the destinies of the behavioristic school which appeared later in America. It is only fair to record, however, that neither Pavlov nor Bekhterev was responsible for what the behaviorists made out of their researches. It is fairly certain they would not have subscribed to the principle that the conditioned reflex has rid psychology of its task of studying conscious data.

In developing his theory of conditioned reflexes, Pavlov found that the time-order of events is an essential factor. Even after a thousand trials, an animal will not become conditioned if the normal stimulus is presented before the conditioning stimulus. Moreover, after the conditioned reflex is well established, it is necessary to give it an occasional "re-enforcement" by following up the conditioning stimulus with the normal one. If, after the conditioned response has worn out, the conditioning stimulus is again presented, a new phenomenon, called "conditioned inhibition," is observed. In this state, the animal will fail to respond to either the normal stimulus or the conditioning stimulus.

By conditioning the animal to a given stimulus — for example, a certain pitch of sound — and then building up conditioned inhibitions to all stimuli that differ only slightly from this one, the investigator can get a measure of the fineness of discrimination possible to the animal. In this manner, a brute may be made to differentiate between shades of color, tonal pitches, geometrical forms, and so forth. The work of Bekhterev and Pavlov was important insofar as it furnished confirmation, on the physiological level, of the law that stimuli are linked together in consciousness by a bond of temporal contiguity. Thus the relationship between certain psychological data and their organic basis was better understood.

Edward Thorndike developed the "trial and error" principle of Lloyd Morgan and made an effort to apply the precise measurements of the laboratory to the reactions of normal animals. He secured a certain number of facts that could be expressed quantitatively and compared them with other facts. His favorite experiment was the escape problem. Fish learned to withdraw from the sunlight; chicks to find their way out of mazes; cats, dogs, and apes to manipulate strings and bars in order to liberate themselves from cages. Such devices allowed Thorndike to make measurements in terms of definite units of action. He was able to estimate the number of correct and incorrect performances involved in the successful completion of an escape task. From a long series of observations he derived a group of curves which were quite like the jagged and sloping learning curves that Ebbinghaus had obtained. Because of the similarity, Thorndike was led to infer that there is no evidence of a reasoning capacity in animals. The argument from analogy, it should be noted, resulted in a true conclusion, namely, that animals do not possess intellectual insights in solving their problems; but, it was drawn from the premise that the curves of human learning, which supplied the basis of the comparison, do not give evidence of intellectual insights. This premise is true only on condition that the learning process in human beings is confined strictly to the operation of the senses.

The point about the matter, however, is that animals do not think. They do not solve their problems ideationally, as human beings do. According to Thorndike, they learn by trial and error. That is to say, they merely fumble around with a stimulus or a situation and, after making several attempts and committing many blunders, they finally learn to complete a given task with a fair amount of success. But there is no evidence that they observe abstract relations or use ideas, that they draw inferences, or have any notion of what is involved in a choice. Aristotle once said that man's hand is his most intellectual tool. Aquinas repeated the observation. Stanley Hall turned it around by declaring that man's intellect is handmade. But never has the prehensile organ of an ape given any token of intellectual patterning in its movements. Its skills are either purely animal accomplishments or habits that have been imposed by the ingenuity of man.

Thorndike further inferred that the development of habits of learning is like the genesis of muscular skills where use and disuse condition the ease and promptness with which the muscles are employed. He also noted that an animal strives to continue those actions that are emotionally satisfying, just as it endeavors to alter or leave off those actions that are emotionally unsatisfying. Thorndike attempted to apply what he discovered about animal learning to the tasks of human education. For intellectual insight and volitional control, which surely have some part in man's early acquisition of habits, he substituted his "law of use and disuse" and its related "law of satisfaction." His account of the habit-forming process is a purely sensistic one.

Robert Yerkes made a specialized study of primates. In 1927, he helped establish a primate laboratory at Yale University. He also summarized the extensive literature that had been written on the anthropoids, including descriptions of their sensitive capacities, their ability to perceive form, distance, and movement, their power of learning, and their emotional life. He employed a method of so-called multiple choice in which an animal is trained to distinguish, among several concrete situations, the particular response which bears a relation to other situations. For example, in the presence of several doorways, the animal must learn to push

open the door to the right of any door that is left standing
ajar. Crows could manage the feat, but could not learn to
push open the second door to the right. As the tasks got
closer to genuine abstract types of generalization, the animal
became more incompetent to solve them. Thus, oddly
enough, no brute, however sharp-witted, could learn not to
attempt the opening of a door that had been successfully
opened on an immediately previous trial.

For over forty years Yerkes gave his best efforts to the
work of analyzing the gorilla, the orangutan, the chimpanzee,
and the gibbon. From womb to tomb he observed their
complicated ways of behavior. It was a Herculean task but
the results were written into the annals of science as a new
chapter in animal psychology. His findings clearly show
that the primates have a temperamental pattern which is
distinctly their own; that their faculties are capable of improvement; that their instincts are highly organized, and
their social sense very keen. Still, the differences that set
them off from human beings are clearly marked. "As our
knowledge and understanding of anthropoid life increases"
concludes Yerkes, "so also does our thankfulness that we are
man."

From experiments on the different phases of animal life,
most of the facts that have supplied the genetic approach to
psychology have been developed. One of the problems of
special attraction to the investigator is the question of the
inheritance of instincts. *William McDougall* studied the
ability of several generations of rats to learn the proper avenue
of escape from a tank of water. Care was taken to choose
rats which were typical for each generation, so that the experiment would not be influenced by an undue special selection.
The results showed that a certain amount of improvement in
the rate of learning occurred within the span of sixteen
generations.

After 1908, McDougall championed the position that the fundamental analysis of both human and animal nature should be made in terms of inherited instincts and inherited tendencies. These are to be interpreted as distinct patterns of behavior, transmitted from generation to generation, and furnishing each individual with a psychological equipment that is largely hereditary. Because of his emphasis on the purposive value of instincts and native tendencies in the development of the individual, McDougall's psychology is described as hormic in character.

If patterns of behavior can be inherited, it follows that the organization of the neuromuscular system by which such behavior is exhibited is somehow predetermined in the germinal tissue of the organism. Such a view has been accepted by many authors. Other investigators, however, like *Samuel Detwiller* and *Zing Kuo* conducted experiments that illustrate the influence of one part of the growing organism on another. Their work indicated that environment, both internal and external, contributes something to the structural and functional development of the individual. After a careful survey of the whole problem, in which the evidence for both positions was thoroughly examined, *Leonard Carmichael* declared that heredity and environment are not antagonistic agencies; that, in fact, it is neither expedient nor scientific to separate them as factors in the expansion of our psychological powers.

6

How the Psychopathologists Helped

Philippe Pinel is usually given credit for having been the first investigator to attempt a study of the problem of insanity from a scientific point of view. He regarded mental disease as a medical problem and sought to make a thorough reform of the crude methods with which insane patients were treated.

His techniques, however, were physiological rather than psychological in approach. He saw to it that patients were given proper nourishment and an adequate amount of rest. In great measure, the splendid system of public and private hospitals for the insane throughout the world owes its existence to the pioneering work of Pinel at the Bicêtre in Paris. His treatise on the medicophilosophic aspects of insanity was one of the first books of its kind.

Emil Kraepelin was the first scholar to introduce a comprehensive classification of the various forms of insanity. In his records, he aimed at integrating psychological symptoms with physiological ones. From the complicated descriptions of earlier physicians, Kraepelin devised a list of distinct types of mental disease which he regarded as analogous to certain types of physical disease. Three kinds were given special consideration: (*a*) "primary dementia," which usually appears at the age of adolescence and is characterized by a withdrawal from reality, exaggerated daydreaming, and incongruous emotional responses; (*b*) "paranoia," marked by an abnormal centering of everything on the patient's self, with delusions of grandeur or delusions of persecution developing as a result; (*c*) "manic-depressive" insanity, whose symptoms are revealed by recurring cycles of violent passional outbursts and correspondingly deep states of melancholia and inactivity.

The influence of Wundt, under whom he studied as a young man, is apparent in the work of Kraepelin. The rigid and elemental manner in which he classified the psychological symptoms of insanity often made it necessary to combine several of his types in the diagnosis of a single case. This became confusing when more and more symptoms of mental abnormality were brought to light by medical investigation.

Jean Charcot developed a theory of mental abnormality from earlier studies that had been made on hypnotism. The curious slumberlike states that Mesmer had explained as phenomena of animal magnetism were now accounted for on a new clinical basis, and the word "mesmerism" was supplanted by the more acceptable term "hypnotism." For a brief period, the hypnotic sleep was used in surgical operations, but was soon displaced by the discovery of ether in 1846. Charcot was of the opinion that the hypnotic condition was identical with hysteria which, in turn, was pictured as a neurosis due to organic weakness. To substantiate his theory, he pointed to the actual sameness of symptoms found in both states: the fact that all sorts of suggestions are acted upon, the rigid cataleptic condition that overtakes the muscles, and so on. Charcot's psychological description of these states was made in terms of the activity of the subject's ideas. Thus, in the normal person, there is a unified stream of thought; but in the abnormal person, the stream scatters and his ideas become dissociated.

In support of this view, *Pierre Janet*, the pupil of Charcot, propounded the theory that in a healthy individual there is always a normal "psychic tension." Through some disability, this tension is lost, so that either a dissociation of ideas occurs, with a possibility that one or more of them may become fixed; or a general feeling of incompetence develops, accompanied by morbid anxiety. Janet was inclined to doubt his master's opinion that hypnosis and hysteria really are identical phenomena. He agreed that the hysteric patient has suffered some form of mental dissociation. The result is a splitting of personality due to the efforts of the patient to push unpleasant ideas and emotions out of his consciousness.

In America, *Morton Prince* followed through the teachings of Charcot and Janet in his studies on the breakdown of personality patterns. Under the pressure of untoward circumstances from without and within, an individual may exhibit alternate mental states, each of which possesses a distinct portion of the individual's past feelings and memories. First one and then the other state is lived through; and often what happens in one state is unknown to the individual when he is passing through the other state. Prince had an unusual sample of dissociated personality in the case of Sally Beauchamp. His investigations put the so-called Dr. Jekyll and Mr. Hyde types of humanity in a new and more understandable light.

Charcot and his followers at the Salpêtrière were vigorously opposed by a rival school that had been set up at Nancy. *Ambroise Liébeault* was a quiet practitioner who had settled at Nancy and for over twenty years had used hypnotism as a therapeutic measure. He proposed the idea that hypnosis is simply a matter of suggestibility on the part of the person to be hypnotized. The idea did not make much stir until a fellow townsman, *Hippolyte Bernheim*, became interested in it: hypnotic phenomena are nothing out of the ordinary but simply the result of suggestion. Bernheim also denied that hypnosis is an abnormal state like hysteria. The verdict of time favored the Nancy school; and the controversy was fortunate inasmuch as it dismissed, once and for all, the notion that hypnosis is not a proper subject of scientific inquiry. Charcot brought the ghost of hysteria into the open. Janet improved the uses of hypnosis. Prince showed the effects of repressed ideas and emotions on personality. The next step was a serious investigation of the unconscious; and the stage was being set for a new and soul-stirring act in the drama of modern mind healing. Of Sigmund Freud's unique role of master psychoanalyst we shall speak in another chapter.

The spirit of the great psychopathologists in the nineteenth century marches on in our contemporary students of mental hygiene. One of the outstanding names in the history of medical psychology is *Adolf Meyer*. His point of view is interesting because of its philosophic implications. Meyer is the champion of a new kind of approach which he calls "psychobiologic." It is the science of man as a mental and physical whole. The central idea arises from a mistake that the investigators have been making all along. Why should one think that in order to be scientific one has to break down human beings into countless units, mental and physical? Such orientation, which is atomistic for both body and mind, springs from the false metaphysics of Descartes.

The older thinkers, like Thomas Aquinas, were wiser; for they considered body and mind as a unit. Further, this is really the only common-sense way of looking at things. If you examine a man's life history, from cradle to grave, you get the impression that he is one being, made up of physical and mental elements that are blended into unity. Yes, man is a unit, a psychobiologic integer. Only when you look at human beings in this light can you grasp the meaning of their behavior, both normal and abnormal; and even if you fail to grasp it perfectly, at any rate it becomes less shrouded in mystery than it was before. Such is Adolf Meyers' vision of man in his nature; and it is safe to predict that the future of clinical medicine will be largely shaped by concepts such as his. The breadth and humanity of his outlook is well represented in the writings of *Gregory Zilboorg*, one of the clearest thinkers in the field of psychiatric literature.

At the same time that Meyers was giving a new direction to research in psychosomatic medicine, an event of importance occurred which was to have a bearing on the whole course of mental hygiene. *Clifford Beers* was sent to a hospital for the insane shortly after his graduation from Yale. What he went through during his period of confinement and how his cure was brought about was later revealed to the world in a book entitled *A Mind That Found Itself*. It is one of the most widely read autobiographies of modern times. Beers became a crusader of mental hygiene. He believed, as a result of his experiences, that there was a desperate need of measures which would forestall as well as alleviate the sufferings of disordered minds. He founded a National Committee of Mental Hygiene in the United States and set on foot a movement that has now reached into all parts of the civilized world. The society has devoted its efforts both to the advance of scientific methods in treating the insane and to the spread of knowledge that will help prevent and cure dreaded illnesses of mind. Its medium of publication is *Mental Hygiene*.

To the men who pioneered in the work of caring for the mentally sick, a special tribute must be paid. Most of them were physicians. They brought their inspiration from the bedside, from the hospital wards, from the medical laboratories, and from their wide experience with the most unfortunate group of human society, the mentally distrait. Theirs was a work of patient and often thankless toil since the very nature of their interests called for unusual gifts of understanding when confronted with human beings who had lost their hold on reality. They worked against enormous odds, trying to wage a sane battle against the insane thoughts, passions, and behavior of their patients. Discouragement was their meat and drink, but they toiled on in the hope that some small ray of light would be shed on the dark corners of the human mind.

CHAPTER 17

THE FIELD OF PSYCHOMETRICS

I

Mental Tests and the Experimental Method

The common opinion that mental testing is not an experimental form of psychology is false. The fact is that the work of the psychometrists, which represents some of the best research done in psychology, could neither exist nor develop except by the employment of an experimental method. There is this difference, however, which may be observed: that, whereas the mental tester aims at securing scores from a large number of individuals, the laboratory psychologist is more interested in a particular phenomenon which he can attack with a greater precision of technique than is possible to the psychometrist.

Moreover, mental powers exhibit an enormous range of differences; so that the material of psychometric investigation exists at a level which is too complex to be satisfactorily handled by the usual laboratory methods. This is not to say that the work of the psychometrists was not influenced by the men of the laboratory. On the contrary, especially at the beginning, there was a great deal of compenetration of the two spheres; and signs are not absent at present that they are growing closer to each other once more. Indeed, the excellent results produced by the mental testers may well be interpreted as a challenge to other psychologists to produce work equally significant for the deeper understanding of human nature and its properties.

2

Trail Blazers in Mental Testing

One of the first investigators to study the abilities of children was the Paris physician *Edouard Séguin*. This was about the middle of the last century. Séguin's interest centered on the feeble-minded; and his work lay mainly in the development of their powers of motor control. He taught them, among other things, to walk along straight lines and to climb ladders. He also tried to increase their alertness by the use of strong sensory stimuli, such as bright colors and highly flavored foods. He constructed a "form board" made out of wood, in which three holes, one square, one round, and one triangular, had been cut. The children were asked to fit corresponding wooden pegs into these holes. Séguin published the results of his unique method in 1843. His success was so great that he was requested to organize the instruction of the feeble-minded children in some of our early American institutions.

The real father of the test movement in France, however, was *Alfred Binet* whose work is comparable to that of Galton in England. The latter, in a sense, is prior to all other psychometrists by virtue of his studies of individual differences; yet Binet actually had more to do with the development of mental tests than Galton or any other investigator. This was due in large part to the fact that the French psychologist was seeking a definite goal, namely, the measurement of the intellectual faculty; whereas Galton experimented mainly with simple sense-abilities, hoping, of course, that the information which he thus gained by his over-all methods of testing would have some significance for "intellect." So, too, in comparison with the work of Ebbinghaus, the contributions of Binet to psychometrics are more important. The classical researches of the former were designed rather as a test of memory skill than as an analysis of memorial consciousness as such.

In 1905 Binet was given the task of segregating the school children of Paris into groups according to their intelligence, so that instruction suitable to their actual capacities might be devised. Working with *Théodore Simon*, he prepared a set of tasks which were arranged in varying levels of difficulty. Each level was standardized by taking the type and amount of difficult material which could be just mastered by the majority of pupils at a given age. The measurement of intelligence was made in terms of chronological maturity as well as of the average performance that might be expected of all the individuals of a given age. The tests called for the use of rational insights, instead of the simple discriminations made in Galton's technique.

Among the problems which Binet proposed, we find such tasks as naming coins, repeating a series of digits or a set of phrases, judging weights, the comprehension of concrete and abstract differences, and so on. Binet made a further revision of his tests, so that about 75 per cent of the children, at a particular chronological age, could accomplish all the tasks through a given level of difficulty. So strong was the interest created by this kind of research that the attention of the psychometrists soon came to be centered almost entirely upon the question of intelligence and its measurement. Binet is also remembered for having founded the first journal in French devoted to the problems of psychology: *L'Année Psychologique* which was started in 1894.

3
Early American Workers

Psychological testing found a friendly reception in America. Indeed, it became as much a part of the picture of American psychology as the experimental analysis of consciousness was to German psychology; or philosophic speculation to British psychology; or predilection for the abnormal to French psychology. This means that the trend in psychological research in America is properly evaluated, not only by reference to the structural approach which started with Wundt, but also by its connections with the dynamic and functional approach which stemmed from Brentano's act psychology and Darwin's genetic concepts.

We have already mentioned the work of *James McKeen Cattell* in the field of capacity psychology. He is undoubtedly the most important figure in the early days of mental testing in America. But he worked upon Galton's assumption that simple tests of sensory and motor powers would reveal the most important facts bearing on the adjustment of human beings to life, and particularly to life as it involves the getting of an education. This assumption was discarded as Binet's work became better known in America with *Henry Goddard's* translation of the Binet-Simon revised tests and his adoption of them in his Vineyard, New Jersey, school for the feeble-minded. This was in 1908. Three years later, Goddard produced his own revision of the Binet scale. At this time, something of the great researches of *Wilhelm Stern*, who pioneered in Germany in the field of individual differences, also became known in America. Stern helped to give greater clarification to the concept of intelligence and was the first to employ the term "mental quotient."

4

Testing Comes of Age

Perhaps the most outstanding name in the field of American psychometrics today is that of *Lewis Terman*, who made a thorough revision of the Binet-Simon tests and replaced certain items, which referred to unfamiliar French objects and situations, with other items that were more familiar to American children. This "Stanford Revision," so called after the University in California where Terman worked for many years, is the most widely employed measure of intelligence that has been produced to date. Terman adopted Stern's mathematical description of intelligence as the quotient between mental and chronological age. By mental age here is meant the highest age level in the scale at which an individual can pass all the tests.

For "mental quotient" Terman substituted "intelligence quotient," now commonly referred to as "I. Q." According to its intelligence quotient, a child will have a rating of 1.00 if normal and less than 1.00 if subnormal. Terman also made a special study of superior children and he outlined certain methods by which they can be allowed to develop their additional ability by courses that had been disregarded in the ordinary school training. His three-volume work on the genetic analysis of genius is a fascinating thing and marks an advance in the mental-testing movement. Terman's plan was to follow through the life story of these superior children to see if they fulfilled the promise that they gave in youth. We go to great pains to solve the mystery of meteors and comets that come within range of our earth. Yet how much more important are the human meteors and human comets, the Aristotles, da Vincis, Newtons, Beethovens, and Einsteins. "Let us find out, if possible, how such golden eggs are laid and nurtured."

The value of the "mental-age" concept was called into question by some of the testers. In 1914, *Robert Yerkes*, whose work in animal research has already been described, and *James Bridges* sought to replace the concept of mental age with a "point scale" of fractional credits for the successful completion of any part of a task regardless of whether all simpler tasks, up to this level, had been finished or not. In the same year, *Rudolph Pinter*, working in collaboration with *Donald Paterson*, declared for the importance of nonlanguage tests in determining natural ability. They complained that the aptitude of an individual to express himself in proper language exerts a great influence in such tests as the Stanford revision. Since the employment of language or the power of communication depends to a great extent on the quality of the training that one receives at home and in school, it is not necessarily a measure of natural ability. The nonlanguage tests are called "performance tests" and consist of form-boards, puzzle pictures cut into irregular shapes, and so forth. Pinel, as we remember, had designed similar tests for his feeble-minded patients.

During the First World War, several representative American psychologists worked together in the preparation of both language and nonlanguage group tests. These were given to nearly two million soldiers. Prominent in this gigantic task was the group headed by Robert Yerkes. Critics who misunderstood the practical nature of the tests declared that such a wholesale method of attacking mental levels could issue only in sterility. A flood of indignation swept the country when it was made known that the average American soldier had a mental age of fourteen years. But gradually the solid fruits of the testers became apparent. Though far from perfect in their efforts, they were able to draw many statistical conclusions regarding the intelligence level of different occupational groups and of widely separated racial stocks.

5
Factorial Psychology

By far the most prominent figure in the development of English psychometrics is *Charles Spearman*. His work is all the more significant because it has been done in the spirit of an Aristotelian investigator. Nothing was wrong with the traditional concept of faculties, declared Spearman. But things definitely went amiss when the scientific psychologist undertook to measure the abilities of man on the false assumption that one faculty can adequately represent all the rest. Mental tests, according to Spearman, are not direct measures of mental ability. Thus the solving of a particular logical problem, presented in a test, does not constitute a criterion of one's general ability to reason.

The only facts that the tests present are statistical. Intelligence, for example, is not directly observed. The best we can do is to measure it indirectly in much the same way as physical temperature is indirectly measured by the height of a column of mercury. Therefore it was proposed by Spearman that mental ability should be expressed in statistical terms. By comparing the results of several different kinds of tests, the general quality of an individual's performance can be determined. This general ability is known as "g" factor. It is derived from a hierarchy of correlations and is regarded by Spearman as a distinct characteristic of mind which partly determines the individual's performance in each of the different tasks.

On the other hand, the results of the separate tests may differ greatly from each other; and these differences represent variations in quality between the individual's special abilities which are "s" factors. On a basis of this kind of measurement, some persons exhibit a high general level of performance, others a moderate general level but a high level in one or more special abilities. "P" factor manifests itself as a broad form of mental inertia, making it difficult for the subject to pass rapidly from one kind of psychological activity to another. In the characterological dimension, there is an apparently independent factor which has been labeled "w" factor. Those who possess it in a high degree tend, as a rule, to act on reasoned motives rather than on impulse. In regard to special abilities, investigators claim to have discovered moderately broad factors in the fields of mathematics, language, music, and mechanics.

6
What Is Intelligence?

Spearman, Terman, and a host of other lesser lights have worked for years in perfecting their mental tests. Every kind of special aptitude has been searched out, measured, discussed, and brought before the psychometrists for overhauling and refurbishing. All these special aptitudes — and each represents some kind of intellectual perfection — have been studied just as thoroughly as science makes possible. Yet the major factor responsible for so much care and effort, the *pièce de résistance* of psychometric analysis, is unknown. The testers have not succeeded, up to now, in answering the simple query: what is intelligence? They have run up and down the scale in setting human beings into groups. They have computed I. Q.'s of idiots, geniuses, and all the in-betweens. Still, what intelligence is, in itself, nobody seems to know. It has been described in various ways, as an ability to adapt oneself or to size up a situation or to fit into a gap or to make a success of things. But these definitions just touch the surface. According to Terman, the best formula that has been proposed to date is the old traditional one that comes down from Aristotle through the schoolmen: the ability to do abstract thinking. At any rate, the precise nature of intelligence has not as yet been brought to light by experiment — even by the ingenious experiments of the mental testers.

7

Psychometrics and the Doctrine of Faculties

The orientation of research work in psychometrics toward an implicit recognition of the faculty theory is best seen when we examine some of the more important conclusions that emerge from it. Briefly, modern testers are fairly well agreed on the following points: (a) that there are established differences in the way that man operates; (b) that each difference represents a general tendency to act in a particular way; (c) that all such general tendencies are native, and must be developed, by actual practice and by the formation of habits, before they reach their perfect nature; (d) that in their progressive movement toward perfection, general tendencies show the effects of environmental influences, training, and so forth; (e) that general tendencies vary from one person to another.

Now, the Aristotelian and Thomistic concept of faculty is nothing more than the broad factor of the psychometrist; that is to say, a power of performing certain operations which are grouped together because they have some obvious connection with each other. If, then, we substitute the term "faculty" for the term "general tendency," in the above conclusions, we have five experimentally verified propositions that are in perfect harmony with the traditional notion of man's abilities. It may be added, here, that Thomas Aquinas preferred to use the word "power" rather than "faculty" in his analysis of human capacities. Moreover, since the powers of man are, in the strict philosophic sense, proper to his nature, Aquinas also refers to them as "properties." Thus, in the same way as the powers of matter are the natural properties of nonliving things, or the powers of protoplasm are the natural properties of living things, so the powers of man are the natural properties of his soul and the instruments by which he exhibits his nature to the cosmic world.

8

The Fruitfulness of Psychometric Research

To have a genuine experimental science of human nature it is necessary, first, that its generalizations be true inductions from experimental evidence; second, that they specifically concern human nature in its psychological aspects; third, that they hang together by sharing a few simple concepts, in much the same way as the generalizations of mechanics are unified under such heads as space, time, mass, and so on. By these criteria, the work of the psychometrists has been productive of excellent results. True, the measuring of factors or faculties has not added a great deal to psychological analysis itself. Rather, the goal of the testers has been the compilation of metrical data and the application of mathematics to the quantitative aspects of human acts and human abilities. Nevertheless, the solid achievements of psychometrics obviously operate on the principle that man possesses basically differentiated faculties. Only so long as the science of mental measurements recognizes the truth of this possession can it proceed fruitfully to the construction of its mathematical formulas.

CHAPTER 18

BEHAVIORISTIC PSYCHOLOGY

I

The Spirit of Rebellion

Like other and similar movements, the behavioristic way of looking at psychology did not mushroom into being over night but was largely the result of antecedent factors. It had its historical roots in the findings of the Russian reflexologists, in comparative work on animals, and in the researches of the functionalists, all of which were more or less in the spirit of objective approaches to mental data. But more than this! There was the positive dissatisfaction with the methods of introspective analysis which, in the hands of men like Titchener, had definitely limited the scope of psychological research. The introspectionists, it was said, were more interested in technical performances than in experience as ordinary human beings have it. Their revelations were only for the initiate.

Could not psychology be regarded simply as the study of human behavior? This, it seemed to many researchers, was a broad enough concept to cover the work of both the introspectionists and the objective investigators. Surely there can be no fundamental antagonism between behavior and consciousness — as though a man or an animal must be unconscious in order to behave. Unfortunately, the liveliness of opposition to introspective technique did actually result in the development of this sort of antagonism, so that when the official position of the behaviorists was finally declared in 1912, it clearly meant to rule out all introspection and all reference to consciousness.

2

The Father of Behaviorism

John Watson gave the first well-crystallized statement of what the behaviorists meant to do in psychology. He very bluntly said that the method of introspection was a detriment to psychological research. Such a method yields only a descriptive account of consciousness; and it furnishes no means of verifying what it asserts. There are cases on record, Watson maintained, where different observers reported contradictory introspections, and with no objective means by which these disagreements could be resolved. Moreover, the language of introspection is not like that in which scientific facts are usually stated. Hence, no direct relationship can be established between the data of introspection and scientific facts, as such.

There is only one solution to this dilemma: "the elimination of states of consciousness as proper objects of investigation in themselves." Only by cutting the Gordian knot and throwing out subjective data altogether, can we remove the barrier which hinders psychology from taking its rightful place in the hierarchy of natural sciences. Such was the avowed position of the first systematic behaviorist; and it was not long before Watson had a large band of enthusiastic followers in America, where the school was born.

3

The Outside Way of Looking Inside

At the time of Watson's declaration of war, the study of behavior had been growing more and more important in the general expansion of psychological research. The animal experimentalists had to depend entirely on such a method; and it was the basic outlook of those who became interested in the problems of individual differences and mental measurements. In the early animal studies that were made during Darwin's time, a common practice had sprung up of referring to conscious states in order to explain the "purposes" and "feelings" of animal life. Then a series of disputes followed between investigators. One group accused the other of anthropomorphic equivocations; that is to say, of reading human meanings into animal life, of vitiating objective situations by subjective interpretations, of making unwarranted general statements that gave a false tenor to the programs of research.

The criticisms that were aimed at the animal psychologists soon came to be leveled against the students of human nature. Watson, for example, was dissatisfied with the results of functionalism, as a psychological approach, even though he himself was trained in that tradition. He called the work of William James into question; nor did he spare his own teacher, James Rowland Angell, who was John Dewey's early colleague. What Watson especially reprobated in these men was the fact that they adopted a biological point of view, yet continued to use introspection. For, by the Watsonian standards, these were irreconcilable elements. The separation between consciousness and behavior must be absolute and complete; and the only way of securing this end is by restricting one's observations to instrumental measurements and mathematical calculations of the sort that are employed in the other exact sciences. The declared aims of behaviorism, therefore, meant the entrance of a new method into psychology, a method that would prevent investigators from making intentional or unintentional allusions to consciousness in records that should be entirely objective.

4
The Principle of Reflex Action

Watson thought he saw the key to all human and animal behavior in the reflex. There is nothing that man does which cannot be accounted for as a pattern of chained reflexes; that is, as a series of connected neurological responses. To explain the development of these connections, Watson at first proposed the quantitative factors of "frequency of response" and "recency of response" as sufficient to describe all integrating phenomena. Later, however, he became convinced that, in the experiments which he performed on the learning process of children and animals, the errors could be repeated more often than the correct response which solved the problem.

Accordingly, Watson adopted the principle of the conditioned reflex. By virtue of this principle, the correct acts of the performer become conditioned to the stimulus situation with which they coincide. Errors are eliminated because the actions by which they are corrected — for instance, backing out of a cul-de-sac in a maze — are adjusted to their stimulus situation. Thus, when the cul-de-sac is arrived at, on subsequent trials, there will be a developed tendency to back away from it.

5
Intellectual Behavior

The process of thinking, as Watson explained it, is simply "a form of general bodily activity." As such, it can be described without referring to internal conscious states or to subjective imagery of any sort. It occurs within the dimension of linguistic movements, since most human problems are solved in terms of verbal symbols. Because the conventions of society prevent the individual from constantly talking out loud, the activity of speech, in the economy of thought, has been reduced to a subvocal level. From a behavioristic standpoint, then, the muscular reflexes of the larynx and chest are the important factors in the thinking process. There are other outward movements that go along with our vocalizing efforts, such as the shrugging of the shoulders, nodding the head, and possibly some slight visceral responses.

As a result of purely objective analysis, Watson concluded that it might be better to give up the term "thinking" and use the phrase "implicit behavior" in its place. Thought, in short, is no longer to be regarded as a psychological datum. As the behaviorist sees it, it can be explained entirely by physiological concepts. Translated into the language of Aristotle, thought would be a product of the faculty which is "kinetic according to place"; that is to say, the power of local movement.

6

Disciples of Watson

One of the first enthusiasts of the Watsonian psychology was *Edwin Holt* who, in 1915, proclaimed its founder as "the one great luminary of the psychological sky." The subsequent history of the behavioristic movement can hardly be called a fulfillment of Holt's dream of grandeur. To Watson's views, he added some of the psychoanalytic theory; and this may have had something to do with the sympathetic reception which Freudianism received at the hands of the behaviorists. I shall have occasion to refer to Holt again in a later section of this chapter.

Albert Weiss also swore early allegiance to the behavioristic cause, thereby involving himself in a great deal of polemic against the tenets of both the functional and structural psychologists. *Walter Hunter* sought to give a behavioristic account of the tabooed subjects of consciousness, sensation, thought, and so forth. *Edward Tolman* interpreted the or-

ganization of behavior as a whole-making pattern and thus
tried to synthesize Watson's work with that of the gestaltists.

Karl Lashley, whose splendid researches in the field of neurology have already been mentioned, left aside his experimental tasks long enough to write a defense of the behavioristic
system. Since many of these men were interested primarily
in animal psychology, it was quite natural that they should
find their medium of expression in the language of behaviorism.
If they studied human nature at all, it was through the analysis
of animal reactions, rather than by a direct approach to man
himself.

7

The Battle Over Instincts

In its total structure, instinct is a very complicated affair
which demands several animal powers for its complete description. Thus, on the cognitive side, there is the estimative
faculty, which is its foundation. On the orectic side, there
are the sensitive appetites and their emotional responses.
On the behavioral side, there is the locomotive power which
exhibits itself in a variety of external movements according
to the needs of the organism. The contention of Watson
that instincts, like all other animal phenomena, may be explained in terms of reflex activity, issued in many a heated
debate in academic circles. Watson's view was championed
by men like *Charles Josey*, *Zing Kuo*, *Jacob Kantor*, and *Luther
Bernard*, who contended that instincts really owe nothing to
consciousness or experience, that a response which is secured
through the animal's possession of native equipment is enough
to account for all the so-called instinctive reactions.

Among the psychologists who strenuously opposed such an
interpretation we find *William McDougall* who devoted much
space in his writings to a discussion of instincts and their
essential purposiveness in animal life. For McDougall, the

notion of instinct cannot be divorced from the notion of conscious striving. Its cognitive character is the very thing that separates it immediately from reflex activity. Thus, while it is innate in tendency, it is also a psychophysical disposition that tends to express itself in a variety of ways, according to past experience, present situations, and future needs.

McDougall's point is well taken since obviously, if consciousness is not admitted, then, from a strictly behavioristic angle, there can be no ground for distinguishing between a reflex and an instinct. The whole drift of McDougall's psychology was an affront to the objective ideals of the behaviorists. Not that he denied the importance of studying observable behavior; but he insisted that no amount of reflex analysis could ever supply for the experience of the introspectionists. To McDougall, the technique of the behaviorists, based on the assumption that consciousness is only a by-product of outer conduct, was just an easy way out. To use a familiar example, it was like beating around the bush instead of plunging in after the quarry.

8

The Progressive Aspects of Behaviorism

It may be remarked here that within the field of locomotor activity the behaviorist has made some definite contributions to psychology. Watson's best work was done with small children. From his observations of the newborn, he presented a most precise and exhaustive account of infantile behavior. He noted a predominance of diffuse activity in the early months of human life as well as a corresponding scarcity of coordinated responses. He used his findings as evidence against the lengthy lists of instincts that had been proposed by the evolutionists. Among the types of coordinated behavior which he studied, Watson saw signs of three distinct patterns of emotional activity: (a) fear, characterized by trembling; (b) rage, distinguished by rigidity; and (c) love, manifested in cooing and smiling. These, he declared, are the real primitive emotions of man; and from them, as fountainheads, all the streams of emotional conduct in later life are derived through a process of conditioning. As an example, Watson pointed to the fact that a child is not inherently afraid of furry objects. But if suddenly startled by a loud noise at the moment that it is handed such an object, the fear response to the sound will become associated with the sight of anything furry. Many unaccountable dreads and dislikes of adulthood have their origin in conditioning experiences of this kind.

9
Oversights in the Watsonian Technique

Child study will always be interesting because it tells us so many vital facts about the early history of human beings and because it provides a means of discovering some of the roots of the complex behavior of adult life. Most of Watson's research was done at Johns Hopkins. Clinics were soon established in other centers. At Yale University, an infantorium was set up under the direction of *Arnold Gesell* which produced some excellent results. This clinic was particularly well equipped for the observation of infant behavior under natural conditions. Complete records were made by motion pictures. The same technique was employed in other centers also. Then the interesting discovery was made that even parents, watching the emotional expression of their children on the screen, could not distinguish between rage and fear if they did not know what stimuli had been used to provoke the emotion. This seemed to reveal an oversight in Watson's methodology. At any rate, it was interpreted to mean that Watson had read into the outer behavior of children certain meanings that were based on his own knowledge of the stimulus situation. Here was an oversight that illustrated one of the fundamental criticisms raised against the behavioristic position: namely, the extreme difficulty of securing a record that is completely objective, even when the observer has made every effort to be impartial.

10

Motorized Consciousness

The extent to which muscular responses may serve to account for particular data of consciousness has been discussed by psychologists over a long period of years. In 1900, *Hugo Münsterberg* presented his "action theory" which postulated a relation between consciousness and the opening of motor pathways in the central nervous system. In this manner, he explained the fact that a person may be keenly aware of a slight stimulus, such as whispering, in the midst of intense stimuli, such as the multiple sounds of an orchestra. In 1916, *Margaret Washburn* gave a somewhat different explication in her "motor theory" of consciousness. She suggested that a certain amount of resistance or blocking of motor pathways intensifies consciousness. This is seen in the early stages of learning a new task or in the conflicting activity which accompanies an emotional outburst.

Edwin Holt attempted to describe the process by which motor responses determine certain characteristics of consciousness. He based his explanations on the principle of the "reflex circle" which states that the random muscular contractions of prenatal behavior become conditioned to the sensory impulses aroused by such contractions. Thus, a sensory impulse leads to a motor impulse which stimulates the same muscle to contract again or to continue its former contraction. The next stage comes when a muscular contraction causes a new kind of sensation to which it becomes conditioned.

For example, the prenatal spasmodic clenching of the fists causes stimulation of the palms which, in turn, causes further clenching movements so that a remarkable "grasping reflex" is developed. After birth, there may be some fairly constant stimulus in the environment to which muscular movement is conditioned. Hence, if a word is repeated while the infant is uttering certain sounds, revocalization will be set up; and there will come a time when the infant pronounces the word whenever it is uttered by another person. This is the beginning of language, according to Holt.

II

Response Psychology

The notion that consciousness conforms to different types of muscular activity has grown, historically, into a systematic way of looking at mental data. It is now described as response psychology. Like the behavioristic approach, the formal interest here is in the motor aspects of human and animal life. Consciousness is admitted as a psychological factor, but there is the definite implication that its existence depends upon the actual achievement of external actions. This is the point of view of men like *Knight Dunlap* and *Herbert Langfeld*.

But perhaps the most systematic exposition of response psychology is to be found in the work of *Robert Woodworth* who collaborated with *Edward Thorndike* in his researches at Columbia. In theory, at least, the aim has been to employ subjective as well as objective methods in getting at psychological facts, though the preponderance of behavioristic techniques is only too obvious, especially in the case of Thorndike. As an adventure into mind, response psychology set out to explain the changes that occur in the central nervous system when "functional connections" are made between stimulus and response or between physical situations and final behavior. As Woodworth expressed it, response psychology is interested in "cause and effect," or what may be called the "dynamics" of behavior.

In 1901, Woodworth and Thorndike tested the benefits which training in one mental capacity would produce on another mental capacity. They discovered that practice in a special task of reading, such as noting every word that contained the two letters "e" and "s," afterwards speeded up the rate of improvement in proofreading. This phenomenon was referred to as "transfer of training," and was explained as a result of the activity of common neural bonds in the two mental functions. This would mean the existence of identical elements in the two functions that help each other. Curiously enough, the more Thorndike and Woodworth investigated the matter, the less transfer value they found even in the best subject matters. Here is a summary of their findings: expectancy of any large improvement due to one study rather than another seems doomed to disappointment. Further, the main reason that good thinkers get more out of special cultural subjects, such as Greek and Latin, is precisely that they are good thinkers, more highly gifted by nature, and therefore bound to gain more from a subject than would a poor thinker. For general training of the mind, experiments show that mathematics is first, followed closely by general science; then Latin and French which are about equal in merit; next economics and stenography; and finally manual training and dramatic art.

12

Failure of Behaviorism as a System of Psychology

Most of the research which has been done in the name of academic behaviorism — and the same is largely true of response psychology — can be reduced either to pure physiology or to animal psychology. In principle, it represents a reaction to introspectionism. As a systematic interpretation, it sees no difference, except one of degree, between men and animals. All its major concepts are reducible to terms of reflexes and stimulus-response bonds. These are the formulas by which it explains all behavior, both human and infrahuman. The fact is that it is concerned, really, not with psychological data as such, but with sensorimotor coordinations; or if it does discuss such data, as in the case of emotional responses, it is interested more in the response than in the emotion.

Behaviorism, from a historical point of view, started out as a reform movement in the right direction: namely, to check the excessive or unbalanced employment of introspective techniques. But it soon showed that it could be just as excessive itself in its negation of any value to introspective procedures. It has stimulated many new kinds of experimental work, especially on the physiological level and in the realm of animal behavior. Yet it has not achieved what it set out to accomplish: the establishment of psychology as a science in its own title. In this respect, it is no better and no worse than most of its sister schools in the field of scientific psychology.

CHAPTER 19

GESTALT PSYCHOLOGY

I

The Pendulum Swings Back

While there is much in common between the approaches of the behaviorist and the gestaltist, there is also a basic differ-ence. Despite the claims of the former, it still remains true that the fundamental way of getting at the contents of con-sciousness and therefore at the data of psychological analysis is through the avenue of introspection. The gestaltist is opposed, on the one hand, to the overrefined methods of the Titchenerian subjectivist in psychology. On the other hand, he is unwilling to commit himself to the ultrascientific demands of the Watsonian objectivist. For him, consciousness has a value that arises from the fact that it provides, in part at least, the subject matter of psychological research; just as introspection has a value from the fact that it furnishes a natural tool for the investigation of this matter.

Behaviorism and gestaltism are alike, however, in their psychophysical outlook. The neurology which forms the ground plan of most of the behavioristic interpretation can also be made the point of departure for gestaltist theorizing. The behaviorist, I should say, has arrived at a well-developed knowledge of sensorimotor phenomena. The gestaltist, in like manner, has advanced our insights into the meaning of perception and has clarified the type of problem solving that can be handled by the senses. Both, too, have a common interest in the facts of comparative psychology.

2
Historical Antecedents

Present-day Gestalt psychology has its counterpart in earlier investigations of perceptual data. Perhaps the closest approach to the modern Gestalt outlook is found in the work of the Austrian school. Most of the men belonging to this group were associated, in one way or another, with Franz Brentano. There was Christian von Ehrenfels, for example, whose theory of form qualities has already been discussed in a preceding chapter. This theory was an outgrowth of Ernst Mach's researches on sensations of spatial and temporal forms. Next came the work of *Alexius Meinong* who gave a more precise elaboration to the concept of form qualities. Meinong also had the distinction of being the first to found a psychological laboratory in Austria, in 1894. His pupil, *Vittorio Benussi*, continued the labors of his master and became the most energetic and original experimenter that Austria produced.

It is not quite true to say, however, that contemporary Gestalt psychology is a direct descendant of the form quality school. Like the latter, it is opposed to the type of mental chemistry that Wundt and Titchener defended. Also, it has the same basic interest in data of the perceptual field. But the father and founder of the Gestalt system, as we know it today, studied under none of the men whom we have just mentioned. *Max Wertheimer* received his early training first under Carl Stumpf at Berlin and later under Oswald Külpe at Würzburg. In 1910, he inaugurated his famous studies on seen movement, in which Wolfgang Koehler and Kurt Koffka, also pupils of Stumpf, participated as observers. Wertheimer's experiments, which were conducted at Frankfurt, really began the movement that we recognize today as gestaltism.

3

The Phi Phenomenon

In 1912, Wertheimer demonstrated that when two parallel lines are presented alternately at an interval of one-fifteenth of a second, there appears to be a movement between the lines even though no visible object is moving — since each line is really seen as a "still" picture. Moreover, from the observer's point of view, there is never any awareness of the stimulus lines as discrete or separate units, but only a consciousness of their spatial and temporal relations as the movement itself. This unique experience was called the "phi phenomenon." Wertheimer denied that it was due to eye movements, since the impression of simultaneous movements in opposite directions can be elicited from two pairs of stimuli. He suggested that the experience is the result of a physiological process: namely, a shift between two separate fields of neural excitation in the cerebral cortex.

Psychologically, movement is perceived not as a congeries of sensations, as the atomists would have it, but simply as an experience. It is, in short, a phenomenon: something to be regarded as a whole, a pattern or configuration, a Gestalt. Above all, it is not a bundle of sensational units, because the perceived whole is really greater than the sum of its parts. To regard it as made up of unit sensations gets us nowhere — unless it be back to the elementaristic and unprogressive outlook of the older psychologists.

4

Further Developments

Like all novel interpretations, the account of Wertheimer was rather simple and naïve at the beginning. *Kurt Koffka* sought to make a more complete synthesis of the psychological factors involved in the Gestalt experience. He was of the opinion that the properties of consciousness are created out of the relations that arise between physiological events as they occur in the nervous system. The properties thus evolved are unitary and indivisible. They are not merely the sum total of the properties of their individual causes. They are "forms" in the psychological sense of the term. Because the accent, in Gestalt theory, is so largely on interconnections between physical, neural, and mental patterns of activity, the gestaltists have been called "relativists" in psychology. In approach, they are fundamentally opposed to the atomic contents of the Wundtians, on the one hand; and to the isolated reflexes of the behaviorists, on the other. Neither do they have any great sympathy for stimulus-response bonds. In place of elementary principles of mental experience, they have substituted the notion of unitary wholes.

Koffka gave many examples to show that there is no one-to-one correspondence between physical stimuli and the resultant data of psychological consciousness. What we experience, so he contended, is only an awareness of change between stimuli. This awareness occurs in a manner that is analogous to the shift of an electric charge between two fields when their difference in potential becomes sufficiently great. Even though the shift begins at one point, it affects the entire potential of each field. The significant thing about Wertheimer's discovery was to show how an experience comes into existence from the relation developed between two stimuli, despite the fact that it does not correspond to either one.

Koffka further declared that the earliest experiences of childhood are "configurative" in character, because the first perceptual responses are made to complex situations, for instance, the distinction of a friendly from an unfriendly face. The child is aware of such situations long before he is able to make a correct discrimination between colors. This fact, according to Koffka, means that we have to throw out the old theory that the dawn of consciousness in early life consists in a succession of separate sensations. Configurations occur in the field of occupational behavior as well as in the perceptual sphere. Thus, it can be shown that for uncompleted tasks there may be as much as 90 per cent greater memory than for completed assignments. With the uncompleted tasks, there appears to be a need for fulfillment whose presence is akin to the perceptual tendency toward "closure" when the incomplete lines of a figure are presented.

Wolfgang Koehler divided the burden of leadership with Koffka in advancing the cause of gestaltism. He presented many illustrations of the principle of configuration from the behavior of the higher apes. In one experiment, a hollow bamboo pole was placed in the cage of a chimpanzee. Outside the cage was a smaller stick within reach; and beyond this, a banana. The animal first tried to rake in the fruit by using either the longer or the shorter stick. Later on, while playing with the two sticks, it accidentally thrust the end of the smaller stick into the hollow end of the larger one. It thus produced a jointed rod which was longer than the pieces taken separately. At once it went to the bars of the cage and raked in the banana. According to Koehler, the promptness with which the action was performed indicated that a new relation had emerged between the physiological predisposition of the animal, on the one side, and the objective spatial factors of length of the conjoined sticks and distance of the banana, on the other. From the psychological point of view, this new relation became known, in Gestalt language, as an "insight." The term, it should be noted immediately, is not to be confused with the true intellectual solution of a problem which is what we traditionally mean by insight. The difference here is the difference between the apprehension of concrete relations, such as the animal in Koehler's experiment could achieve, and the apprehension of abstract relations, which is strictly a function of the reasoning faculty.

With their new concept of "insight," the gestaltists now began to challenge the "trial and error principle with gradual increments of improvement" which Thorndike used to explain the learning process. Instead of a simple response to a definite stimulus, learning became a matter of "insight"; that is to say, of forming the configurations which will give the knowledge wherewith a given problem can be solved. The configurational or whole-making approach to the technique of learning has had some influence on modern education, inasmuch as it developed a preference for studying things by wholes rather than by parts. The trouble with the approach of the response psychologist, so far as the gestaltist is concerned, is that it smacks too much of the old associational way of attacking the riddles of psychology.

5

A Vote of Disapproval

The course of the Gestalt school has not always been a smooth one. Perhaps the most emphatic voice raised against its tenets was that of *Eugenio Rignano*, who called into question both the oneness and the insight value of the whole-making experience, as the gestaltists interpreted it. His controversies with Koehler reached such a pitch that it was finally decided to submit their dispute to an outside court of appeal. Charles Spearman was the man chosen to act as judge; and his verdict took the shape of a widely publicized book on the nature of human intelligence. The mind of man, said Spearman, is essentially a creative faculty. It operates according to a definite pattern which may be expressed qualitatively, first, as an apprehension of experience; second, as an induction of relations wherein ideas are brought together;

third, as a deduction of correlates, in which new ideas are brought into being from already existing ones. Thus the unitary character which the gestaltist finds in his experience of wholes is to be explained by the stress that he lays on apprehended relations.

6

Evaluation

The Gestalt school has one good service to its credit, namely, its redirection of psychological research toward an analysis of consciousness. Further, it has clarified the atmosphere of perceptual investigation by its insistence on a whole-making interpretation of perceptual data. It is an advance, therefore, upon the psychophysical accounts of sensation that had been built up by the followers of Wundt and Titchener. But, as in the case of so many other movements, it has pushed its configurational theory to the point where it is in danger of losing much of its value and significance. Thus it has tried to include all human and animal behavior within the perspective of sense-patterning. The whole man and the whole animal, in fact, are living configurations of the same essential nature, which it is useless to break down into partial aspects for analysis. And so the gestaltist has arrived at a position which is as untenable as that of the behaviorist. Like the latter, he has obliterated the line of demarcation between sensitive and intellectual modes of being.

In the same way that the behaviorist has employed the notions of conditioned reflex to account for human and animal operations without distinction, the gestaltist has applied his theory of patterning and "insight" to both human and animal perception and learning. Starting off as an attempt to explain our experience of movement, it ends by declaring that there is nothing in nature that cannot be accounted for as a configuration. Instead of proceeding from the perceptual level upward to a true explanation of the intellectual phenomena of ideation and judgment, it has sought to bring these specifically human achievements down to a purely physiological or physical level of explication. It has introduced many new avenues of experimental research; but it surely cannot be said to have done what all the modern investigators, from Wundt's time on, have sought to do: namely, to establish psychology as a science universally recognized by the partisans of all lines of investigation.

CHAPTER 20

PSYCHOANALYTIC PSYCHOLOGY

I

The Empirical Approaches to Psychology

The bulk of the research, thus far mentioned in our study of modern psychology, has been associated with some kind of systematic interpretation. From the laboratory of Wundt, the school of content psychology was born; from Titchener's workshop, structuralism came into being; from Watson's researches, the behaviorist point of view took its rise; from Wertheimer's interest in seen movement, the Gestalt way of interpreting was begotten. Two observations may be made at this juncture: first, the work of the various schools has been carried on, for the most part, in a strictly experimental manner, so far as it is possible to apply scientific technique to psychological data; second, the facts brought to light as a result of such experimentation have a value independent of the particular academic meaning that is attached to them.

We come now to another way of looking at psychological matters which, though not experimental in method, is yet empirical, in the best sense of the term. For, psychoanalytic psychology is not, definitely, a laboratory type of science. Perhaps the best way of describing it would be to call it "clinical" in its perspective. The couch, rather than the table, gives a truer picture of its setting; and mental association tests and medical diagnostics, rather than the artifacts of the laboratory, represent the kind of tools that it employs. This, in a sense, is its strength and its weakness: its strength, because it has necessarily to depend on a more psychosomatic approach to human nature, an approach that has been successful for the reason that it orientates itself toward man in his total make-up; its weakness, because it cannot resort to the elaborate instrumental techniques that investigators in their workshops are able to employ in analyzing certain aspects of human nature.

2

The Genesis of Freudian Psychology

To understand the psychoanalytic school in its proper historical background, we must go back, for a moment, to the work of the French psychopathologists. We have mentioned the disagreements that arose between Charcot at Paris and Bernheim at Nancy. For the former, as we recall, hypnosis was nothing short of a downright pathological state of the organism. For the latter, hypnosis could be a perfectly normal condition, produced through the power of suggestion. Charcot was a man of striking personality and an inspiring teacher. His fame went abroad into other lands, and one of the students attracted to his Parisian clinic was the physician *Sigmund Freud*, who had completed his medical course at Vienna.

Freud was particularly impressed with Charcot's use of hypnosis as a method for treating hysteria. He was also to remember a remark Charcot once made to the effect that in most cases of psychoneurosis, one will discover something wrong in the sexual life of the patient. Freud was in France in 1885. The following year he returned to Vienna and started practice with neurotics. At the same time he began an active collaboration with *Josef Breuer* who, more than any other man, was responsible for Freud's brilliant career in medical psychology. In 1895, with Breuer's assistance, he published his findings on hysterical phenomena. Here he appeared to favor Bernheim's interpretation of such states, rather than that of the Paris school. At any rate, he was now definitely of the opinion that abnormal mental manifestations may start from the level of ideas; that is to say, they may be purely psychogenic in origin.

3

The Function of Symbols

Many ideas, said Freud, are the expression of emotional drives. Abnormal conditions develop when there is a repression of the ideas through which affective impulses are ordinarily expressed. It is not simply a case of the drives disappearing under the strain of psychological repression. On the contrary, if they cannot find an outlet in one direction, they will tend to escape by another route. The result is the creation of a mental conflict which persists until the submerged feelings gain expression through some other kind of ideas. Here the familiar laws of association come into play. Thus it will be found, on analysis, that it is through some kind of similarity, contrast, or contiguity that repressed drives are able to gain their freedom. In this manner, a whole world of symbols was built up by Freud to show how instinctive promptings that cannot be admitted into the company of our conscious desires are expressed through dreams, slips of the tongue, humorous remarks, anxieties, pet aversions, and so forth.

4

A Case in Point

All this complicated theory of symbolism became crystallized in the mind of Freud as a result of a clinical analysis, made by Breuer, of one of his female patients. Anna O. was a victim of hysteria. She fell into frequent stupors during which she mumbled broken phrases of speech. Under hypnosis she repeated these phrases in their proper setting. From her connected story thus told, Breuer learned that she was brooding over the illness and death of her father to whom she had been deeply attached. She also displayed many symptoms of hysteria, such as double vision, a feeling that the walls of her room were closing in on her, an imagined inability to use one arm, and an unreasonable aversion to ordinary objects like drinking glasses. During her normal intervals, Breuer discussed these symptoms with her; and it soon became clear that the memory of the father's sufferings and demise had become unbearable to the girl and had therefore been repressed. This intense sorrow, associated originally with her father's tragic end, sought an outlet in ideas that were symbolically connected with her repressed feelings. Because the handling of glasses was reminiscent of the illness of her father, all drinking glasses and even the use of the hand that had administered them, became symbols of her sorrow. The patient was made to "talk out" her experiences, once the clue of the difficulty was revealed.

By this process of "mental catharsis" Anna O. came to realize that her hysterical behavior was an indirect expression of her repressed memories. Her "abreaction" showed itself in a normal discussion of her father's death which thus provided her with an exit for all the pent-up emotions that had caused her unusual psychological tensions. Breuer discussed his findings with Freud. The latter was fascinated and wanted his friend to publish the whole case. There were difficulties, it seems. In the end, Freud took over the record of Anna's experiences and published it in his own and Breuer's name. As his practice widened out, he was able to improve on Breuer's cathartic method and went on eventually to give the medical world a new technique of mental healing. It should be mentioned that Breuer and Freud were not the only physicians to employ the hypnotic coma for purposes of mental therapeutics. Pierre Janet, at this time, was also bringing out some studies in which he demonstrated that hypnosis could be used as a devise for tapping the patient's memory and discovering the origin of hysterical symptoms.

5

The Omnipotence of Sex

As Freud's researches continued, he became more and more convinced of the truth of Charcot's dictum that neurotic troubles were somehow centered in abnormal sexual reactions. But Freud went even further. He now declared that sex is the most fundamental driving power in human life, normal as well as abnormal. The concept of sex, however, in the Freudian theory, is not limited to procreative functions. It also embraces all the instinctive energies that are behind the individual's preservation of self. In the psychoanalyst's language, it is known as "libido." Matched against the outward expression of sexual tendencies, so understood, we find all the repressive and inhibitory customs of civilized society. Through a proper development, by avoiding excessive attachments to the members of one's family, the individual may arrive at a successful compromise between the expression of the sexual drive and the ordinary program of civilized life. Any diversion of an impulse into a channel of activity which is socially acceptable is known as "sublimation." Such a procedure is calculated to do away with the conflicts that would arise between means and ends in the adjustment of emotional tendencies.

As his system took on larger perspective, Freud made excursions into the field of social psychology, with the result that his early views of sex underwent some revision. The concept of libido was broadened out to include the communal

drives on which society is founded as well as the more fundamental and intimate instincts that make for self-preservation.
A further point may be noted. Forty years after his first
exploratory efforts to solve the riddle of the unconscious,
Freud entered another item into the pattern of men's instinctive drives. The main point of analysis, all this time, was love
or eros, and its vicissitudes under the stress and strain of
libidinal urgings. The new force now added was called the
"death instinct." It was pictured as an aggressive force, in
conflict with the ultimate strivings of love. The goal of love
is union; the goal of death is separation. To be properly
adapted to life, man must combine the forces of his love and
death instincts. It is the only situation in which he can
avoid pain and secure any measure of earthly happiness.

6

The Watchman Who Never Sleeps

Though repression is the end result of social factors that
determine the course of action which one shall pursue, its
work is actually accomplished through the presence of a generalized attitude within ourselves which Freud called the
"censor." The fundamental sexual drive, described a moment
ago as a combination of the self-preserving and the race-
preserving instincts, is intimately connected with the censor.
In order to give a more complete description of this relationship, Freud found it necessary to make several divisions
between the "levels of mind." Striking down into its lower
depths, there is the "id" — corresponding to the "subconscious" of Herbert's psychology — made up of a "foreconscious"
and an "unconscious" sector. Next, there is the "ego"
which is the level of rational consciousness. It is on this
plane that conflict takes place, for here is where we
witness the perpetual battle that is going on between passion

and reason. Finally, there is the "superego." This level, in Freud's theory, does not represent conscience; yet it bears a certain analogy to the concept of morality. The rules that it formulates for individual conduct are based, not on objective norms of what is right and wrong, but on considerations of utility, such as the customs and habits and social conventions that one must observe in order to lead a successful life.

The most important and far-reaching differences, among the categories just enumerated, are between the id and the ego. The foreconscious part of the id contains memories that can be revived, such as names, songs, ordinary experiences that do not have any particular conflicting emotional meaning for the individual. The foreconscious is also the residence of the censor whose all-seeing eye is strategically placed so that it can look upward to the conscious level, and downward to the unconscious mind. As the unconscious contents attempt to make their way to the surface, they encounter the censor whose stern duty is to cast them back into their dark and unpleasant prison. There is only one ruse that enables them to "slip by" the censor: namely, to clothe themselves in symbolic form so that their vigilant keeper does not recognize them. Because of this ability to give symbolic expression to unconscious drives, it is entirely possible that a person should be unaware of the true cause of his difficulties on the conscious rational level.

As in the case of his theory of libido, Freud's notion of the unconscious also underwent certain changes and enlargements. Now it included the id, a good portion of the superego, and certain marginal areas of the ego. But it still remains true that the id, in Freud's ultimate intentions, was meant to stand for the sum total of man's instinctive dispositions. In this sense, it is opposed to the activities of reason. Just as the id is always on the alert to make the ego do its bidding, so it strives to subject the instrument of the ego, which is reason, to itself. This teaching, of course, is nothing new. That passions cloud the intellectual faculty and make moral judgments extremely difficult was known to the ancients.

7

The Psychoanalytic Technique

Freud had employed the hypnotic method in probing the unconscious; but he became distrustful of its reliability since it was dependent, to some extent at least, on the suggestions of the hypnotist. It would be better to allow the patient to talk for himself. And so he developed a new approach which he called "psychoanalysis." Free association was the key to the secret chambers of the unconscious. Now Freud would allow the patient to say anything and to talk for as long as he pleased — provided, of course, he stuck to the theme of his personal difficulties. During the long periods that were allowed for self-explanation, Freud remained alert to detect those topics which the patient referred to very frequently, yet avoided as soon as they were mentioned by the analyst.

One of the most fertile sources of information was the dream. The patient was encouraged to relate every detail, however insignificant, that could be remembered from his slumbers. Here was a veritable flood of data that gave an immediate clue to the nature of one's repressions. Freud spent a great deal of care and energy in analyzing the content of the dream. He pointed to its obvious grotesqueness, or lack of meaning, as one of the most significant things about man's dream life. This, he declared, is merely a way of covering up desires which, in conscious life, would be unpleasant, painful, or designed to make us feel ashamed of ourselves. But refusing to think about the things that we want, or deliberately repressing such impulses, does not eliminate the craving. It persists throughout the hours of unconsciousness and forms the latent content of our dreams — in contrast to their manifest content which is the bizarre and obvious thing that we remember. During sleep, the ban is lifted and a vicarious satisfaction achieved.

Further — and this is the typical Freudian part of the interpretation — every repression represents an impeded sexual desire; and so the distortion of the dream is a symbol of sexual impulse. In spite of the fact that the term "sex" or "libido" is used by Freud in the broad meaning of sensitive love of any sort, his theory has been severely criticized on this point by other psychologists. Most students of mind hold to the view that any kind of unpleasant desire, whether it be of an immediately sexual nature or not, may be repressed. There is a general agreement, however, that unsatisfied desires can and perhaps do motivate most of our dreams; and further, that the warped and distorted nature of dream imagery may be due to the intensity of our repressions.

8

Men at Cross-purposes

In 1903, Freud founded the Viennese Psychoanalytic Society. From this center, students and practitioners went forth into all parts of the world. One of Freud's most brilliant pupils was *Carl Jung* who took up cudgels with his master on certain critical points in his theory. He rejected Freud's overemphasis of sex or libidinal impulse and reduced it to the level of the other common drives in life, such as fear, shame, and so forth, any one of which is equally able to produce a mental conflict. Libido now becomes the sum total of all our psychic energies. Jung was particularly noted for his intensive use of the association-reaction tests that had been devised by James Cattell and Emil Kraepelin. He selected stimulus words to cover the different phases of human experience.

When a patient exhibited an undue shyness or hesitancy in his responses, the stimulus word was interpreted to have some special meaning for the conflict from which he was suffering. In this manner, clues to hidden repressions could be brought to light.

Jung was also distinguished for his pioneering work in the field of type psychology. He classified people in two categories. In one group we find the "introverts" who constantly evaluate things in terms of their own private thoughts and feelings; in the other are the "extroverts" whose thoughts and reactions always reflect the force of external influences. Psychologists today are generally agreed that Jung's list is a picture of extremes rather than of means; that the average individual is an "ambivert" who combines within himself the elements of both the extrovert and the introvert categories.

Jung also broke lances with his master on the religious implications of the Freudian theory. He refused to accept the idea that religion antagonizes the individualistic forces of nature by placing an unbearable burden on the demands of sex. He insisted, moreover, that no soul-searching treatment can be complete if it fails to go back to the primitive levels of the human mind. In studying his patients' dreams, he discovered what he called a "racial" unconsciousness, as opposed to individual unconsciousness. He psychoanalyzed the old myths of humanity and laid low a number of superstitions. Though there is much in his system that fails to commend itself to the traditional psychologist, his general outlook was healthy. At any rate, it served as an antidote to the excessively animalistic concept of human nature which one gets from the writings of Freud.

Another of Freud's brilliant pupils was *Alfred Adler*, who, like Jung, came to have some basic disagreements with his teacher. Adler declared that the feeling of inadequacy, rather than libidinal impulse, is the capital driving power in human conduct and in the shaping of human character. This feeling of inadequacy arises from two sources: first, organic immaturity; second, lack of mental development. The infant is overwhelmed at its littleness in a world that is bigger and stronger than itself. However, by a law of compensation, the very presence of such a feeling of inadequacy actually works toward an increase of the child's self-assertiveness. The will to power is checked by the will to community and other educational forces. There is nothing abnormal, therefore, about the experience of inadequacy which is felt in infantile life.

But it happens, sometimes, that the maturing child is unwilling to leave its world of fancy, that it refuses to come to grips with reality, that it fails, in short, to adjust itself to the world of adults into which it is advancing. This state of affairs may give rise to two definite extremes: overcompensation, which results in a complex of superiority; and undercompensation, which develops into a complex of inferiority. In a sense, these two extremes are really one since the abnormal feeling of inferiority may manifest itself in a totally exaggerated mode of behavior in which delusions of grandeur make up for the individual's disappointments and failures in the battle for self-expression.

Serious breaks such as these showed that Freud could not have everything his own way. He tried to rule his flock with an iron hand, but some of his followers were bound to come forward with their own ideas about things. Freud refused to compromise. He favored those who favored him. A revolutionary himself, he denied to others the right to rebel. He exacted a strict conformity to the rules of psychoanalytic science, as he conceived it. Yet he himself often broke the rules or changed them or threw them out altogether. It is not surprising that men of enterprise, like Jung and Adler, found this sort of atmosphere too stifling to live in. Differ-

ences with the master were inevitable. Despite the opposition, however, Freudianism dug in, rooted itself, and spread.
Freud refused to be impressed by the theories of Jung and
Adler but he did listen to his patients and from them he got
points of view that made him remold his own opinions. In
the main, the teaching of Freud has centered around four
cardinal principles: (a) the repression of unconscious tendencies; (b) the appearance of emotional conflicts in physical
symptoms; (c) the reappearance of childhood sexuality in
adult life; (d) the genesis of nervous troubles by damming
up libido, that is, unrelieved sexual energy.

9
Evaluation

Psychoanalysis may be regarded as a genuine psychological
science in the sense that it has properly estimated the scope
of its subject matter as man. It represents an effort to take
into account the individual's entire personality. Moreover,
it is investigative in its method, with the reservation, however,
that its technique is clinical rather than strictly experimental,
as we have pointed out. That such a technique has added
to our human progress may be inferred from the fact that it
has brought within scientific horizons a vast fund of information of which we were heretofore ignorant. The proper use
of such information has established the definite therapeutic
value of Freud's method.

In principle, however, there are many objectionable features
to the Freudian concept of human nature. If sex and instinct
are such dominating and all-pervading features of human life,
there is really no room for the play of reason and will in the
expression of man's life. At bottom, a human being is nothing
more than a higher type of animal. With the loss of insight,
freedom is extinguished; and the conflict between reason and

passion is inevitably doomed to issue in the extinction of all human ideals. It is not enough to say that Freud himself had no intentions of denying free will, that he had a deep respect for reason which he sought to liberate from the forces of instinct. The fact remains that the very conditions he set for the exercise of human conduct put man's will face to face with a tour de force. In practice Freud would say that we are free. Once asked if a man could be held responsible for his dreams he replied: "Whom else would you hold responsible?" But this does not rid his system of its deterministic implications. I doubt that Freud, with all his profound interest in human nature, really understood the metaphysical meaning of that nature. It is quite certain that he mistook the integrated arrangement of man's powers and operations for the soul. He uses the term "Psyche" to describe this arrangement and at times equates it with "Seele." This is surely far afield from the philosophic notion of soul as Aristotle defined it.

Again, morality in the Freudian ethic means simply the mores of the human race in operation: the prevailing sentiments and ruling customs of society at any given time or place. There is the definite suggestion, too, that knowledge by itself can decide all practical questions. Hence, conversion into moral principles, by the admission of an objective difference between good and evil, is quite impossible in the psychoanalytic theory. According to Freud, man owes everything to libidinal energy. There is no room for the higher values of life, and above all, no room for the operation of the movements of divine grace. Unfortunately, Freudianism is not merely a description of unconscious psychological processes; neither is it simply a branch of psychiatry or a method of healing diseases of the mind. It is also proposed as a philosophy of life and a philosophy which, in its theoretic principles, is materialistic, and, in its practical rules, is full of errors regarding the moral nature of men.

But, to come back to our original point, psychoanalysis must also be judged as a technique, a way of treating mental disease, an empirical and scientific method, based on causal principles. As a technique, it is the fruit of a mass of empirical data which brought to light the natural conflict between reason and passion and gave witness, at times, to the transformation of man's self-love into a love of others, of hedonism into altruism. Freud's preoccupation with data of this sort shows that he was really working more in line with the tradition of Aristotle and Aquinas than with the heritage of Democritus and Plato. And so it is necessary to approach his system with a respect for its tremendous achievements — let us say with the same breadth of view and impartial outlook that characterized the Angelic Doctor when he came to examine the writings of Aristotle and his Arabian commentators. A careful study of Freudian literature is required in order to see wherein the scientific findings of an unbeliever and anti-religious man are truly scientific. For if they are such, then, like any other genuine findings of science, they do not, because they cannot, encroach on the principles of the traditional philosophy, much less on the truths of revelation.

Let us give just one example of what we mean before we close this discussion of psychoanalysis. In St. Thomas, there is a clear development of the idea that sensuality is one of the main sources of sin, bearing in its train any number of abuses of reason and will. The findings of Freud point to the same conclusion when they show that infantile sexuality, run amuck and persisted in up to adulthood, brings on mental illnesses and other forms of maladjustment. All along the line, in fact, it is most interesting to observe the natural points of contact between the disorders of "sensuality," as pictured in the writings of the Angelic Doctor, and the excesses of "libido" in the theory of Freud.

CHAPTER 21

TRENDS OF THE MOMENT

I

Further Lands to Explore

The activities of human nature are so numerous and complex that they offer an inexhaustible field for investigation. Perhaps if there were not so many hidden depths to man's being, there would not be so many schools of psychology. The intricacies of his cosmic person, representing every aspect of visible creation in miniature, surely indicate one of the reasons for the existence of systems and academic differences in the psychological realm. And what is more natural than that the investigator who becomes absorbed in one of these multiple facets should either forget the others or interpret the whole in terms of the part! It was in this restricted manner that the psychophysiologists approached the problem of sensation; that the gestaltists became immersed in visual perception and translated their concepts of patterning into ultimate facts of human nature; that the behaviorists concentrated on motor behavior as though that were the final principle by which to explain man's world-embracing being; that the psychoanalysts fixed on libidinal impulses as the all-compelling source of human striving.

To be sure, the schools have emphasized things that were deserving of emphasis and which, in a relative capacity, have served a useful purpose in the progress of psychology as a whole. But the end is not yet, nor ever will be, so long as the mystery of man continues to challenge the ingenuity of the investigator. New points of view are constantly being stressed and new lines of research are opening up. Perhaps, as psychology continues its forward march, it will grow more holistic in outlook. At any rate, it seems true to say that, at the moment, there is less talk of schools and more talk of scholars. In this chapter, we shall try to survey the contemporary scene, catching up the threads that are still lying loose, and preparing ourselves for a final estimate of the work of the moderns.*

2

Psychic Research

First of all, a word about a type of investigation that has a never-failing appeal to the layman, even though its scientific value is far from being established. It embraces a wide range of phenomena such as mind reading and thought transference, clairvoyance or second sight, the production of physical effects by psychic influences, and so forth. One of the difficulties about events of this sort is that not everybody can experience them. The investigator who wants to explore them is at a disadvantage from the start. Another obstacle is the peculiar background, hardly the right one for experiment, against which the psychic events must take place. As a rule, they are anything but out in the open. Still, when all the fraud and sleight of hand has been eliminated, when the mass of dubious fact and questionable data has been peeled off, there may be a core of truth at the center which represents a new horizon of parapsychic experience, a land of promise into which science will enter at some future time.

* It is impossible, at the present time, to know the exact state of affairs in European research. The student will understand that all references to European scholars in this chapter are as of latest report. When the battlefields of Europe are cleared, it is likely that some of the men here mentioned will be missing or retired from their academic labors.

The *Proceedings of the Society for Psychical Research* was founded in London in 1882. It has its counterpart in an American publication of the same name. Both journals have printed papers by a number of scientists of high standing.

What are the results of this sort of research? Let us note at once that in mind reading and mental telepathy at least two people must participate: a sender and a receiver. The case of mind reading may be explained, in part at least, through a power of reading unconsciously expressed motor signals. The case of mental telepathy is more difficult. Here the sender and receiver are separated in a way that would exclude the use of motor signals. The experiments of *Joseph Rhine* at Duke University are attempts to produce scientific proof for the transference of thought, or for the existence of extrasensory perception. According to Rhine, the results of his work must make the psychologist reexamine the ancient doctrine "that nothing can enter the mind except through the gateways of the recognized senses." Clairvoyance, so called, differs from mind reading or telepathy by the fact that the person who has second sight needs no sender. Here the scientist is more sceptic.

As for phenomena that involve the manipulation of matter — table rapping, slate writing, the creation of body plasms, and so on — not much can be said from the scientific point of view. As natural events they have little to commend themselves to the student of mental science. Whether wrought by man's magic or accomplished through some other agency, the psychologist is bound to approach such events with empirical care, since the data of physics and chemistry as well as the action of immaterial psychic influences may be involved. One thing can be said with certainty: that the bulk of phenomena which come under the name of "metapsychic activities" have not been generally accepted and have not been incorporated as yet within the body of psychological science. If they are authentic, this is where they belong and this is where they will be found in the future.

3
In English-speaking Lands

Passing back to the ranks of the more academic investigators, one notes the pleasing fact that out of the forty odd scholars who have been presidents of the American Psychological Association since its foundation in 1892, only fifteen have been associated with particular schools of psychology. This would indicate that the trend of the moment is toward an eclecticism which will undoubtedly prove more healthy for the general status of the science of mind. It is quite impossible to enumerate the names of all the men who are thus striving for a middle position which would see good in all systems but would commit itself to no one in particular. To mention a few investigators who have worked and written in this eclectic spirit, we find *Edwin Boring* at Harvard; *Walter Pillsbury* at Michigan; *John Dashiell* at South Carolina; *Robert Woodworth* at Columbia; *Leonard Carmichael* for several years at Brown and later at Tufts. Some of the middle-of-the-roaders were not always such. Woodworth, for example, apparently has profited by his long years of experience in developing a central position from which he now benignly surveys the vested interests of all the schools. At any rate, a goodly number of our contemporary scholars are making sincere efforts to combine the best features of the subjective and the objective approaches to psychological data. This is surely in the right direction.

In England, *Charles Myers* has been a leader of influence for years. Made director of the first psychological laboratory in the kingdom, at Cambridge, he later headed an institute which devoted its energies to a practical application of psychological principles. The work of *Charles Spearman* continues to grow in importance. Most students are familiar with the long controversy which he has carried on with *Edward Thorndike* on the nature of intelligence. The latter supports the view that intelligence is an aggregate of numerous special abilities which are unrelated except as each depends on facility of learning. The former recognizes a special aptitude for each type of performance, but insists also on a general ability which enters in some degree into every kind of intelligent behavior. Since the issue here involved is in a fair way to being settled by evidence, it can scarcely be called a debate between rival schools in psychology.

4

Totality Psychology

Directorship of the Wundtian laboratory at Leipzig eventually passed into the hands of *Felix Krueger* who, as a student, had interested himself in the study of phonetics and folk psychology. Krueger is commonly reckoned as the father of totality (*Ganzheits*) psychology. Though closely related to the Gestalt theory, it represents an autonomous effort in the field of form psychology. Thus it holds (*a*) that the experience of total quality is prior, in the genetic order, to the experience of partial qualities; (*b*) that the configuration which is experienced at any given moment is itself imbedded in a total feeling background. Feeling, in fact, is a more basic fact than figure or perceptual patterning.

Psychological data can be understood only in terms of their developmental history. Hence Krueger's school speaks of "emotional prime totals" out of which other forms of mental life are produced. The influence of Wundt is apparent here, though it is rather the student of racial psychology than the experimenter in psychophysiology whose spirit is working in the younger Leipzig school. Krueger's vision is not limited to the laboratory. He sees in his psychology an approach to a deeper grasp of the meaning of cultural phenomena and an opportunity for practical consideration of the problems of society.

5
Understanding Psychology

Eduard Spranger at Berlin has also been the representative of a new movement in mental science. His point of view is called "understanding" (*Verständnis*) psychology. Quite obviously, we are dealing here with something closely related to act psychology. Indeed, the influence of *Edmund Husserl*, who had been a pupil of Brentano, is readily discerned in the work of Spranger. Understanding psychology, as its name implies, is concerned with meanings. Now, the meaning of anything is contextual; that is to say, it derives from its contribution to the understanding of a whole. For example, the meaning of a word in a sentence arises from its function in communicating, that is, in carrying out the intention of the speaker or writer.

To understand an individual, it is not enough that we dissect him or regard him apart from the environment in which he moves. We must further see him in his social relationships and envision his present in relation to his past. Spranger's unique theory of personality types has been enthusiastically endorsed by many psychologists. Uncommon, too, is his manner of approach to the science of human nature — an approach which depends more on intuitive analysis than on the devices of the laboratory or the methods of mental testing.

6

Eidetic Psychology

The work of *Erich Jaensch* is also akin to that of the Gestalt school, though he is not an adherent of the latter. Jaensch, a professor at Marburg, was one of the most enterprising of the pupils of Georg Müller. He labored for years on the problems of visual perception, and finally succeeded in awakening the interest of scholars by his findings on the lifelike imagery of children. Jaensch coined the term "eidetic" to describe the peculiarly vivid type of fancy which characterizes the period of infancy. The eidetic image is usually a visual one, which possesses an objective or perceptual nature, even though it is recognized as something purely subjective. It resembles an hallucination in almost every respect except that its possessor knows that it is an image. Thus Jaensch found that many children could describe pictures they had seen as distinctly as if they had the picture in front of them. It was not simply a matter of memory but of actually seeing the images in question. The eidetic predisposition should not be regarded as pathological. It may persist into adult life, where it expresses itself in daydreaming, castle-building, and so forth.

Walther Jaensch, a brother of Erich, studied the relation between eidetic tendencies and the whole psychophysical constitution. In their published researches, the Jaensches distinguished two eidetic types which are clinically connected with two kinds of disease: (*a*) basedowoid type which, while not pathological, is a miniature of Grave's disease, an illness due to overfunctioning of the thyroid gland; and (*b*) tetanoid type, also not pathological in itself, which offers a telescoped picture of tetany, a disease due to the disfunction of the parathyroid gland. The novelty of these classifications and the enthusiasm of the Jaenschian pronouncements have made a considerable impress on current psychology; but only the future will tell how productive of fruit the new way of looking at individual differences will turn out to be. The facts brought to light about eidetic imagery will certainly remain as a definite contribution to psychology. On the other hand, the wholesale reduction of conscious phenomena to imaginal effects is certainly a weakness in the Jaenschian system that is bound to prove fatal. From the philosophic standpoint, such a reduction is scarcely more than a refined form of materialism, on a par with the deterministic concepts of the gestaltists and the atomism of the Wundtians.

Another pupil of Georg Müller who has made some notable discoveries in his field is *David Katz*, professor at Rostock. Katz, like the Jaensches, has been interested in child psychology. He is especially remembered for his demonstration of the curious way in which color perception is affected by the conditions under which the color is seen.

In commenting on the modern German research along the lines of individual differences, reference must be made to the labors of the Swiss psychiatrist *Hermann Rorschach* who devised an unusual test for getting at the personality difficulties of his patients. The test consists of ten irregular ink blots which stand out against a white background. Five of the blots are in black and grey and five contain color. The subject is given one card at a time and is allowed to look at the blot as long as he likes. The examiner groups together the responses under such headings as form, detail, wholeness, originality, color, movement, and the like. Dominant trends of personality are then inferred. Unoriginal replies, and those involving animals, are interpreted to mean low intelligence. Whole-making responses, good form, and movement signify high intelligence. Introverts give many-detailed answers. The emotionally unstable are fond of colors. At first many criticisms were raised against the test, on the grounds that it lacked objective norms; but respect grew as its results were confirmed by later clinical findings. Insights into the personality defects of the feeble-minded and delinquent have also been revealed by its use. In the hands of a trained examiner, it is undoubtedly of great diagnostic value.

7
Personalistic Psychology

Mention was made on a previous page of the work of *Wilhelm Stern* in the field of individual differences. Among the Germans, he was a pioneer on the problem. Stern was a pupil of Hermann Ebbinghaus and was distinguished for the many lines of activity in which he interested himself. He introduced and developed intelligence tests in his native land. He also gave much of his time and labor to the study of children. In the sphere of applied psychology his name stands among the German leaders. Somewhat in the manner of William McDougall, Stern used his scientific training in psychology as a stepping stone to what he called a philosophy of "personalism." A person is a manifold in one. He exhibits unity in multiplicity and thus reconciles within himself the categories of existence and value.

The orientation here is significant, since it means that, for Stern, person is central in mental science as well as in mental philosophy; so that psychology, both scientific and philosophic, must be resolved ultimately into a study of human nature as a person. Stern's system accepts the individual as the primary whole of psychological reality. It is sympathetically concerned with philosophic standpoints, at the same time that it admits the definite contributions of the experimentalists. Actually, of course, it has led to less laboratory research than Krueger's developmental psychology or Jaensch's eidetic approach; but its practical influence will probably turn out to be larger than that of either of these systems. Already Stern has a fairly numerous band of followers in America.

8

European Functionalism

In Switzerland we find another psychologist of wide reputation. *Edouard Claparède* has developed an outlook which very much resembles Dewey's in its functional approach to the data of consciousness. The application of its principles to the problems of education makes the similarity all the more obvious. Claparède founded the Rousseau Institute for the study of children; and many fine pieces of research have been carried on there under his direction. As a functionalist, Claparède has found much to criticize in the old associational way of looking at mental phenomena. He is of the opinion that association itself does not account for the control of associative tendencies, so much in evidence in the intellectual activities of reading, adding, and so forth. The control, according to Claparède, must arise from the factor of interest.

Sleep is one of the most vitally important functions, and Claparède's account of it is interesting. He finds that it cannot be explained merely as the result of intoxication from the by-products of fatigue. It must also be regarded as a positive response of the organism which amounts to an instinctive form of activity. For many years, Claparède has served as secretary of the International Congress of Psychology. A man of peace-loving habits, he believes that the long debates that have engaged scholars since the foundation of psychology as a science represent wasted effort. How much better to fund all these energies and direct them into creative channels!

9
Italian Research

Vittorio Benussi has already been described as a member of the Austrian school of psychologists; yet he was a professor for many seasons at Padua. *Sante de Sanctis* taught psychiatry and experimental psychology at Rome. He was a close student of dream phenomena before Freud entered this field. His chief contributions, perhaps, have come in the sphere of child psychology. He devised one of the earlier test scales for indicating the degrees of mental deficiency.

Friedrich Kiesow taught at Turin for many years. He was a pupil of Wundt and also worked with the physiologist Mosso, known to students for his experiments with the ergograph and his researches on fatigue in human muscles. Part of Mosso's laboratory was given over to Kiesow in 1895. After years in these borrowed headquarters, he was able to open a larger and more adequate laboratory of his own. His workshop soon became the scene of a varied program of experiments on sensations of taste, touch, and bodily position, and on different types of images and feelings.

In his theoretic outlook, Kiesow has preserved the approach of his master Wundt. While he admits that the gestaltists have undertaken a very important line of study in opening up avenues to a deeper insight into perceptual data, he contends that such research has by no means done away with the fact of elementary sensations or with the need of continuing an analysis of psychophysical phenomena.

10
Progress in France

French psychologists have always remained strongly attached to associationalistic ways of explaining mental data.

Today, there is a growing tendency to combine this principle with the hormic approach which Henri Bergson illustrated in his philosophic writings. The guiding genius of experimental work in France has been *Henri Pieron* who succeeded Binet at the Sorbonne, took over the editorship of *L'Année Psychologique*, and in 1923 was appointed to Ribot's chair at the Collège de France. The fact is that Pieron's work has not been along Binet's line of intelligence testing but rather in the field of physiological psychology. He particularly interested himself in a study of brain injuries.

Even before Watson conceived of a systematic behaviorism, Pieron had defined psychology as a study of behavior. It would be a mistake, however, to identify his point of view with that of Watson and his followers. Pieron sees no reason why the analysis of sensations and imagery should be excluded from the total range of human activity, as investigated by the scientific psychologists. He insists only that introspective data be registered in objective and socially intelligible forms before they be regarded as proper subject matter for scientific study. The expression in understandable language of one's impressions suffices to make them amenable to scientific inquiry. All such verbally clothed experience is objective behavior. The only question here is the degree of intelligibility and the reliableness of a given type of evidence. In any case, there is no sharp line to be drawn between objective and subjective methods in psychology.

Another psychologist of prominence is *Georges Dumas* who, though not an experimentalist, has been a writer of wide interests and the editor of a large handbook entitled *Nouveau Traité de Psychologie* to which the best French scholars have contributed. As professor at the University of Paris, his own lectures and writings have been largely occupied with emotional life. The point of view of Dumas and his collaborators is basically introspective; and despite the difficulties involved, the method has proved fruitful: first, because of the suggestions it has offered for an objective approach; second, because of the initiative it has developed in the pursuit of psychological studies.

Generally speaking, students of the science of mind in France have been strongly attached to biological principles in their approach to mental phenomena. At the same time, they manifest a predilection for social settings in their studies of the activities of the individual. Their concern for the abnormal has already been pointed out. From the days of Charcot and earlier, they have leaned heavily on psychopathology. For this reason, the dynamic aspects of the Freudian system appear much less revolutionary to the French than to most English-speaking psychologists.

II

Russian Psychology

In closing this brief review of contemporary trends, a word must be said about the official psychology of Soviet Russia. As is well known, the entire communistic movement of the Soviet rests upon the philosophy of *Karl Marx* and is academically referred to as the philosophy of dialectical materialism. The influence of this way of thinking on the progress of mental science is doubly apparent: first, in the attempt to clarify the facts of psychology by relating them with the principles of the Marxian philosophy; second, in the employment of Marxian concepts as norms for the pursuit of new researches in the field of psychology. Thus dialectical materialism claims to have a place for consciousness as a new fact or quality which emerges when the physical processes of nature have reached a certain degree of complication. For this reason, the modern Russian investigator rejects both the exclusively subjective and the exclusively objective approach to the data of psychology. Introspection is not to be debarred; but its findings always need the confirmation of objective methods since the latter are more closely related to the fundamental processes of physical nature.

Moreover, the individual must be studied from the social as well as the biological standpoint inasmuch as he is a product of both kinds of environment. Further, his history is incomplete without some consideration of the economic class to which he belongs and the work which he will be called upon to perform in the world. So he must be analyzed in terms of his vocational value, that is to say, of his performances in reference to society as a whole. Because of this fact, the study of class psychology is both fundamental and practical. As an example of attitudes of this kind in the field of psychology, we must mention the name of *Konstantin Kornilov* who, at last report, was director of the department of experimental psychology at the University of Moscow.

12

The Perspective of Seventy Years

The invention of scientific psychology is simply an effort to apply the technique of the laboratory or the clinic to the problems of the psychological organism. Wundt's ambition was to put psychology on an equal footing with physics and chemistry. His goal, sad to say, has not yet been reached. Careful research is not wanting, nor faith in the experimental method. But great discoveries that would vitalize the science of mind and open up new fields of investigation, releasing new energies and knitting together the efforts of the investigators, have not yet come to light. Why?

Perhaps, in the first place, because there have never been any really great psychologists who could bring unity into the diverse trends that have separated scientists into schools from the days of Wundt. In the second place, because there are difficulties intrinsic to the subject matter of psychology. Exact measurements can never be applied to mind in the same way that they are applied to matter. In the third place. because of internal conflicts within the science of mind itself, Thus psychology, as a science, has not only failed to discern its proper subject matter; it has also failed to see that, as a science, it must leave the problems of philosophy alone.

It is a significant thing that all the great movements in psychology — Wundt's psychophysiological researches, intro-spective structuralism, the functional movement, the Gestalt system, behaviorism — have been mainly philosophic move-ments based on experimental techniques. Theoretical papers have appeared in abundance, written in the philosophic manner, but by men untrained in the philosophic disciplines. What has obviously been forgotten is that it requires as much care and expertness in the production of a good philosopher as of a good scientist.

In an earlier chapter, we tried to point out what the rela-tion between philosophic and scientific knowledge should be, so far as psychology is concerned. We shall bring our story to a close by some further remarks on the condition of sci-entific psychology today, especially in its bearing on the philosophy of human nature as Aristotle and Thomas Aquinas conceived it.

CHAPTER 22

THE THOMIST TAKES STOCK

I

Main Streams

As we reflect on the course of psychology down through the ages, we see that three great trends of thought have dominated its historical development from the days of the Greeks. These trends represent the three ways in which the facts of both common and special experience may be philosophically interpreted. We have pointed them out many times in these pages. They are: the tradition of Democritus which is the spirit of materialism; the tradition of Plato which is idealistic in its outlook; and the tradition of Aristotle which is a combination of the two. In one respect, these three ways of looking at human nature are epistemological attitudes: that is to say, they depend on the manner in which we interpret the human mind and its knowledge. Yet in another and more ultimate meaning, they depend on what we make of human nature, as such. The point here will be clear when we say that man, in his entitative make-up, is more basic than man in his cognitive achievements.

According to the Democritean tradition, only matter is a valid object of knowledge. In terms of the philosophy of nature, and more particularly, the philosophy of human nature, man is knowable because he is matter, whole and entire, body and soul. According to the Platonic tradition, only mind is a valid object of knowledge, because only mind is real; and whatever reality matter possesses it has by virtue of an essence and a being communicated to it by mind. According to the Aristotelian tradition, both mind and matter are knowable because both are real, and man is knowable because he is a form immersed in matter. If he knows his soul it is through his body; and if he knows his body it is through his soul. His soul is not a by-product of the body; neither is his body an aspect of the soul. Actually, man is a synolon in which both body and soul are joined as essential elements. Judged by this standard, the modern Cartesian is really a very old Platonist. His psychology is grounded on psychophysical principles that divorce mind and matter in exactly the same way as Plato divorced them. Similarly, the modern positivist is a very old Democritean. His psychology springs from the same kind of atomism that characterized the Greek materialists. He may be more refined than they; certainly he is not less deluded.

2

The Study of Human Nature

It is the tradition of Aristotle, not of Plato or of Democritus, which is emerging today with new depth and vigor when confronted with the impartial evidence of the investigators. More than ever before, we realize now that the observed facts of consciousness must be correlated with the physiology of human life if they are to be correctly understood. Furthermore, from serious reflection on the content and meaning of these same experimental data, it is obvious that the mechanistic concept of the soul as a property of cortical substance, or the Cartesian notion of it as an immaterial entity whose whole nature is to think, must be ruled out. Ideas of this sort simply do not fit the evidence. If any solid advance is to be made in the field of psychophysical analysis, it must proceed on the principle that the soul of man, like the first actuality of all other cosmic creatures, is a form united substantially with matter.

This being the case, psychology cannot limit itself to the phenomena of consciousness, but must extend its technical observation to the *whole man:* his acts, his powers, his habits, and his entire personality. It must be a science of human nature if it is to be a science at all. It must be a science of man as man if it is to contribute to the advance of knowledge by its investigation of a special area of reality. Assured against both excess and defect by the correctness of its investigative principles, it need set no boundaries to the daring of its plans for research. With its subject matter accurately fixed upon, it can proceed with assurance to the construction of proper techniques for attacking its special problems. In addition, it can so divide the labor of research as to secure, from all sides, a real cooperative analysis, and thus be a balanced development, of all its particular problems. From this point on it is the task of philosophy, utilizing the data of scientific experience as well as commonsense observation, to establish the ultimate *ratio* of human nature, and to show forth the fixed ontological principles that underlie man's mobile and sensible being.

3
Modern Issues

The present position of modern psychology, both as a science and as a branch of philosophy, can be easily summarized. It derives, in part, from the heavy emphasis laid on the physical sciences, beginning with Francis Bacon and growing stronger with the discovery of new ways and means of probing nature, until it reached its saturation point with the gross mechanism of the nineteenth century; in part, from the utter contempt of the men of the Renaissance for the culture of the medievals and for the philosophy of the Aristotelian and Thomistic tradition; in part, from the basic misconception of metaphysics which grew out of Descartes' critical doubt and his false reconstruction of reality.

The decline of metaphysics may be best seen in the reappearance, in modern times, of the two traditions which Aristotle and Thomas opposed singly but reconciled in their mean. Thus materialism became rampant once more when sense knowledge grew paramount; that is to say, when the doctrine of intellect, as a power *sui generis*, radically distinct from the senses, was denied. It was inevitable that with the departure of man's reason, the empirical teachings of philosophers like Hume, Locke, Mill, and Spencer should gain an entrance. These had their counterpart in the positivism of Comte and his disciples; and in the grossly atomistic concepts of men like Büchner and la Mettrie.

On the other hand, there were extremely idealistic tendencies in the philosophy of Descartes which led eventually to a denial of reality as knowable. Some of the subjectivists, such as Kant and his disciples, held that man's intellect could reach only the laws of the thinking subject; which means that it could have no knowledge of the speculative principles that would ensure the absolute value of reality. Other subjectivists, especially Hegel and the Hegelians, were more logical in their conclusions and rejected all reality beyond the thinking subject.

Between these extremes there is a doctrine and a tradition which is empiric or objective and idealistic or subjective at the same time; which has the authentic ring of common sense, yet is profound in its analysis of reality. In man, it places an intellect and a power of abstraction that is able to discover the essence and perfection of the objects of sensible experience. Beginning with something that is exterior to mind, something that is individual and material, this mind is able to construct a world of intelligibility wherein it walks and searches, analyzes and infers, until it strikes on the highest laws of being; and these it proclaims with metaphysical certainty. But if it is able to rise from sensible to intelligible reality, is it not because the human intellect is the property of a matterless form united to matter? Thus, the problem of what human nature can do in its thinking is ultimately the result of what human nature is in its being. Epistemological truth is conditioned by psychological truth; so that, if we do not know what man is in his nature and essence, how can we ever hope to learn what man is in his wisdom and knowledge?

4

Troubles of the Scientist

The story of psychology from the days of Wundt and Fechner is largely a tale of the rise and fall of systems. Something is wrong somewhere with the science of psychology, as a whole. I have already pointed out many mistakes in the approach of the individual investigators and many errors of interpretation on the part of certain schools. Here I should like to be more general in my remarks. The root of the trouble, it seems to me, lies in the failure of the investigators to appreciate the proper scope of their discipline. They cannot agree on the subject matter of psychology. Apparently, they have overlooked or forgotten the fact that, in order to build up a true science of mind, one must study, not this or that particular function of consciousness to the exclusion of other data, not somatic processes as a substitute for psychic processes, not the evolutionary tendencies of the organism or its motor responses to stimuli, but *man*, in all his various manifestations.

I would go a step further and say that the failure of the investigators is also due to their inability to appreciate the true nature of the subject matter of research. On what grounds, for example, does the behaviorist proceed *as if* man were merely an animal? Or by what antecedent evidence does the structuralist or the gestaltist proceed *as if* all man's conscious activities were reducible to a complexus of sensations or perceptions? Such methodological principles may be quite legitimate for the physiologist, or even for the animal psychologist; but, for the student of human nature, they are wholly false and unwarranted.

If it be admitted, as I think we can admit, that psychology has the potentialities of becoming a well-established science, this does not mean that it can do so without the aid of philosophy, or in spite of such aid. Aristotle could have foretold the confusion and polemic of modern psychology had he known the false metaphysical premises with which the majority of investigators begin their studies, or the equally false metaphysical conclusions with which many end their labors. Mere acquaintance with the facts of the laboratory does not warrant the making of philosophic pronouncements on the nature of man; yet acquaintance with the nature of man is required if the observer of the facts is to understand them properly, even in their scientific aspects, and if he is to exercise the correct perspective on them in their relation to the whole of psychological knowledge.

5

The Anthropological Approach

Where the schools have run amuck, in so many instances, is in extending to the whole of man's psychological life what is demonstrably true of only a part of it. We have already noted how, for the behaviorist, reflex action explains everything; for the gestaltist, perceptual patterns, with isomorphic structures in the nervous system, tell the whole story of man's conscious life; for the disciples of Jaensch, the eidetic image is the supreme fact in the development of human personality; for the Freudian, the interplay of instincts is the final principle of all human achievement. But reflexes, percepts, images, and instincts are only particular problems in the whole of man's psychological life.

What we need today, as Aquinas would contend, is really less of psychology and more of anthropology, using the term "anthropology" in its traditional meaning to signify the study of man. For that is what psychology should be: the study of man, as man, not as a concatenation of reflexes, or a sum of perceptual configurations, or a series of imaginal processes, or a complexus of instinctive responses. Such things are simply isolated events in the history of human nature, and they have no meaning except in relation to the whole nature. Further, the study of man, as man, means the study of man as a be-souled organism, or as a creature composed of matter and spirit, whose operations fall within the dimensions of scientific analysis, but whose fundamental nature is the proper study of philosophy.

Just as there is no one idea deep enough to exhaust the contents of reality, no one term or proposition which completely describes it, so there is no single formula to express, in all its richness of meaning, the notion of human nature. One representation of it is, however, more full and more exact than another. If we are looking for an idea that expresses the central aspect of philosophic psychology, then the concept of man as a creature composed of body and soul is as faultless as any. Of course, such a concept is really very complex. Accordingly, it is allowable, for the sake of clear understanding, to consider its different facets as though they were separate realities.

In this way we are justified in studying the acts, powers, and habits of man, one by one, as though they were discrete properties of human nature; but all such accidental entities derive their significance from the fact that they are rooted in the substance of man. All, therefore, must be analyzed and interpreted, eventually, in terms of this central substance which is, itself, a composition of matter and form. From the principle of a substantial union between body and soul, as from a fountainhead, spring all the peripheral truths that complete our scientific knowledge of man. These truths, from their position of dependency on the central principle, can touch only the accidents of our being. We may designate them "truths of the structural order," in the sense that powers are accidental parts of a nature; or we may call them "truths of the operational order," in the sense that the movements of powers are accidental manifestations of a nature.

The point is that structures and operations do not constitute a nature but presuppose it. This being the case, it is of capital importance that we understand the fundamental constituency of man's essence if we are to theorize about the meaning of his attributes. Understanding his essence, we can understand the arrangement and distinction of the acts and powers that flow from it and exhibit it, phenomenally, to scientist and philosopher alike. Thus it becomes as wrong for the scientist as for the philosopher to say or imply that man does not share some of his acts and powers with the plant and animal kingdoms, or that he is not essentially distinct, by other acts and powers, from both these orders of being.

· Putting the matter more concretely, I should say that it shows greater conformity with the demands of scientific evidence to regard man as the proper subject of vegetative, sensitive, and rational functions, and to look upon his soul as the basic operational principle by which he lives, feels, and thinks, than to attempt a monistic or falsely dualistic solution of the problems of human psychology. The investigator who recognizes the human person as something compounded of mind and matter will find no difficulty in grasping the significance of the data which he studies in the laboratory or the clinical chambers. For one who shares with Aquinas the view that man is a single substance, made up of contrasted psychic and somatic elements, there can be no idealistic fear that psychology will end by materializing the spirit of man; just as there can be no positivistic fear that psychology will vanish into the realm of the unknowable by dematerializing the body of man.

6

Where Things Have Gone Awry

As we bring our historical account to a close, I should like to make a short summary of the present position of psychology in its scientific aspects. Such a stocktaking is designed chiefly to correct false attitudes and may be regarded as part of the interpretative function of the Thomist.

The first mistake is in the point of view that the sole subject matter of scientific psychology is either consciousness and its phenomena, or behavior and its phenomena. Obviously, the Cartesian wedge is still doing its work effectively when it can divide investigators into such widely opposed camps. A dichotomy of this sort not only fails to recognize the difference between the psychological, as such, and the physiological; but it also fails to see that man reconciles both within the depths of his human nature. And even in the field of consciousness alone, or of behavior alone, there is the further failure to distinguish between phenomena that are rational in kind and phenomena that are simply sensitive or vegetative in character.

The second mistake is in the investigator's complete abandonment of philosophic criteria for his work. Out of this abandonment comes the loss of the precious concept of soul, and its ensuing loss of the concept of human nature. Of course, I do not mean to say that it is the scientist's business to investigate the soul or the nature of man, for these are philosophic problems. But surely, if the scientist cannot successfully prosecute his work and build up his science without a truthful knowledge about human nature, then such knowledge must be presupposed to his investigations. At any rate, he must not theorize in a way that would negate the correct philosophic analysis of man.

We are forced to conclude, then, that the regrettable state of affairs in the science of psychology today is due, in no small measure, to bad philosophic influences. Such can be shown to be the case, historically, I believe. Thus under the influence of Kant, on the one hand, and of Comte, on the other, the scientists have been completely bogged down by their special preferences, either for the informations of subjective consciousness alone, or for the data of objective behavior alone. And so we witness a convergence, from idealistic and positivistic streams, of concepts that mark the investigator as a false dualist, if he is not already an out-and-out materialistic monist.

With the disappearance of the notion of substance, the notion of soul vanished out of reality. This made it relatively easy to discard the idea of consciousness in favor of the idea of behavior. Without a soul, psychology is like a temple without a deity, or a home without a family spirit. Of course, phenomena constitute the proper area of investigation for the scientist, in psychology as in any other discipline. But concentration on phenomena alone, as events have shown, tends to reduce psychology to the level of pure physiology. This is true in the case of the Wundtian as well as the behaviorist, of the gestaltist as well as the response psychologist.

Moreover, the prejudice created by the extraordinary progress of the experimental sciences, as contrasted with the sterility of philosophic discussion at its worst, has filled the minds of scholars with a distrust of speculation. This attitude has been strengthened by the fact that nonpsychological sciences depend on a method that is strictly objective, whereas psychology must fall back on the data of introspection in order to resolve its major problems. The latter circumstance has led men gradually to think that the temper of psychological investigation is at basic loggerheads with any kind of external observation; with the result that they either have concentrated too much on the phenomenally conscious aspects of their subject matter, or else have given themselves up exclusively to the study of objective behavior.

7

Man in Truth and Reality

Finally, let me urge once more the point that not every philosophy is useful to the science of psychology, but only that analysis which expounds the truth of human nature. Such, I take it, is the analysis which was formulated over two thousand years ago by Aristotle, which was subsequently taken over, refined, and developed by Aquinas, and which is now known as the "traditional psychology". This is the position which denies the idealistic creed that psychology is nothing but a philosophy of spirit: and, with equal vigor, denies the positivistic position that psychology is simply a physiological discipline.

Every investigator, at some time or other, is confronted with the task of passing judgment on his work. His research programs can be marred and distorted and his conclusions invalidated by wrong philosophic premises which, wittingly or unwittingly, he has accepted as a basis of his inductive procedures. Now, the psychologist is a student of human nature; and human nature fairly bristles with problems that require the combined efforts of the scientist and philosopher, if adequate solutions are to be reached.

It is difficult to see how the investigator can avoid assuming some definite philosophic attitude toward the subject matter which he is studying. In this case, the subject matter is man, regarding whom there can be but one satisfactory attitude. It is the position which recognizes in every human being, regardless of race or age, a creature possessed of soul and body; a cosmic entity made out of spirit and matter; an organism quickened with a principle of rational life; a corporeal substance that not only vegetates with the plants and senses with the animals, but also, and more importantly, reflects on its own intellectual nature, and stretches out, by its faculty of divine love, toward a Creator Who is supremely perfect.

BIBLIOGRAPHY

I. Philosophic Psychology:

  1. General:

    a. Ueberweg, Friedrich, *History of Philosophy* (trans.), London, Hodder and Stoughton, 1874, 2 vol.

    b. Erdmann, Johannes Eduard, *History of Philosophy* (trans.), London, Macmillan, 1890, 3 vol.

    c. Turner, William, *History of Philosophy*, Boston, Ginn, 1903.

    d. Gilson, Etienne, *The Unity of Philosophical Experience*, New York, Scribner, 1941.

  2. Ancient:

    a. Robin, Léon, *Greek Thought* (trans.), New York, Knopf, 1928.

    b. Jaeger, Werner Wilhelm, *Paideia: The Ideals of Greek Culture* (trans.), New York, Oxford, 1939.

    c. Burnett, John, *Early Greek Philosophy*, London, A. & C. Black, 1930, 4th ed.

  3. Medieval:

    a. de Wulf, Maurice, *History of Mediaeval Philosophy* (trans.), New York, Longmans, 1935, 3rd English ed., 2 vol.

    b. Gilson, Etienne, *The Spirit of Mediaeval Philosophy* (trans.), New York, Scribner, 1940.

  4. Modern:

    a. Höffding, Harald, *History of Modern Philosophy* (trans.), London, Macmillan, 1890, 2 vol.

II. Scientific Psychology:

  1. General:

    a. Boring, Edwin G., *A History of Experimental Psychology*, New York, Appleton, 1929.

      b. Müller-Freienfels, Richard, *The Evolution of Modern Psychology* (trans.), New Haven, Yale University Press, 1935.

      c. Spearman, Charles, *Psychology Down the Ages*, London, Macmillan, 1937, 2 vol.

2. Special:
      a. Murchison, Carl (ed.), *A Handbook of General Experimental Psychology*, Worcester, Mass., Clark University Press, 1934.

      b. Garrett, Henry E., *Great Experiments in Psychology*, New York, Appleton, 1941.

BIBLIOGRAPHICAL INDEX

Abelard (1079–1142), 54

Ach, Narziss (1871–   ), 155, 164

Adler, Alfred (1870–1937), 231–33
The Practise and Theory of Individual Psychology (trans.)

Adrian, Edgar Douglas (1889–   ), 175
The Basis of Sensation

Albert the Great (1193?–1280), 55, 59, 83, 85

Alexander of Hales (?–1245), 57

Anaxagoras (B.C. 500?–428), 20

Anaximander (B.C. 611?–547?), 18, 28, 32

Angell, James Rowland (1869–   ), 171, 204
An Introductory Study of the Structure and Function of Human Consciousness

Anselm (1033–1109), 54
Monologium (trans.)

Aquinas, V. Thomas

Aristotle (B.C. 384–322), 1, 2, 3, 4, 5, 6, 7, 13, 19, 20, 23, 24, 25, 26, 27–38, 39, 55, 62, 66, 69, 80, 85, 89, 93, 96, 100, 108, 109, 122, 126, 144, 146, 158, 184, 196, 199, 206, 234, 235, 250, 251, 252, 254, 256, 261
Treatise on the Soul (trans.)
Treatise on Memory and Reminiscence (trans.)
Treatise on Sense and the Object of Sense (trans.)

Augustine (354–430), 46–51, 89
Confessions (trans.)
The City of God (trans.)

Aveling, Francis (1875–1941), 164
Psychology: The Changing Outlook

Avencebrol (Salomon ben Gabirol) (about 1020–1070), 56, 57

Averroes (Ibn Roschd) (1126–1198), 56

Avicenna (Ibn Sina) (980–1037?), 55, 56

Bacon, Francis (1561–1626), 32, 59, 88, 94, 119, 253
Novum Organon (trans.)

Bacon, Roger (1214?–1294), 59

Bain, Alexander (1818–1903), 114
The Emotions and the Will

Baird, John Wallace (1869–1919), 162, 163

Ballard, Philip Boswood (1865–   ), 145

Beers, Clifford Whittingham (1876–   ), 190
A Mind That Found Itself

Bekhterev, Vladimir Mikhailovich (1857–1927), 182
General Principles of Human Reflexology (trans.)

Bell, Charles (1774–1842), 122
The Nervous System of the Human Body

Benussi, Vittorio (1878–   ), 215, 246

Bergson, Henri (1859–1941), 51, 112, 247
Time and Free Will (trans.)
Creative Evolution (trans.)

Berkeley, George (1685–1753), 86, 93, 98, 99, 100, 108, 109
A Treatise Concerning the Principles of Human Knowledge

Bernard, Luther Lee (1881–   ), 207
An Introduction to Social Psychology

Bernheim, Hippolyte (1840–1909), 189, 223, 224

Bessel, Friedrich Wilhelm (1784–1846), 123, 124

Binet, Alfred (1857–1911), 152, 193–95, 247
   The Development of Intelligence in Children (trans.)
Boethius (480?–524?), 53
Boll, Franz (1867–1924), 129
Bonald, Louis Gabriel de (1754–1840), 110
Bonaventure (1221–1274), 58–9
Boring, Edwin Garrigues (1886–   ), 162, 239
   The Physical Dimensions of Consciousness
Braid, James (1795–1861), 121
Brentano, Franz (1838–1917), 148, 165, 195, 215, 241
Breuer, Josef (1842–1925), 122, 223, 224, 225
Bridges, James Winfred (1885–   ), 196
   A Point Scale for Measuring Mental Ability (with Yerkes, Bridges, Hardwick)
Broca, Paul (1824–1880), 123, 177
Brown, Thomas (1778–1820), 108
   A Treatise on the Philosophy of the Human Mind
Büchner, Ludwig (1824–1899), 107, 254
   Man in the Past, Present and Future
Bühler, Karl (1879–   ), 152
Burch, George James (1852–?), 176

Cabanis, Pierre Jean (1757–1808) 94
Calkins, Mary Whiton (1863–1930), 163
   A First Book in Psychology
Cannon, Walter Bradford (1871–   ), 166, 178
   Bodily Changes in Pain, Hunger, Fear and Rage
Carmichael, Leonard (1898–   ), 186, 239
   Elements of Human Psychology (with Warren)
Cattell, James McKeen (1860–1944), 168, 172, 195, 230

Charcot, Jean Martin (1825–1893), 122, 187, 188, 189, 223, 226, 248
Cicero, (B.C. 106–43), 40
Claparède, Edouard (1873–1940), 245
   Experimental Pedagogy and the Psychology of the Child (trans.)
Comte, Auguste (1798–1857), 111, 254, 260
   A General View of Positivism (trans.)
Condillac, l'Abbé Etienne Bonnot de (1714–1780), 94, 100
Cousin, Victor (1792–1867), 111

Dalton, John (1766–1844), 129
Darwin, Charles (1809–1882), 114, 132, 133, 134, 135, 166, 169, 195, 204
   The Origin of Species
Darwin, Erasmus (1731–1802), 113
   Zoonomia: or, The Laws of Organic Life
Dashiell, John Frederick (1888–   ), 239
   Fundamentals of General Psychology
Democritus (B.C. 460?–362?), 4, 21, 28, 92, 118, 126, 235, 251, 252
De Sanctis, Sante (1862–   ), 246
Descartes, René (1596–1650), 46, 86, 87–90, 95, 96, 100, 104, 116, 190, 254
   Principles of Philosophy (trans.)
   The Passions of the Soule (trans.)
   Meditations (trans.)
Detwiler, Samuel Randall (1890–   ), 186
Dewey, John (1859–   ), 170, 171, 181, 204, 245
   How We Think
   Democracy and Education
   Human Nature and Conduct
Driesch, Hans (1867–1941), 180, 181
   The Science and Philosophy of the Organism (trans.)
Dumas, Georges (1866–   ), 247
Dunlap, Knight (1875–   ), 211
   Elements of Psychology

Durandus of St. Pourçain (?–1332?), 81

Ebbinghaus, Hermann (1850–1909), 143, 144, 145, 146, 159, 172, 183, 193, 244
Memory

Ehrenfels, Christian von (1859–1932), 149, 215

Empedocles (about B.C. 500–430?), 20, 28, 32

Epicurus (B.C. 342?–270), 39

Erigena, John Scotus (?–875?), 54

Fechner, Gustav Theodor (1801–1887), 117, 129, 130, 131, 140, 145, 166, 168, 255

Fichte, Johann Gottlieb (1762–1814), 105

Flourens, Pierre (1794–1867), 122, 123, 177

Franz, Shepherd Ivory (1874–1933), 178, 179
Nervous and Mental Re-education

Freud, Sigmund (1856–1939), 7, 40, 46, 122, 164, 189, 222–35, 246, 248, 257
A General Introduction to Psychoanalysis (trans.)
The Interpretation of Dreams (trans.)
The Ego and the Id (trans.)

Fritsch, Gustav (1838–1891), 123

Fullerton, George Stuart (1859–1925), 168
The World We Live In

Galen (131–201), 40, 41

Gall, Franz Joseph (1758–1828), 95
On the Functions of the Brain and of Each of its Parts (trans.)

Galton, Francis (1822–1911), 135–37, 168, 169, 193, 194, 195
Inquiries into Human Faculty and Its Development

Galvani, Luigi (1737–1798), 121

Gesell, Arnold Lucius (1880–   ), 209
The Mental Growth of the Pre-school Child

Geulincx, Arnold (1625?–1669), 90

Goddard, Henry Herbert (1866–   ), 195
Feeble-Mindedness
The Kallikak Family

Goethe, Johann Wolfgang von (1749–1832), 126

Golgi, Camillo (1844–1926), 175

Goltz, Friedrich (1834–1902), 180

Gorgias (B.C. 485?–380?), 22

Gotch, Francis (1853–1913), 176

Haeckel, Ernst Heinrich (1834–1919), 107, 169
The Evolution of Man (trans.)

Hall, Granville Stanley (1844–1924), 169, 170, 172, 184
Adolescence

Hall, Marshall (1790–1857), 121

Haller, Albrecht von (1708–1777), 120

Hamilton, William (1788–1856), 108, 109
Lectures on Metaphysics and Logic

Hartmann, Eduard (1842–1906), 106

Hartley, David (1705–1757), 113
Observations on Man

Head, Henry (1861–1940), 178, 179
Aphasia and Kindred Disorders of Speech

Hegel, Georg Wilhelm Friedrich (1770–1831), 105, 107, 254
The Phenomenology of Mind (trans.)

Helmholtz, Hermann (1821–1894), 128, 129, 131, 132, 139, 149
Treatise on Psysiological Optics (trans.)
Popular Lectures on Scientific Subjects (trans.)

Heraclitus (flourished B.C. 500), 18, 19, 24, 28, 32

Herbart, Johann Friedrich (1776–1841), 105, 106, 134
Outlines of Educational Doctrine

Hering, Ewald (1834–1918), 131, 132

Hippocrates (B.C. 460–359 or 377?), 41

Hitzig, Eduard (1838–?), 123

Hobbes, Thomas (1588–1679), 91, 92, 100, 113
Leviathan

Holmes, Gordon Morgan (1876–   ),
    178
Holt, Edwin Bissel (1873–   ), 206,
    210, 211
    *The Freudian Wish and its Place in
    Ethics*
Hume, David (1711–1776), 86, 93, 98,
    100, 107, 108, 109, 113, 117, 143,
    254
    *An Enquiry concerning Human
    Understanding*
    Of the Passions
Hunter, Walter Samuel (1889–   ),
    206
Husserl, Edmund (1859–1938), 241
    *Ideas: General Introduction to Pure
    Phenomenology* (trans.)

Jaensch, Erich (1883–1940), 242
    *Eidetic Imagery and Typological
    Methods of Investigation*
Jaensch, Walther (1889–   ), 242,
    244, 257
James, William (1842–1910), 165, 166,
    167, 170, 171, 172, 204
    Psychology
    Talks to Teachers
Janet, Paul (1823–1899), 111, 122
Janet, Pierre (1859–   ), 188, 189,
    226
    Psychological Healing (trans.)
Jennings, Herbert Spencer (1868–
    ), 180, 181
    Behavior of the Lower Organisms
    *The Biological Basis of Human
    Nature*
Josey, Charles Conant (1893–   ),
    207
    The Social Philosophy of Instinct
Jouffroy, Théodore (1796–1842), 111
    Introduction to Ethics (trans.)
Jung, Carl (1875–   ), 230–31, 232,
    233
    Psychological Types (trans.)
    Studies in Word Association (trans.)

Kant, Immanuel (1724–1804), 51, 99,
    100, 101–5, 117, 149, 254, 260

    Critique of Pure Reason (trans.)
    Critique of Practical Reason (trans.)
    Critique of the Faculty of Judgment
    (trans.)
Kantor, Jacob Robert (1888–   ),
    207
    A Survey of the Science of Psychology
Katz, David (1884–   ), 243
    The World of Color (trans.)
Kiesow, Friedrich (1858–   ), 246
Koehler, Wolfgang (1887–   ), 7,
    215, 218, 219
    Gestalt Psychology
Koffka, Kurt (1886–1941), 215, 216,
    217, 218
    The Growth of the Mind
Kornilov, Konstantin (1879–   ),
    249
    *Psychology in the Light of Dialectic
    Materialism* (in *Psychologies of
    1930*)
Kraepelin, Emil (1856–1926), 187, 230
    Clinical Psychiatry (trans.)
Krueger, Felix Emil (1874–   ), 240,
    241, 244
Külpe, Oswald (1862–1916), 150, 151,
    152, 161, 215
    Outlines of Psychology (trans.)
Kuo, Zing Yang (1898–   ), 186, 207
    Human Behavior

Ladd, George Trumball (1842–1921),
    171
    Elements of Physiological Psychology
Lamennais, Félicité Robert de (1782–
    1854), 110
LaMettrie, Julien Offray de (1709–
    1751), 94, 100, 254
    Man a Machine (trans.)
Lange, Carl (1834–1900), 166
    The Emotions (with James)
Langfeld, Herbert Sidney (1879–
    ), 211
Langley, John Newport (1852–1925),
    176
    The Autonomic Nervous System
Lashley, Karl Spencer (1890–   ),
    178, 179, 207
    Brain Mechanisms and Intelligence

Lavoisier, Antoine Laurent (1743–1794), 121

Leibniz, Gottfried Wilhelm von (1646–1716), 51, 86, 96, 97, 100, 104
New Essays Concerning Human Understanding (trans.)

Leucippus (flourished B.C. 5th century), 21

Liébeault, Ambroise Auguste (1823–?), 189

Lindworsky, Johannes (1875–), 156, 157
Theoretical Psychology (trans.)

Locke, John (1632–1704), 92, 93, 99, 113, 116, 254
An Essay Concerning Human Understanding

Loeb, Jacques (1859–1924), 180
Comparative Physiology of the Brain and Comparative Psychology

Lombroso, Cesare (1835–1909), 134
Crime, its Causes and Remedies (trans.)

Lotze, Rudolf Hermann (1817–1881), 127, 128

Lucretius (B.C. 96–55), 40, 92

Mach, Ernst (1838–1916), 143, 149, 181, 215
The Analysis of Sensations (trans.)

Magendie, François (1783–1855), 122

Maimonides (1135–1204), 57
Guide for the Perplexed

Maine de Biran, Pierre (1766–1824), 110
The Influence of Habit on the Faculty of Thinking (trans.)

Malebranche, Nicholas de (1638–1715), 90

Marbe, Karl (1869–), 152

Marx, Karl (1818–1883), 248
Capital (trans.)

McDougall, William (1871–1938), 164, 185, 186, 207, 208, 244
An Introduction to Social Psychology
The Frontiers of Psychology

McGeoch, John Alexander (1897–1942), 146

Meinong, Alexius (1853–1920), 215

Mendel, Gregor Johann (1822–1884), 134

Mesmer, Franz Anton (1734–1815), 121, 122, 187

Messer, August (1867–), 152

Meumann, Ernst (1862–1915), 145
The Psychology of Learning (trans.)

Meyer, Adolf (1866–), 189, 190

Michotte, Albert Eduard (1881–), 155, 156

Mill, James (1773–1836), 113
Analysis of the Phenomena of the Human Mind

Mill, John Stuart (1806–1873), 114, 254
A System of Logic

Moleschott, Jacob (1822–1893), 107

Moore, Thomas Verner (1877–), 152
Cognitive Psychology

Morgan, Conway Lloyd (1852–1936), 114, 181, 183
The Animal Mind

Müller, Georg Elias (1850–1934), 144, 145, 146, 176, 242, 243

Müller, Johannes (1801–1858), 125, 126, 127, 128, 130, 139
The Physiology of the Senses (trans.)

Münsterberg, Hugo (1863–1916), 210

Myers, Charles Samuel (1873–), 239
An Introduction to Experimental Psychology

Occam, William (?–1349?), 51, 82

Parmenides (flourished B.C. 6th century), 19, 24, 28

Pascal, Blaise (1623–1662), 90
Pensées (trans.)

Paterson, Donald Gildersleeve (1892–), 197

Paul, Saint, Apostle (1?–67?), 45–46

Pavlov, Ivan Petrovich (1849–1936), 181, 182
Conditioned Reflexes (trans.)

Philo, (about B.C. 20—about A.D. 54), 41, 42

Pieron, Henri (1881–   ), 247
The Principles of Experimental Psychology (trans.)

Pillsbury, Walter Bowers (1872–   ), 239
The Fundamentals of Psychology

Pinel, Philippe (1745–1826), 186, 187

Pintner, Rudolf (1884–1942), 197
Intelligence Testing

Plato, (B.C. 427?–347), 2, 5, 20, 23, 24–26, 28, 30, 96, 98, 235, 251, 252
Timaeus (trans.)
Phaedo (trans.)
Phaedrus (trans.)

Plotinus, (205?–270?), 42, 46, 50
Enneads

Preyer, Wilhelm (1841–1897), 133

Priestley, Joseph (1733–1804), 113

Prince, Morton (1854–1929), 188, 189
The Unconscious

Protagoras (B.C. 481?–411), 22

Prüm, Emile (1857–   ), 155, 156

Purkinje, Johannes Evangelista (1787–1869), 175

Pyrrho (B.C. 365?–275?), 40

Pythagoras (B.C. 582—aft. 507), 18, 22, 28

Rahn, Carl Leo (1881–   ), 161, 162

Ramón y Cajal, Santiago (1852–1934), 175

Reid, Thomas (1710–1796), 107, 108
Essays on the Active Powers of the Human Mind

Rhine, Joseph Banks (1895–   ), 238
New Frontiers of the Mind

Ribot, Théodule Armand (1839–1916), 146, 147
The Diseases of Personality (trans.)

Rignano, Eugenio (1870–1930), 219
The Psychology of Reasoning (trans.)

Romanes, George John (1848–1894), 133
Animal Intelligence

Rorschach, Hermann (1884–1922), 243
Psychodiagnostics (trans.)

Schelling, Friedrich Wilhelm Joseph von (1775–1854), 105
Transcendental Idealism (trans.)

Schopenhauer, Arthur (1788–1860), 106, 107
The World as Will (trans.)

Scotus, Duns (1265?–1308), 80, 81

Séguin, Edouard (1812–1880), 193
Idiocy: and its Treatment by Physiological Method (trans.)

Selz, Otto (1881–   ), 156

Sherrington, Charles Scott (1861–   ), 166, 175
The Integrative Action of the Nervous System

Simon, Théodore (1873–   ), 194

Socrates (B.C. 469–399), 20, 22–23, 24, 26, 28

Spearman, Charles Edward (1863–   ), 137, 197, 198–99, 219, 240
The Nature of "Intelligence" and the Principles of Cognition
The Abilities of Man: their Nature and Measurement

Spencer, Herbert (1820–1903), 115, 169, 254
The Factors of Organic Evolution

Spinoza, Baruch (1632–1677), 86, 90–91, 95, 100, 104, 116
Ethic Demonstrated in Geometrical Order (trans.)

Spranger, Eduard (1882–   ), 241
Types of Men (trans.)

Spurzheim, Johann Gaspar (1776–1832), 95

Stagirite, V. Aristotle

Steffens, Lottie (1872–   ), 145

Stern, Ludwig Wilhelm (1871–1938), 195, 196, 244
Psychology of Early Childhood (trans.)
General Psychology from the Personalistic Standpoint

Stumpf, Karl (1848–1936), 148, 149, 215

Terman, Lewis Madison (1877–   ), 195, 196, 199
The Intelligence of School Children
Measuring Intelligence

Thales (about B.C. 640–546), 18

Thomas Aquinas (1225?–1274), 1, 2, 3, 4, 5, 6, 7, 28, 29, 55, 59, 60, 61–79, 80, 81, 83, 85, 86, 89, 93, 96, 100, 116, 117, 137, 144, 146, 153, 154, 166, 184, 190, 200, 235, 250, 254, 257, 259, 261

Treatise on Man (trans. part I, *Summa Theologica*)

Treatise on the Passions (trans. part I–II, *Summa Theologica*)

Treatise on the Union of Soul and Body (trans. book II, *Summa contra Gentiles*)

Thorndike, Edward Lee (1874–   ), 146, 183, 184, 211, 212, 219, 240

Principles of Teaching

The Original Nature of Man

Adult Learning (with Bregnan, Tilton, Woodyard)

Titchener, Edward Bradford (1867–1927), 152, 158–62, 165, 171, 215, 220, 222

Experimental Psychology

Lectures on the Experimental Psychology of the Thought-processes

Tolman, Edward Chace (1886–   ), 206

Purposive Behavior in Animals and Men

Tylor, Edward Burnett (1832–1917), 134

Primitive Culture

Vogt, Karl (1817–1895), 107

Lectures on Man (trans.)

Volta, Alessandro (1745–1827), 121

Voltaire, François Marie Arouet de (1694–1778), 86, 94

Waller, Augustus (1816–1870), 175

Ward, James (1843–1925), 147

Psychological Principles

Washburn, Margaret Floy (1871–1939), 210

The Animal Mind

Watson, John Broadus (1878–   ), 7, 203–6, 207, 208, 209, 240, 243, 246, 247, 249, 250, 255, 260

Psychology from the Standpoint of a Behaviorist

Weber, Ernst Heinrich (1795–1878), 117, 124, 125, 127, 130, 172

Weismann, August (1834–1914), 135, 136

The Germ-plasm: a Theory of Heredity (trans.)

Weiss, Albert Paul (1879–1931), 206

A Theoretical Basis of Human Behavior

Wells, Honoria Marian, 156

The Phenomenology of Acts of Choice

Wertheimer, Max (1880–1943), 215, 216, 217, 222

Wheeler, Raymond Holder (1892–   ), 163

The Science of Psychology

Whytt, Robert (1714–1766), 121

Wirth, Wilhelm (1876–   ), 160

Wolff, Christian von (1679–1754), 100, 101

Woodworth, Robert Sessions (1869–   ), 152, 211, 212, 239

Dynamic Psychology

Psychology

Wundt, Wilhelm (1832–1920), 117, 131, 139–43, 144, 148, 150, 158, 160, 162, 165, 166, 168, 172, 187, 195, 215, 220, 221, 222

An Introduction to Psychology (trans.)

Elements of Folk Psychology (trans.)

Yerkes, Robert Mearns (1876–   ), 184, 185, 196, 197

Almost Human

The Great Apes (with A. W. Yerkes)

Young, Thomas (1773–1839), 128

Zeno (B.C. 336?–264?), 39

Zilboorg, Gregory (1890–   ), 190

Mind, Medicine and Man

SUBJECT INDEX

"Abreaction," Freudian, 225
Abstraction, 9, 23, 35, 36, 70, 71, 104
Academicians, 4
Act, 29
  and potency, 18, 24
Action, life of, 72–73
"Action Theory," 210
Adam, 15, 47
Adolescence, 169
Ambivert, 231
American Journal of Psychology, 170
American Psychological Association, 170, 239
A Mind That Found Itself, 190
Anabolism, 132
Animals, experiments on, 180
Animal spirits, 88
Animism
  primitive, 15
  causes of, 16
Associationism, 92, 113, 114, 118, 140, 141
Aristotelian tradition, 5
Aristotelian synthesis, 27–38
Attention, 160
Autonomic nervous system, 176

Basedowoid type, 242
Beauchamp, Sally, 189
Brain physiology, 123, 177–78
Body-soul problem, 30, 31, 63, 64, 65, 87, 131, 140, 261, 262

Cardiograph, 179
Carolingian schools, 54
Catabolism, 132
Categorical imperative, 103
"Censor," Freudian, 227
Cerebral localization, 95
Clairvoyance, 237, 238

"Closure," 218
Color pyramid, 159
Common sense
  Scottish school of, 109, 110
  traditional meaning of, 109
Complex
  inferiority, 232
  superiority, 232
Conceptualists, 61, 83
Consciousness, 259
  atoms of, 159
  dimensions of, 162
  motorized, 210, 211
  stream of, 167
  utilities of, 171
"Cosmos," 18
Crusades, 54

Darwinian hypothesis, 32, 114, 115
"Death instinct," 227
Democritean tradition, 5, 21, 251 252
De Rerum Natura, 40
Desire, life of, 72–73
Determining tendencies, 155
Dialectical materialism, 248
Diaries, 67
Dreams, 229, 230, 234
Dynamism, idealistic, 105

"Ego," Freudian, 227, 228
"Eidos," 69
Elan vital, 112
Eleatics, 28
Emotions, 72, 88, 92, 103, 147, 166, 204
  concupiscent, 72
  irascible, 72
Emotional infantilism, 147
"Emotional prime totals," 240
"Empirical" psychology, 101

Empiricism, 86, 110
  British, 91–94
  French, 94
Empiriological order, 9
Encephalograph, 179
"Entitative habit," 74
Epicureans, 39, 40
Esse est percipi, 98
Eugenics, 136
Evolution
  early Greek, 20
  and psychology, 32, 114
Experience, 10–11
  appeal to, 77
  types of, 10–11
Experiment in psychology, 12, 124–27,
  131, 132, 143–46
Extrovert, 231

Factor
  "g," 198
  "p," 198
  "s," 198
  "w," 198
Faculty, 36, 74, 75
  modern concept of, 100
  Thomistic concept of, 200
Fathers of the Church, 5, 52, 53
"First actuality," 29
"First matter," 29
"First perfection," 29
"Foreconscious," Freudian, 227
Form board, 193
Form qualities, 149
Form, substantial, 29, 30

Genesis, book of, 15
Genetic approach in psychology, 132,
  133, 134
Genetics, modern, 134
Germ plasm, continuity of, 135
Gestalt psychology, v. psychology
Gnostics, 52

Habit, 74, 75, 114
Heredity, 134
Hylomorphic doctrine, 29, 30, 62, 63,
  64
Hylozoists, 15

Hypnosis, 121, 122, 134, 188, 223, 225,
  226

"Id," Freudian, 227, 228
Ideas
  birth of, 70, 71
  Lockian, 93
  Platonic, 24
"Ideomotor Theory," 88, 167
Illumination, doctrine of, 50
Imageless thought, 151–52, 158
  and Thomistic teaching, 152–54
Implicit behavior, 206
Individual differences, 135, 136
Individuation, principle of, 80
"Insight," 219
Instinct, controversy over, 207, 208
Intellect, 193
  agent, 35, 70, 81, 82
  possible, 35, 70
  practical, 37, 108, 109
  theoretic, 37, 108
  and sense, 76
Intelligence, meaning of, 199
"Intelligence quotient," 196
Intentional species, 33
Introspection, 14, 110
Introvert, 231
Involuntary muscles, 176

James-Lange theory of emotion, 166

Kinesthesis, 147, 206
Knowledge
  goals of human, 8
  household of human, 3
  intellectual, 70, 71
  moments of human, 3, 4, 5
  order of human, 71
  origin of human, 66, 67
  philosophic, 4
  role of human, 3
  scientific, 5
  sense, 67, 68, 69
  stages of human, 3, 111
  theological, 4

"Law of Conservation," 107
"Law of Filial Regression," 136

"Law of Satisfaction," 184
"Law of Use and Disuse," 184
"Laws of Association," 34
L'Annee Psychologique, 194, **247**
Learning, 145
  stages in, 115
Liberum arbitrium, 54, **74**
"Libido"
  Freudian, 226, 230
  Jungian, 230
Life
  Aristotelian notion of, 31, 32, 66
  grades of, 32, 33, 65, 66
"Local signs," 127

Magnetism, animal, 121
Man, 75, 252, 253
  Aristotelian, 29–31
  Augustinian, 47–49
  Cartesian, 87–88
  Thomistic, 63–65, 261, 262
Manic-depressive psychosis, 187
Manicheans, 52
Materialism, in psychology, 21, 92,
   252, 253, 256
Matter
  and form, 29
"Mental catharsis," Freudian, 225
Mental Hygiene, 191
Mental quotient, 195, 196
Mental suggestion (Mesmer), 121
Mental telepathy, 237, 238
Mental tests, 168, 192–201
Mesmerism, 188
Metaphysics, decline of, 254
Metapsychic activities, 238
Methods in psychology
  constant stimuli, 130, 145
  learning, 144
  minimal change, 130
  right and wrong cases, 145
  right associates, 145
  trial and error, 181, 183, 219
"Microcosmos," 18
Mind
  Cartesian, 87
  levels of, 227
  Thomistic, 87
Mind, 114

Monism, 100
  idealistic, 100, 258
  materialistic, 100, 258
  pantheistic, 100
Monads, doctrine of, 96

Nativistic theory, 126
Natural selection, 132, 133
Neo-Platonism, 42, 57, 83
Nerves
  motor, 122
  sensory, 122
Neurone, 175
Nominalists, 61
Noumenal order, 9
Nouveau Traité de Psychologie, 247

"Occam's razor," 82
Olfactory prism, 159
Ontogenesis, principle of, 169
Ontological order, 9
Orexis, 161
Overcompensation, 232

Panthelism, 106
Parallelism, theory of, 131, 140
Paranoia, 187
Parapsychic experience, 237
Parsimony, principle of, 82
Passions, v. emotions
Perception, extrasensory, 238
"Perennial philosophy," 28
Performance tests, 168, 197
Peripatetics, 4, 57
Perseveration tendencies, 145
Person
  definition of, 53
  patristic notion of, 53
  Thomistic notion of, 75, 76
Personal equation, 123, 140
Personalism, 244
Phantasm, 34, 35, 69
Phenomenalism, 100, 143
Philosophische Studien, 142
Phi phenomenon, 216
Philosophy
  certitude of, 11
  decline of scholastic, 83–85
  etymological meaning, 18
  modern, 86

Philosophy (*Cont.*)
  moral, 8
  role of, 6, 7
  and Revelation, 78
  and science, 9
  and superstition, 38
Phrenology, 95
Physiological zero, 132
Place sense, 125
Platonic tradition, 5, 24–30
Platonism, 4, 5, 42, 46
Platonists, 4, 42
Point scale, 196
Positivism, 5, 6, 7, 111, 112
Potency
  and act, 18, 24
Powers, v. faculties
Preestablished harmony, doctrine of, 96–97
Primary dementia, 187
Prior entry, 141
Psychic research, 237–39
Psychic tension, 188
Psychoanalysis, 222–35
Psychobiology, 190
Psychology
  anthropological approach, 256, 257
  definition of, 13
  "empirical," 101
  empirical approach, 77, 78, 222
  kinds of
    act, 148–57
    animal, 180–86
    Arabian, 55, 56
    Aristotelian, 27–38
    Augustinian, 46
    behavioristic, 202–13, 250, 256
    capacity, 168
    Cartesian, 86–89
    character, 231, 232
    comparative, 133, 180–86
    content, 139–43
    Democritean, 21
    early Christian, 42–43
    early Greek, 17
    early medieval, 40, 41, 54–60
    Eclectic, 39, 40
    eidetic, 242–44
    factorial, 192–201

    folk, 143
    Franciscan, 57, 58
    Freudian, 222–35
    functional, 165–72, 245
    Gestalt, 215, 214–21, 222, 240, 242, 256, 260
    individual differences, 135–38
    Jewish, 55, 56, 57
    Kantian, 101–3
    Occamistic, 82
    Oriental, 16
    patristic, 52
    Pauline, 45
    personalistic, 244, 245
    Platonic, 24–6
    psychoanalytic, 222–35
    response, 211, 212, 260
    Russian, 248, 249
    Scotistic, 80, 81
    Scottish, 107–9
    Socratic, 22, 23
    Sophistic, 22
    structuralistic, 158–62
    Thomistic, 61–79, 252, 253, 256–62
    totality, 240, 241
    type, 231
    understanding, 241
    Wundtian, 139–43
  naturalism in, 170
  philosophy of, 11
  pioneers of, 15
  positivistic approach, 2
  present position of, 253
  psychophysical approach, 129, 130
  psychosomatic approach, 29
  "rational," 101
  science of, 11, 144, 253
  special task of, 6, 7
  study of man, 257
  traditions in, 21, 251
  and Christianity, 42, 43
  and natural sciences, 120
  and practical knowledge, 7
  and Revelation, 43
  and superstition, 38
Psychometric research, 135–38, 192–201
  and faculties, 200
Pythagoreans, 24, 41

Quatrocento, 82

"Rational" psychology, 101
Reason, life of, 35
  and Revelation, 78, 79, 80
Recollection, doctrine of, 48
Reflex
  characteristics
    frequency, 205
    inhibition, 176
    recency, 205
    refractory period, 176
    summation, 176
  circle, 210
  conditioned, 182
  grasping, 211
Relativists in psychology, 217
Reminiscence, 145, 146
Renaissance, 83
Revelation
  and philosophy, 78, 79, 80
Rousseau Institute, 245

Science
  beginnings, 84
  certitude of, 11
  forerunners of modern, 59, 60
  and philosophy, 9
Selbstbeobachtung, 139
Self-determination, 156
Sensation, 33, 68
  attributes of, 140, 162
  units of experience, 130
Sense
  dianoetic, 34
  exterior, 33, 69
  interior, 34, 69, 70
  knowledge, 33–34, 66–69
  life of, 33
  and intellect, 76
Sense appetites, 34, 72, 73
Sensibles
  common, 67
  incidental, 67
  proper, 67
Sensism, 94
Sensists, 91
Sex, omnipotence of, 226

Sleep, 245
Society for Psychical Research, Proceedings of, 258
Sophists, 28
Soul
  creation of, 77
  immortality of, 25, 36, 76, 77, 78, 82, 97, 99
  nature of, 47, 65, 99
  and body, 30, 31, 63–65
"Species," 69, 81
Stoics, 39
"Subconscious," Freudian, 227
"Sublimation," Freudian, 226
"Superego," Freudian, 228
Symbols, Freudian, 224
Synapse, 175
Synesthetic phenomena, 137

Taste tetrahedron, 160
Telepathy, mental, 238
Terminism, 83
Tetanoid type, 242
Thomistic synthesis, 61–79
Thomistic theses, 80
Thought transference, 237
Time
  discernment, 141
  sensory, 141
  will, 141
Tonal pencil, 159
Topos eidon, 35
Touch pyramid, 159
"Traditional philosophy," 29
"Traditional psychology," 29
Transfer of training, 212
Treatise on the Soul, 27
Tropism, 180

Unconscious, 46, 106, 107, 227, 228
  racial, 231
Undercompensation, 232
Ultrarealists, 61

Viennese Psychoanalytic Society, 230
Virtues, cardinal, 25, 26
Vital phenomena, 32

Volition, studies in, 155
Voluntary muscles, 176

Weber Law, 124
Weber-Fechner Law, 130, 142

Will, 36, 37, 73, 74
  freedom of, 37, 49, 73, 74
Wundtian tradition, 139–43

Zoroastrian doctrine, 52